AF849028

FOREIGN DIRECT INVESTMENT

FOREIGN DIRECT INVESTMENT

HARRISON G. BLAINE
EDITOR

Nova Science Publishers, Inc.
New York

Copyright © 2009 by Nova Science Publishers, Inc.

All rights reserved. No part of this book may be reproduced, stored in a retrieval system or transmitted in any form or by any means: electronic, electrostatic, magnetic, tape, mechanical photocopying, recording or otherwise without the written permission of the Publisher.

For permission to use material from this book please contact us:
Telephone 631-231-7269; Fax 631-231-8175
Web Site: http://www.novapublishers.com

NOTICE TO THE READER

The Publisher has taken reasonable care in the preparation of this book, but makes no expressed or implied warranty of any kind and assumes no responsibility for any errors or omissions. No liability is assumed for incidental or consequential damages in connection with or arising out of information contained in this book. The Publisher shall not be liable for any special, consequential, or exemplary damages resulting, in whole or in part, from the readers' use of, or reliance upon, this material. Any parts of this book based on government reports are so indicated and copyright is claimed for those parts to the extent applicable to compilations of such works.

Independent verification should be sought for any data, advice or recommendations contained in this book. In addition, no responsibility is assumed by the publisher for any injury and/or damage to persons or property arising from any methods, products, instructions, ideas or otherwise contained in this publication.

This publication is designed to provide accurate and authoritative information with regard to the subject matter covered herein. It is sold with the clear understanding that the Publisher is not engaged in rendering legal or any other professional services. If legal or any other expert assistance is required, the services of a competent person should be sought. FROM A DECLARATION OF PARTICIPANTS JOINTLY ADOPTED BY A COMMITTEE OF THE AMERICAN BAR ASSOCIATION AND A COMMITTEE OF PUBLISHERS.

LIBRARY OF CONGRESS CATALOGING-IN-PUBLICATION DATA

Foreign direct investment / Harrison G. Blaine (editor).
p. cm.
ISBN 978-1-60456-921-6 (hardcover)
1. Investments, Foreign. 2. Investments, Foreign--China. I. Blaine, Harrison G.
HG4538.F6182 2008
332.67'3--dc22

2008027618

Published by Nova Science Publishers, Inc. ✦ New York

CONTENTS

PREFACE

Foreign direct investment (FDI) is defined as "investment made to acquire lasting interest in enterprises operating outside of the economy of the investor." The FDI relationship consists of a parent enterprise and a foreign affiliate which together form a Multinational corporation (MNC). In order to qualify as FDI the investment must afford the parent enterprise control over its foreign affiliate. The UN defines control in this case as owning 10% or more of the ordinary shares or voting power of an incorporated firm or its equivalent for an unincorporated firm; lower ownership shares are known as portfolio investment.

Foreign direct investment (FDI) plays an extraordinary and growing role in global business. It can provide a firm with new markets and marketing channels, cheaper production facilities, access to new technology, products, skills and financing. For a host country or the foreign firm which receives the investment, it can provide a source of new technologies, capital, processes, products, organizational technologies and management skills, and as such can provide a strong impetus to economic development. Foreign direct investment, in its classic definition, is defined as a company from one country making a physical investment into building a factory in another country.

Despite the geographical and cultural distance between Brazil and Japan, both countries have been traditional partners for over a century collaborating in a wide variety of activities. By focusing on foreign direct investment by Japanese companies in Brazil, Chapter 1 provides an extensive background of the evolution of the Japan-Brazil economic relationship. It contains two waves of investments during the 1950s and 1970s, the stagnation period during the 1980s and the beginning of 1990s, the current situation for Japanese investments including the celebration of the centenary of Japanese immigration to Brazil where some businessmen suggest it as a start point of the third wave of investments. Finally, a survey conducted by a Japanese bank that presents a view of Brazil as a promising destination for Japanese overseas business operations.

There are many determinants of FDI, including factors related to market access and demand, risk factors including (though not exclusively) political and legal stability, the desire to gain access to natural resources and policy-related variables. For policy-makers, the ability to influence inward investment flows may extend to all of these areas, for example, in relation to deregulating market access, promoting a high growth strategy (to extend market size) and liberalising access to raw materials. Alternatively, government potentially has a more direct influence over variables such as exchange rate policy, environmental protection, infrastructure, taxation, together with human resource quality and availability. Hence, it is not surprising that a strategic approach toward the attraction of FDI might focus upon these factors.

Chapter 2 concentrates upon labour market flexibility as a key determinant of FDI, both in terms of its relative importance vis-à-vis other attractors of inward investment, but also in terms of the significance of the constituent characteristics of this aggregate variable. The UK economy is a good case study for an evaluation of this type, as it embodies both a relatively flexible labour market, certainly in terms of its regulatory framework, and is consistently one of the leading recipients of FDI.

Drawing upon a primary dataset, generated through a government-funded study, the chapter examines the drivers for FDI, disaggregated according to sector, business strategy type and technological risk. It additionally examines the potential for policy conflict and misdirection, due to a lack of targeting upon those specific characteristics most attractive to inward investors.

As explained in Chapter 3, an important aspect of the current WTO regime is to standardize patent systems across countries, thus strengthening patent protection in the developing countries. In a North-South trade model, the authors analyze the effect of a stronger Southern patent protection on the Northern firm's incentive for foreign direct investment (FDI), when the Southern labor market is unionized. If there are firm-specific unions in the South, the incentive for inward FDI is higher under weak patent protection than under strong patent protection if the Southern firm is sufficiently cost inefficient. However, if there is an industry-wide union in the South, the incentive for inward FDI is always higher under strong patent protection in the South. The unionization structure plays an important role in determining the effect of patent protection on inward FDI.

Chapter 4 studies the impact of core labor standards on foreign direct investment in Latin America and the Caribbean. One of the potentially key attractions developing countries hold for foreign investment is their lower average wage costs. In particular, the authors study if lax enforcement of labor standards is a criterion that really counts for investors in deciding whether and where to invest? This thorny issue has been at the center of much of the debates on north-south free trade agreements (like NAFTA and more recently CAFTA). Clearly, foreign investors care about much more than labor costs. Capital costs matter as well, as do current demand conditions for the firm's output and expectations of future profitability. Even if the argument is refined to a ceteris paribus argument that – other things equal – investors prefer to invest in where labor costs are lower, there is an important debate about whether stricter observance of labor standards will in fact lead to higher labor costs. In addition to its specific focus on Latin America and the Caribbean, this paper departs from previous studies on foreign direct investment and core labor standards in a number of ways. Rather than examine foreign direct investment in the aggregate, it examines, to the extent possible with available current data, a sectoral breakdown of FDI. The purpose of disaggregating FDI flows is to determine whether broad economic sectors (manufacturing/non-manufacturing) are more sensitive to the enforcement of core labor standards than others. Also, the authors do not use ratification of ILO core labor conventions as a variable or proxy for enforcement of these standards. While widely used in other models, this study argues that ratification is likely to have little or no link with enforcement efforts in the case of Latin America and the Caribbean. Therefore, in contrast to previous studies that have used mainly measures of ratification, the authors show that enforcement and labor market conditions demonstrate to be more important for the region. The authors also analyze whether some core labor standards are more important than others in influencing foreign investment decisions. In particular, the paper examines whether indicators of collective bargaining, unionization and civil rights seem to be more relevant to investment patterns than child labor, for example. This contrasts with the majority of studies that either examine the impact of only one core standard or – in the case in which the impacts of multiple standards are examined –treat the standards one-by-one.

After receiving more than two decades of heavy foreign direct investment (FDI) inflows since China's economic opening in 1979, two globalized delta economies (GDEs) in China, namely, the Yangtze River Delta region in east China and the Pearl River Delta region in south China, have not only become the two fastest growing regions in China but also served as the engines of rapid growth. Chapter 5 examines first, the mobilization of FDI inflows and its agglomerative patterns in the two GDEs at the city level along with the regional output growth and trade performance; second, the similarity structure in manufacturing production by industry groups at the city level and its structural adjustments overtime; and third, the patterns of inter-city and intra-regional competition being derived. Specifically, production agglomerations and the subsequent industry output complementarity or specialization patterns at the city level would be investigated via the industry specialization (complementarity) index and clustering patterns among cities. The formation of industry and city clusters, the inter-city competitive patterns, and any implications on intra-regional competition in the two delta regions are explored and discussed.

Chapter 6 examines the behavior of a risk-averse multinational firm (MNF) under exchange rate uncertainty. The MNF has an investment opportunity in a foreign country. To hedge the exchange rate risk, the MNF can avail itself of customized derivative contracts that are fairly priced. Foreign direct investment (FDI) is irreversible and costly expandable in that the MNF can acquire additional capital at a higher unit price after the spot exchange rate has been publicly revealed. The MNF as such possesses a real (call) option that is rationally exercised whenever the foreign currency has been substantially appreciated relative to the domestic currency. The ex-post exercise of the real option convexifies the MNF's ex-ante domestic currency profit with respect to the random spot exchange rate, thereby calling for the use of currency options as a hedging instrument. The authors show that the MNF's optimal initial level of sequential FDI is always lower than that of lumpy FDI, while the expected optimal aggregate level of sequential FDI can be higher or lower than that of lumpy FDI. The authors further show that currency hedging, no matter perfect or imperfect, improves the MNF's ex-ante and ex-post incentives to make FDI, a result consistent with the complementary nature of operational and financial hedging strategies.

Chapter 7 will review what is known as the Pollution Haven Hypothesis. This hypothesis states a firm will move its production facilities to countries with relatively weak environmental regulations in order to capitalize on the lower production costs. Given the proliferation of environmental agreements both at the national and international level, their impact on international flows of investment capital is certainly of interest.

Over the years, a variety of approaches have been taken to empirically prove the Pollution Haven Hypothesis. These range from straightforward statistical comparisons to within-region studies to cross-border studies. Unfortunately, at this time there is no clear consensus as to the effects of more stringent environmental regulations on the flows of FDI.

One key issue is preventing this research from establishing a clear conclusion. That is, the difficulty in quantifying environmental regulations. The challenge here lies, first, in the subjective nature of measuring laws on the books. Beyond that, measuring the application of the laws on the books is even more elusive. A common approach is to use a proxy. However, finding a suitable one is difficult. Until a generally agreed upon approach can be found for dealing with the immeasurable nature of environmental regulations, true evidence of the Pollution Haven Hypothesis will continue to elude researchers.

Chapter 8 documents evidence of differential speed of labour demand adjustment among exporters, foreign multinationals (henceforth MNEs) and domestic non-exporting firms from the UK manufacturing industry. The findings show that MNEs exhibit the fastest speed of employment adjustment to its optimal level, followed by exporters and then domestic non-exporters. Interestingly, the long-run adjustment of labour demand with respect to factor price and demand shocks is less pronounced amongst MNEs and exporters, consistent with the view that firms engaged in international commerce activities generate more skilled jobs that are more costly to dispose of. Moreover, exporting intensity also seems to matter; MNEs with limited export-market commitment are found to have more rigid labour adjustment in response to output and wages shocks in the long run. These findings may allay fears on the footloose nature of MNEs in the sense that jobs in MNEs (followed by exporters) are expected to be more secure on average in response to any shocks affecting long-run labour demand.

Chapter 9 sets up a demonstration model to testify the adaptability of the Dunning's theory of FDI in China at first, the result indicated that China is still in the second phase of the whole process. And then the paper analyzed the effect of FDI on Chinese economical growth by utilizing the co-integration and error correction model. Empirical results show that there was a stable positive equilibrium relationship between Outflow FDI and China's economic growth in the long or short run. Through the Granger causality test, it was found that China's economic growth was the reason for Outflow FDI, and conversely, the conclusion wasn't true.

In: Foreign Direct Investment
Editor: Harrison G. Blaine, pp.1-20
ISBN: 978-1-60456-921-6
© 2009 Nova Science Publishers, Inc.

Chapter 1

FOREIGN DIRECT INVESTMENT OF JAPANESE COMPANIES IN BRAZIL

Mário Henrique Ogasavara*
Department of Japanese Studies, Faculty of Arts & Social Sciences
National University of Singapore
Block AS4, Level 3, 9 Arts Link, Singapore 117570

Abstract

Despite the geographical and cultural distance between Brazil and Japan, both countries have been traditional partners for over a century collaborating in a wide variety of activities. By focusing on foreign direct investment by Japanese companies in Brazil, this chapter provides an extensive background of the evolution of the Japan-Brazil economic relationship. It contains two waves of investments during the 1950s and 1970s, the stagnation period during the 1980s and the beginning of 1990s, the current situation for Japanese investments including the celebration of the centenary of Japanese immigration to Brazil where some businessmen suggest it as a start point of the third wave of investments. Finally, a survey conducted by a Japanese bank that presents a view of Brazil as a promising destination for Japanese overseas business operations.

Introduction

The official diplomatic relations between Brazil and Japan began with the signing of the Treaty of Amity, Commerce and Navigation in November 1895 and was sealed with the immigration of more than 250,000 Japanese to Brazil. The immigration began in 1908 with the arrival of the ship *Kasato Maru* at the port of Santos (São Paulo state). Currently, Brazil is the site of for the largest Japanese community outside Japan, estimated at more than 1.3 million people (MOFA, 2008). They constitute a priceless asset in strengthening bonds between Brazil and Japan, and such human ties have served as the foundation of the bilateral relationship over the past century (CNI & Nippon Keidanren, 2007).

---

* E-mail address: marioga@nus.edu.sg

In terms of the economic relationship between the two countries, particularly for foreign direct investment (FDI), there is a considerable presence of Japanese investment in Brazil. Japanese FDI in the country had two waves of investments in the 1950s and 1970s and rapidly grew until the beginning of the 1980s. During the period 1951-1980, Brazil was ranked the third largest recipient of Japanese FDI only behind the U.S. and Indonesia (MOF, 1983). In the past, both countries found each other an indispensable partner in the area of major raw materials investment, known as "national projects" (Nippon Keidanren & CNI, 2000). After this period, however, Brazil had considerably decreased its relative importance as a host country for Japanese FDI. On one hand, this decline was due to the high inflation rates, foreign debit problems, economic and political instability in Brazil during the 1980s and early 1990s. On the other hand, Japan experienced a period of economic recession after the bubble burst, which shifted the interest of Japanese companies to invest in other markets, particularly Asia.

Nevertheless, according to the databank series of Toyo Keizai (2006), Brazil has played a distinctive role in Japan's investments in the region, representing 65.4% of the total number of Japanese subsidiaries established in South America, and 28.7% in Latin America. Furthermore, as of recently, Brazil is once again gaining importance as a host country of Japanese FDI, because of Mercosur's[1] market potential (Nippon Keidanren & CNI, 2000), and because country being one of the four emerging economies known as BRICs (Brazil, Russia, India, and China), which over the next 50 years could become a much larger force in the world economy (Wilson & Purushothaman, 2003).

This chapter presents an extensive background of the evolution of the relationship between Japan and Brazil, including the two waves of investments and the stagnation period mentioned above. A current situation is analyzed together with the recent trends involving the celebration of the centenary of Japanese immigration to Brazil. A number of Japanese companies are investing in Brazil once again and according to some businessmen this is the beginning of a new boom of investments to the country. Finally a view of Brazil as a potential destination for overseas operations of Japanese companies is discussed with the findings of the survey conducted by the Japan Bank of International Cooperation.

Evolution of Japanese FDI in Brazil

According to Delanghe (1999), the 1930s is considered the true beginning of Japanese investment in Brazil[2], particularly when a number of Japanese companies related to the cotton textile industry started to establish subsidiaries in the country. At that time, even though the Japanese-Brazilian relations started more than forty years earlier and the first Japanese migrants arrived in Brazil twenty-seven years earlier, the trade relationship between both countries was insignificant. Delanghe (1999) argued that the 1935 Japanese private sector trade mission to Brazil, organized under the auspices of the Tokyo Chamber of Commerce

---

[1] The Common Market of the South (*Mercado Comum do Sul*). Members of Mercosur are Argentina, Brazil, Paraguay, and Uruguay. Currenlty, Bolivia, Chile, Colombia, Ecuador, Peru, and Venezuela have associate member status.

[2] In 1927 Tozan Agricultural Co. established a local representative in Brazil,Casa Tozan,which founded at the same year an experimental farm in Campinas (São Paulo state) under the name Fazenda *Monte Deste*. In 1933 a bank was established under the name Casa Bancária Tozan Ltda. (Delanghe, 1999).

and Industry and headed by Hirao Hachisaburo,[3] was the true starting point of significant Japanese-Brazilian trade and investment relations. After the 1935 economic mission to Brazil, there was a dramatic increase in Japanese-Brazilian trade. Japanese imports from Brazil, consisting almost entirely of raw cotton, jumped from 158,098 pounds in 1935 to 1,683,333 pounds in 1936 and 2,122,106 pounds in 1937, while Japanese exports to Brazil showed a small but respectable increase from 246,852 pounds in 1935 to 349,609 pounds in 1936 and 647,472 pounds in 1937 (Suzuki, 1995).

But the mere ability to ship the cotton was not enough, which resulted in development by Japan of a whole structure to increase production, purchase, process, bale, stock, and so on (Delanghe, 1999). Consequently, some Japanese trading firms (*sogo shosha*) quickly opened offices in Brazil in order to mediate most of the trade between Japan and Brazil. One example is Tomen Corporation in 1937 (*Tomen Corporation do Brasil*) and another is Mitsui & Co., which established in Rio de Janeiro a branch office, Nipo-Brasileira Ltda, in 1938. Furthermore, a number of Japanese cotton textile companies started to set up subsidiaries in the Brazilian market, such as Japan-Brazil Raw Cotton Co. (*Brazcot Ltda* in 1936 and Marumaru & Co. in 1941); Japan-South Manufacturing Co. (*Bratac*) and Toyo Raw Cotton Co. (Mori & Co.[4]) in 1937. These Japanese cotton textile companies usually created other subsidiaries related to the field of banking including Brazcot Ltda (*Casa Bancária Brazcot Ltda*) in 1936, and Bratac (*Casa Bancária Bratac* de Carlos Y. Kate[5]) in 1937. In order to maintain and promote the trade and foreign direct investment, two important organizations were founded in Brazil: the Japan-Brazil Chamber of Commerce was established in Rio de Janeiro in January 1938, and the Japan Chamber of Commerce was created in São Paulo in August 1940 (Handa, 1976).

The First Wave of Japanese Investments: The 1950s

Although some Japanese cotton textile companies, banks and trading companies opened subsidiaries and offices in Brazil in the 1930s as stated earlier, in fact the "first wave" or "first boom" of investments started in 1950s. During the World War II, despite the fact that there was no direct conflict between Japan and Brazil, diplomatic relations were broken off when President Getúlio Vargas signed the Decree number 18,811 on 6 June 1945, which officially formalized the war against Japan (Nunes, 2006). The diplomatic relations were reestablished when the San Francisco Treaty reinstating the sovereignty of Japan was made known in September 1951, but was put into effect in Brazil in subsequent year (Uehara, 1999).

In the middle of 1950s, Brazil began to attract attention of Japanese companies, both as a potential market for manufacturers and as a supply source of raw materials (Nakasumi & Yamashiro, 1992). As occurred in the 1930s, many cotton textile industries established ventures in Brazil including Toyo Bohseki in 1955 (*Toyobo do Brasil*); Kanegafuchi Bohseki in 1956 (*Kanebo do Brasil*); and Tsuzuki Bohseki in 1960 (*Indústria Têxtil Tsuzuki*). In addition, a number of Japanese companies from different industries started its operations in

[3] President of the shipping company Kawasaki Shipbuilding Co.

[4] In 1938, Mori and Co. changes into Algodoeira do Sul Ltda. and in 1940 it changes into *Nanbei Menka Kaisha* (Delanghe, 1999).

[5] In 1940 Casa Bancária Bratac de Carlos Y. Kate changes into Banco América do Sul Ltda and in 1947 it changes into Banco América do Sul S/A (Handa, 1976).

the country: Pilot Pen Corporation (*Pilot Pen do Brasil S.A.*) and Fuji Bank (*Banco América do Sul*) in 1954; Ishikawajima-Harima (*Ishikawajima do Brasil*) and Ajinomoto in 1956 (*Ajinomoto do Brasil*); Yanmar Diesel in 1957 (*Yanmar Diesel Motor do Brasil*); and Toyota Motors in 1958 (*Toyota do Brasil*), which was the Toyota's first vehicle plant outside Japan (Exame, 1999).

According to Ozawa et al. (1976), this first wave of manufacturing investments in the 1950s exhibited two unique features. First, compared to the Japanese standards at that time, the investments made in Brazil were of substantial size. Second, Japanese companies only established full- or majority-owned subsidiaries.

There were some explanations that justified the interest of Japanese companies in setting up large scale investments in a geographical and cultural distant country such as Brazil. First, in the 1950s Brazil became an important export market for Japanese manufacturers, and the future of Brazil looked particularly promising because of a rich endowment of natural resources (Ozawa et al., 1976). In 1954, Brazil represented 4.8% of the total of Japanese exports and 3.1% of imports (Horisaka, 1997).

Second, the new industrialization policy implemented in Brazil emphasized import substitution under the "law of similars" (*Lei dos Similares*). Under this law, once a particular item was produced in Brazil in "sufficient quality and quantity", and registered with the government as a product similar to its imported counterpart, it would be protected from imports. Consequently, a number of foreign firms quickly decided to set up location production in order to produce "similars" and to be qualified for import protection (Ozawa et al., 1976).

Third, Brazil provided innumerous incentives to foreign capital by introducing a measure called SUMOC Instruction 113 in 1955 (Tonooka, 1998). This measure allowed foreign firms to import equipment for their ventures and are permitted to convert the value of machinery in foreign currency into Brazilian currency at special rates. The measure benefited all foreign investors, but it was particularly a plus to Japanese industry. Under SUMOC Instruction 113, the foreign investor was allowed to ship out used machinery, and this provision was most suitable for Japan's textile makers who were, at that time, operating with idle machinery at home (Ozawa et al., 1976). The Japanese textile companies transferred used machinery from Japan and installed it in most of their subsidiaries in Brazil, which proved to be very attractive in the short term and provided long-run advantages (Tonooka, 1998). It enabled many Japanese textile manufactures to reduce excess capacity in cotton textiles at home and facilitated their expansion into the production of synthetic textiles then emerging as a new-growth sector (Ozawa et al., 1976).

Finally, the presence of a large community of Japanese immigrants and their descendents living in Brazil served as a powerful magnet for Japanese investment (Hollerman, 1988). The justification for Hollerman's argument implies that due to the diligent character of the members of the Japanese immigrant community and its descendents, most of them have become respected individuals in the Brazilian society. In this sense, the Japanese-Brazilian could provide a strong base of operation for the Japanese interests in the country and consequently this enabled Japan's approach to business in Brazil to be readily arranged. Moreover, the fact that Japanese immigrants were welcomed and well treated in Brazil provided a basis for psychological security for Japanese companies. In contrast to some Asian countries that inflamed local antagonisms, touching off anti-Japanese demonstrations (Ozawa et al., 1976).

The Second Wave of Japanese Investments: the 1970s

In the first half of 1960s, Brazilian economy suffered a high inflation rate, a decline in the industrial activities, and political chaos, which discouraged Japanese investments (Tonooka, 1998). At that time, Japanese firms did not have a great experience level of operating overseas subsidiaries, and certainly a few or none experience in countries with political and economic instability (Yokota, 1998). However, in the late 1960s and during 1970s, with the return of political and economic stability, the relation between Brazil and Japan gained more impulse with the large joint projects with the state-owned enterprises, in the area of major raw materials investment known as "national projects" (Nippon Keidanren & CNI, 2000), resulting in the second wave of Japanese investments in Brazil.

During this period, Japanese companies invested in Brazil's basic industries including petrochemicals, aluminum, pulp and paper, industries whose development is stressed in the country's Second Plan for National Development known as II PND (*Segundo Plano Nacional de Desenvolvimento*). A number of Japanese firms willingly accepted minority ownership by investing in collaboration, as joint-ventures, with the Brazilian state-owned enterprises mostly in iron and steel, and petrochemical complex (Ozawa et al., 1976). Some examples of joint projects include the Japanese consortium Japan Brazilian Pulp and Papers Resources Co. that established *Cenibra* in 1974; an international steelmaking consortium with the participation of Brazil's state enterprise Siderbrás (51%), Italy's Finsider (24.5%), and Japan's Kawasaki Steel (24.5%) that set up *Companhia Siderúrgica de Tubarão* in 1976; and another Japanese consortium Nippon Amazon Aluminum Co. started *Albrás* in 1978 (Uehara, 1999).

Furthermore, some groups of Japanese firms, normally consisting of a major chemical company and a trading company, started to set up minority-owned joint ventures with the Brazilian government. An example was *Petroquisa*, a state-owned enterprise, which involved many partnerships with Japanese companies in different ventures (Ozawa et al., 1976) such as high pressure polyethylene (Sumitomo Chemical Co. and C. Itoh & Co., 30% of ownership); low/medium pressure polyethylene and polyvinyl chloride (Mitsubishi Chemical Ind. and Nissho-Iwai Co., 33% of ownership); acrylonitrile (Mitsubishi Rayon Co. and Mitsubishi Corp., 33% of ownership); and polyisoprene rubber (Kuraray Co. and Mitsubishi Corp., 30% of ownership). At that time, the characteristic of establishing a partnership with local government was extremely different from the entry market strategy implemented by American companies which usually focused on the acquisition of local companies in Brazil (Uehara, 2006). Additionally, these Japanese investments involving minority-owned joint ventures with state-owned enterprise distinguished completely from the entry mode strategies exhibited in the first wave of investments in the 1950s, which was characterized by establishing only full- or majority-owned subsidiaries (Ozawa et al., 1976).

Another important joint investment related to the "national projects" was the establishment of the Japanese-Brazilian Program for the Cerrado Development or PRODECER in 1974 (*Programa Nipo-Brasileiro para o Desenvolvimento dos Cerrados*). According to Tonooka (1998), this program became strategically important for Japan after the embargo exports of soybeans and related products from the U.S. PRODECER was a cooperation project involving JICA (Japan International Cooperation Agency) and the Brazilian government aiming at expanding the agricultural production in the *Cerrado* region (Nunes, 2006). This region corresponds to almost the size of the Amazon and was envisioned together by the Brazilian and Japanese governments as the world's largest agricultural frontier. It took four years from the initial proposal to the beginning of the soy production and to reach the Japanese and other international markets. As a matter of figures, this joint project resulted in a great development and expansion of soybean cultivation in the region. By 1976 Brazil was the eighth largest soy producer in the world, which after the Japanese investments, the country became second only behind the U.S. Moreover, as of 1997, Japan is the third largest consumer of Brazilian soy in the world (Siqueira, 2003).

In addition to the implementation of "national projects", many Japanese companies received a special tax credit from the Brazilian government to expand their productive capacities. These including among others US$14.7 million by *Ishikawajima do Brasil*, US$2.2 million by *Yanmar do Brasil*, US$3.1 million by *NEC do Brasil*, and US$8.7 million by *Nisshinbo do Brasil* (Ozawa et al., 1976)

Furthermore, Amorim (1991) considered the establishment of Manaus Free Trade Zone (*Zona Franca de Manaus*) in 1967 as another aspect that contributed to the second wave of Japanese investments in Brazil. This free trade zone in the Amazon region attracted many foreign companies by giving some incentives such as tax-free for imported and industrialized products. Several Japanese companies set up operations in this region (Nunes, 2006) such as Toshiba Corp. (*Semp-Toshiba*) and Matsushita Electric Industrial Co. (*Panasonic da Amazônia*) in 1967, Yamaha Corp. in 1970 (*Yamaha Motor do Brasil*), Sharp Corp. (*Sharp do Brasil*) and Honda Motors Co. (*Honda Motor do Brasil*) in 1971, Fujitsu (*Fujitsu do Brasil*) and Sony Corp. (*Sony Componentes*) in 1972, and Fuji Electric in 1975 (*Fuji Electric do Brasil*).

According to Tonooka (1998), a number of Japanese companies from different industry sectors established subsidiaries in Brazil during the second wave of investments. In the food sector, Nissin Corp. and Ajinomoto Co. started a joint venture in 1965 (*Nissin Ajinomoto Alimentos*); Yakult Honsha Co., Ltd. opened a manufacturing plant in 1966 (*Yakult Indústria e Comércio*); and Marubeni Corp. established a joint venture with a local company in 1967 (*Cia Iguaçu de Café Solúvel*). In the textile sector, Nisshinbo Industries set up in 1972 *Nisshinbo do Brasil* and Daiwabo Co. in 1973 started *Daiwa do Brasil Têxtil Ltda*. Other machinery companies established subsidiaries in Brazil including Mitsutoyo Corp. in 1972 (*Mitsutoyo Sul Americana*); Rinnai Corp. in 1975 (*Equipamentos NGK-Rinnai*); NHK Spring Co. in 1976 (*NHK-Fastener Brasil*); and Brother Industries in 1977 (*Brother International Corp do Brasil*). In the electric-electronic sector, other Japanese firms started operations in Brazil such as NEC Corp. in 1968 (*NEC do Brasil*); Rohm Co. in 1972 (*Rohm Indústria Eletrônica*); Yokogawa Electric Corp. (*Yokogawa Elétrica do Brasil*), TDK Corp. (*TDK do Brasil*), and Alps Electric Co. (*Alps do Brasil*) in 1973; Furukawa Co. (*Furukawa Industrial*) and Fujikura Ltd. (*Fujikura Representações no Brasil*) in 1974; and Kyocera Corp. in 1978 (*Yashica do Brasil*).

The trade between Brazil and Japan increased from US$ 57 million to US$ 1.7 billion between 1964 and 1974. In terms of Japanese FDI outflows, as shown in Table 1 (the evolution 1951-1970 and 1971-1980) and Table 2 (1951-1980), Brazil became the third most important host country of Japanese investments after the U.S. and Indonesia (MOF, 1983).

Table 1. Total Japanese outward FDI, 1951-1970 and 1971-1980 (in million dollars)

Rank	1951-1970	US$ million	Rank	1971-1980	US$ million
1	USA	701	1	USA	8,177
2	England	544	2	Indonesia	4,182
3	Saudi Arabia - Kuwait	326	**3**	**Brazil**	**2,619**
4	**Brazil**	**288**	4	Australia	1,954
5	Indonesia	242	5	England	1,466
6	Canada	211	6	South Korea	1,104
7	Australia	210	7	Hong Kong	1,067
8	Thailand	91	8	Iran	997
9	Brunei	86	9	Singapore	904
10	Taiwan	85	10	Liberia	786

Source: Financial Statistics of Japan, Ministry of Finance Japan 1983

Table 2. Total Japanese outward FDI, 1951-1980 (in million dollars)

Rank	1951-1980	US$ million
1	USA	8,878
2	Indonesia	4,424
3	**Brazil**	**2,908**
4	Australia	2,165
5	England	2,009
6	South Korea	1,137
7	Hong Kong	1,095
8	Iran	1,002
9	Singapore	932
10	Canada	920

Source: Financial Statistics of Japan, Ministry of Finance Japan 1983

Japanese Investments in the 1980s

Foreign direct investment from Japan to Brazil continued to growth until the beginning of 1980s. In 1983, the country was still considered a top destination of Japanese investments, ranked as the fourth largest recipient of Japanese FDI with the amount of US$410 million (MOF, 1991). However, from the middle of 1980s until the beginning of 1990s, the trade relations between both countries declined and the amount of Japanese investments in Brazil decreased significantly on average 13% per year from 1984 to 1987 (MOF, 1991). As shown in Table 3, when taking into consideration the total amount of Japanese outward FDI from 1981 to 1990, it places Brazil as the sixteenth largest recipient of Japanese foreign investments which is far behind from the figure presented during the period from 1971 to 1980 (Table 2).

Table 3. Total Japanese outward FDI, 1981-1990 (in million dollars)

Rank	1981-1990	US$ million
1	USA	121,650
2	England	20,590
3	Panama	15,567
4	Australia	13,898
5	Netherlands	12,519
6	Hong Kong	8,755
7	Cayman Islands	7,148
8	Indonesia	7,117
9	Singapore	5,617
10	Luxemburg	5,502
11	Canada	4,735
12	Germany	4,191
13	Liberia	4,041
14	Thailand	4,027
15	France	3,771
16	**Brazil**	**3,653**

Source: Financial Statistics of Japan, Ministry of Finance Japan 1991

The decrease of Japanese investment flows to Brazil was a result of both endogenous and exogenous factors (Amorim, 1991). First, during this period Brazil had foreign debt problems, high inflation rates, economic recession, and political-economic instability. Second, Japanese companies experienced a change in priorities shifting from the management of raw materials and natural resources to the assignment of securing market for their products (Uehara, 1999). In addition, with the appreciation of the yen, Japan focused on investments in the North American and Asian markets.

Japanese Investments in the 1990s and 2000s

Few new Japanese companies were established in the early 1990s in Brazil. Most of them were small scale investments focusing on the establishment of many representative offices rather than production plants (Shiffer, 2002). The decline in new start-ups reflects the Brazilian economy crisis. However, after the period of recession, the Brazilian economy had changed remarkably since 1994, when Fernando Henrique Cardoso was elected as the President of Brazil by launching the Real Plan (*Plano Real*) thereby introducing a new currency called *real*. Many deep regulatory and structural changes were made by encouraging initiatives to redress fiscal problems, promote privatization of state-owned enterprises, and open up and liberalize the economy. In addition, after a period of hyperinflation which reached 2,000% level per year, the inflation rate dropped dramatically from July 1994 onward. By 1997 the inflation rate reached standard international levels and the hyperinflation was over.

As a result, the Brazilian economy achieved a notable recovery in a short period, resulting increasing flows of foreign direct investment in Brazil. The total FDI inflows reached US$ 4.4 billion in 1995 (almost four times the figure in 1993), rising to US$ 15.3 billion in 1997, and then to US$ 27.6 billion in 1999. During the period 2000 to 2006, Brazil received, on average, total FDI inflows of US$ 20.9 billion per year. In 2007 flow of FDI reached a new record volume of US$ 33.7 billion with an increase of 51.6% comparing to the previous year (BACEN, 2008).

Consequently, the country became one of the most attractive host countries for FDI in the world. Brazil was the second in the ranking of FDI inflows in developing countries between 1997 and 1999, and was the fifth most attractive recipient of FDI in the world between 1997 and 1998 (JETRO, 2001). Based on a FDI Confidence Index developed by A.T. Kearney (Table 4) with responses from global executives spanning seventeen industry sectors in sixty countries across all six continents, Brazil was the second in 1998, the forth between 1999 and 2000, and in 2001 was the third world's most attractive destination of FDI (A.T. Kearney, 2004). Although the country was not listed as the top ten in 2002 and 2004, since 2005 Brazil is once again gaining attention as an important destination for international investment flows (A.T. Kearney, 2005, 2007).

Table 4. FDI Confidence Index (1998-2007)

Rank	1998	1999	2000	2001	2002*	2003	2004*	2005	2007**
1	U.S.	U.S.	U.S.	U.S.	China	China	China	China	China
2	**Brazil**	China	U.K.	China	U.S.	U.S.	U.S.	India	India
3	China	U.K.	China	**Brazil**	U.K.	Mexico	India	U.S.	U.S.
4	U.K.	**Brazil**	**Brazil**	U.K.	Germany	Poland	U.K.	U.K.	U.K.
5	India	Mexico	Poland	Mexico	France	Germany	Germany	Poland	Hong Kong
6	Mexico	India	Germany	Germany	Italy	India	France	Russia	**Brazil**
7	Poland	Australia	Mexico	India	Spain	U.K.	Australia	**Brazil**	Singapore
8	Argentina	Poland	Italy	Italy	Canada	Russia	Hong Kong	Australia	UAE***
9	Australia	Germany	Spain	Spain	Mexico	**Brazil**	Italy	Germany	Russia
10	Germany	France	Australia	France	Australia	Spain	Japan	Hong Kong	Germany

Source: A.T. Kearney Inc – FDI Confidence 2004, 2005, 2007

Notes: * In 2002 Brazil was ranked as the 13th, and 2004 as the 17th; **There was no report launched in 2006; *** United Arab Emirates.

Furthermore, a recent survey carried out by the UNCTAD (United Nations Conference on Trade and Development) entitled "*Foreign direct investment prospects promising for 2005-2008*" (UNCTAD, 2005) revealed the important role that Brazil plays as an attractive location for foreign investors. According to this survey depicted in Table 5, Brazil is the fourth most attractive location for global business based on responses from experts, and the fifth when considered the responses from the world's largest transnational corporations.

Table 5. Most Attractive Global Business Locations in 2005-2008

Rank	Responses from Experts	Responses from TNCs [a]
1	China	China
2	U.S.	India
3	India	U.S.
4	**Brazil**	Russia
5	Russia	**Brazil**
6	U.K.	Mexico
7	Germany	Germany
8	Poland	U.K.
9	Singapore	Thailand
10	Ukraine	Canada

Note: [a] Transnational Corporations
Source: UNCTAD FDI Prospects, 2005-2008

In response to the changes in the Brazilian economy and the positive perspectives in terms of being considered an important and attractive host country for foreign investors, the Japan-Brazil Economic Committee formed by Japan Federation of Economic Organizations (*Nippon Keidanren*) and the National Confederation of Industries - CNI (*Confederação Nacional das Indústrias*) organized a meeting in the year 2000 called "*Brazil-Japan: Alliance for the 21st Century*". The objective of this meeting was to revitalize the economic relations between Brazil and Japan, and to build a stronger partnership between the private sectors of the two countries in order to explore new challenges and opportunities for trade and investment in the new century (Nippon Keidanren & CNI, 2000). Four years later, Nippon Keidanren launched a business report requesting for early start of intergovernmental study of the Japan-Brazil economic partnership agreement (Nippon Keidanren, 2004).

The new Brazilian scenario with a higher political and economic stability and a lower inflation has been generating more credibility for Japanese investors after two decades of low FDI level in the country. Brazil is a major power in Latin America, with a GDP of US$ 1,295 billion which is an economy equal in scale to that of all ten ASEAN countries combined (GDP of US$ 1,203 billion), but a population three times smaller than ASEAN-10 countries (IMF, 2007). As the key nation of Mercosur it is striving to strengthen the political and economic unity of the region (Nippon Keidanren, 2004), and this also means that establishing operations in Brazil enables a company to target the entire Mercosur market of 237 million people with an aggregate GDP of US$ 1,575 billion (IMF, 2007).

In addition, by being one of the so-called BRICs economies, Brazil is gaining importance and business interest as a target market for Japanese overseas investments. The president of Global Foods & Amino Acids Co. of Ajinomoto Co., Takuzo Kitamura, gives his perception of these emerging countries "Ajinomoto is fortunate to already have business bases in the so-called BRICs, which are expected to be the important countries of the 21st century… we intend to build our next Lysine plant in Brazil to cover these emerging markets" (Ajinomoto, 2004, p.8). One of the world's leading heavy machinery manufacturers, Mitsubishi Heavy

Industries (MHI) mentioned about future investments in the BRICs "MHI will be created in Brazil, India, Singapore and Korea over the next few months as a part of MHI's improvement and reinforcement of its overseas bases to meet the needs of today's rapidly globalizing economy... The selection of the four sites in question reflects expectations of strategic merits to be reaped from new developments in the global economy. These include the emerging presence of the BRICs" (MHI, 2004). Toyota Motor Corp. also pointed out the importance to invest in BRICs markets "BRICs are of crucial importance to Toyota, whose aim is to raise its share of the global market to 15 percent from its current 10 percent... BRICs have been drawing growing attention from multinational corporations... Toyota intends to boost production in Brazil in accordance with a plan to optimize operations in Latin America" (Asahi Shimbun, 2004).

In the late 1990s, there were some new investments of Japanese manufacturing companies already operating in Brazil, particularly the case for investments in the Toyota and Honda automobile assembly lines (Shiffer, 2002). Since 1958 Toyota was engaged in producing the same Land Cruiser model called *Bandeirante*. After forty years Toyota Motors established a new manufacturing plant to produce the world successful model *Corolla* in 1998 (Exame, 1999). Honda Motors, which was limited to produce motorcycles in Brazil, opened a new manufacturing plant to produce the model *Civic* car in 1997 (Exame, 1999). Moreover, many other Japanese suppliers for the automobile industry established new manufacturing plants in Brazil including Yazaki Corporation (*Yazaki do Brasil*), Sanoh Industrial Co., Ltd. (*Hisan do Brasil*), and Takata Global Group (*Takata do Brasil Autopeças*).

Table 6. Japanese FDI in Brazil (1991-2007)

Year	Total FDI		Japanese FDI		
	US$ million	Annual % Change	US$ million	Annual % Change	% Total FDI
1991	1,102.2	-	214.1	-	19.4%
1992	2,061.0	87.0%	69.4	-67.6%	3.4%
1993	1,290.9	-37.4%	25.6	-63.1%	2.0%
1994	2,149.9	66.5%	83.5	226.2%	3.9%
1995	4,405.1	104.9%	40.9	-51.0%	0.9%
1996	7,665.5	74.0%	192.2	369.9%	2.5%
1997	15,311.0	99.7%	342.1	78.0%	2.2%
1998	23,270.8	52.0%	277.8	-18.8%	1.2%
1999	27,571.9	18.5%	274.3	-1.3%	1.0%
2000	29,876.4	8.4%	384.7	40.2%	1.3%
2001	21,041.7	-29.6%	826.6	114.9%	3.9%
2002	18,778.3	-10.8%	504.5	-39.0%	2.7%
2003	12,902.4	-31.3%	1,368.3	171.2%	10.6%
2004	20,265.3	57.1%	243.2	-82.2%	1.2%
2005	21,521.6	6.2%	779.1	220.4%	3.6%
2006	22,231.3	3.3%	647.5	-16.9%	2.9%
2007	33,704.6	51.6%	464.6	-28.2%	1.4%

Source: Banco Central do Brasil (Central Bank of Brazil), Census of foreign capitals in Brazil

In terms of volume of Japanese FDI in Brazil during the 1990s and 2000s, although there were low level of investments in the 1990s and many up-downs in terms of annual changes, since year 2000 Japan started to increase again its participation in the country (Table 6). The average of Japanese investments during the 2000s (US$ 652 million/year) is almost four times higher that invested in the 1990s (US$ 169 million/year). In 2003, Japanese FDI reached US$ 1.37 billion that corresponded to 10.6% of the total investments in Brazil at that time. This increase was a result of one large investment made by Mitsui & Co. This trade company invested US$ 800 million in order to acquire 15% ownership of *Valepar S.A.*, the holding company of the *Companhia Vale do Rio Doce* (CVRD), a Brazilian iron ore and mineral resources company (Segalla, 2006).

Is the Beginning of the Third Wave of Japanese Investments?

In year 2008, Brazil and Japan are moving towards the celebration of the Centenary of Japanese Immigration to Brazil. Throughout the year a number of cultural, social, political and economic events will be carried out in both countries aims at improving bilateral relation as a whole. The events include trade missions, symposiums on economy and trade, arts exhibitions, film festivals, theater presentations, concerts, and sporting. Moreover, both countries are going to issue commemorative coins to this "Japan-Brazil Year of Exchange" (Manzini, 2008).

The president of JETRO-Brazil, Yuji Watanabe, believes that the "Year of Exchange" is the beginning of the "third wave" of Japanese investments in Brazil (Okubaro, 2007). Watanabe argues that Japanese companies are interested in Brazil because they are competing in a global scale level and firms need to look for new opportunities and ways in order to not be acquired by its competitors. An example is the investment planned by Nippon Steel. Through a joint venture with local affiliate *Usiminas*, Nippon Steel plans to invest US$ 5-6 billion and begin construction of a steelworks facility in Brazil within the year in order to achieve a global production reach, countering inroads by giant international steelmaking Arcelor-Mittal into fast-growing markets in Asia (Nikkei, 2008). Another large investment is the establishment of a joint venture between Sumitomo Metals and the French company Vallourec. By investing US$ 1.6 billion they will build an integrated steel plant in Brazil, including blast furnace and seamless pipe milling facilities. Brazil was chosen as the location for the new joint venture because the country has good access to growing markets, including North America, the Middle East and Africa, and due to the low cost of raw material and energy (Japan Times, 2007a).

In addition, according to Watanabe the "third boom" of Japanese investments will take place because Brazil had played an important role in the area of renewable sources of energy, which is the world's largest exporter of bioethanol (Okubaro, 2007). Recently some Japanese companies started to invest in this area. Mitsui & Co. and Petrobrás set up a joint venture *Participações Nipo-Brasileira em Complexos Bioenergéticos S.A.* to implement bioethanol-related projects, including to export the product to Japan (Japan Times, 2008). Additionally, both companies are planning to construct forty new ethanol processing plants, a project evaluated at US$ 8 billion to target the production to be exported only to Japan (Japan Times, 2007b). Marubeni Corporation invested US$ 40 million to set up a joint venture with Agrenco Group called *Agrenco Bio-Energia Ltda* which operates bio-energy complexes and produce bio-diesel fuel and soybean meal. Marubeni aims at securing a supply source for bio-diesel fuel, global demand for which is expected to increase, in view of rising fossil fuel prices and growing concerns about the need to protect the environment. Moreover, Marubeni intends to secure a supply source for soybean meal, set to enjoying growing demand, mainly in Asia (Marubeni, 2007). In the energy sector, there are projects developed by Mitsui & Co. including an US$ 1 billion investment on Malhas Project, a gas pipeline network in Southeastern and Northeastern areas of Brazil; and investment of US$ 900 million for REVAP (*Refinaria Henrique Lage*) refinery modernization project (Okubaro, 2007).

Finally, President Luiz Inácio Lula da Silva has signed in 2006 a decree adopting Japan's digital television system in the country instead of the standards used in Europe and the U.S. The ceremony was attended by both communications ministers Hélio Costa of Brazil and Heizo Takenaka of Japan. The Japan Ambassador to Brazil, Ken Shimanouchi, considered the digital television as the symbol of the "Japan-Brazil partnership in the 21st century" (Otta, 2007). It is expected an increasing of Japanese investments in Brazil related to high-technology industry, including the establishment of a semiconductor plant in Brazil (Gusmão, 2008). However, some issues have to be implemented in order to accomplish such kind of investment. Toshiba Corp. has just announced to stop its plan to build a semiconductor plant in Brazil due to the lack of local skilled workers and a network of suppliers for a high-technology plant (Alencar, 2008). In addition, it is still unclear whether or not other countries in South America will follow the Brazilian steps and adopt the Japanese standard (Otta, 2007).

Brazil as a Promising Destination of Japanese FDI

The Japan Bank of International Cooperation (JBIC) has conducted each year since 1989[6] surveys to identify the current and future trends involving overseas business operations and foreign direct investment by Japanese manufacturing companies that have solid record of overseas business operations. The results of JBIC survey are published annually in a report called: "*Survey report on overseas business operations by Japanese manufacturing companies*".

The survey covered Japanese manufacturing companies that have three or more overseas affiliates, including at least one production base. Overseas affiliates in this survey are defined as the first-tier overseas affiliates or companies incorporated overseas in which Japanese parent companies have 10% or more equity stake, and the second-tier overseas affiliates or companies incorporated overseas in which the first-tier Japanese overseas affiliates have more than 50% equity stake. Questionnaires were sent to Japanese companies by mail with an average 61.9% of effective response (based on the last five years' survey). In line with the collection of questionnaires responses, JBIC conducted follow-up telephone interviews and carried out face-to-face interviews by visiting companies and public organizations (JBIC, 2007).

[6] Started by Export-Import Bank of Japan.

Table 7. Promising Destination for Overseas Business Operations over the Medium Term (next three years)

Rank	1997	1998	1999	2000*	2001*	2002	2003*	2004*	2005	2006	2007
1	China	China	China	China	China	China	China	China	China	China	China
2	U.S.	U.S.	U.S.	U.S.	U.S.	Thailand	Thailand	Thailand	India	India	India
3	Indonesia	Thailand	Thailand	Thailand	Thailand	U.S.	U.S.	India	Thailand	Vietnam	Vietnam
4	Thailand	Indonesia	India	Indonesia	Indonesia	Indonesia	Vietnam	Vietnam	Vietnam	Thailand	Thailand
5	India	India	Indonesia	Malaysia	India	Vietnam	India	U.S.	U.S.	U.S.	Russia
6	Vietnam	Philippines	Vietnam	Taiwan	Vietnam	India	Indonesia	Russia	Russia	Russia	U.S.
7	Philippines	Malaysia	Malaysia	India	Taiwan	Korea	Korea	Indonesia	Korea	**Brazil**	**Brazil**
8	Malaysia	Vietnam	Philippines	Vietnam	Korea	Taiwan	Taiwan	Korea	Indonesia	Korea	Indonesia
9	**Brazil**	**Brazil**	U.K.	Korea	Malaysia	Malaysia	Malaysia	Taiwan	**Brazil**	Indonesia	Korea
10	Taiwan	U.K.	**Brazil**	Philippines	Singapore	**Brazil**	Russia	Malaysia	Taiwan	Taiwan	Taiwan

Notes: *Brazil was the 14th in 2000, the 13th in 2001, the 16th in 2003, and the 13th in 2004.

Source: Japan Bank for International Cooperation, JBIC Review, No. 1 (2000) p.20; JBIC Review, No.6 (2002) p.43; JBIC Review No.7 (2003) p.56; JBIC Review No.9 (2004) pp.43; JBIC FY2007 Survey: Outlook for Japanese Foreign Direct Investment (2007) p.13.

Table 8. Promising Destination for Overseas Business Operations over the Long Term (next ten years)

Rank	1997	1998	1999	2000	2001	2002	2003	2004	2005	2006	2007
1	China	China	China	China	China	China	China	China	China	China	India
2	India	U.S.	U.S.	U.S.	India	U.S.	India	India	India	India	China
3	U.S.	India	India	India	U.S.	India	U.S.	Thailand	Vietnam	Russia	Russia
4	Vietnam	Indonesia	Thailand	Thailand	Thailand	Vietnam	Thailand	Vietnam	Russia	Vietnam	Vietnam
5	Indonesia	Thailand	Vietnam	Indonesia	Vietnam	Thailand	Vietnam	U.S.	Thailand	U.S.	**Brazil**
6	Thailand	Vietnam	Indonesia	Vietnam	Indonesia	Indonesia	Russia	Russia	U.S.	Thailand	Thailand
7	**Brazil**	**Brazil**	**Brazil**	Malaysia	**Brazil**	**Brazil**	Indonesia	Indonesia	**Brazil**	**Brazil**	U.S.
8	Philippines	Philippines	Malaysia	**Brazil**	Taiwan	Russia	Korea	**Brazil**	Indonesia	Indonesia	Indonesia
9	Malaysia	Malaysia	Philippines	U.K.	Malaysia	Malaysia	**Brazil**	Korea	Korea	Korea	Mexico
10	Myanmar	U.K.	Mexico	Taiwan	Korea	Korea	Malaysia	Taiwan	Malaysia	Malaysia	Turkey

Source: Japan Bank for International Cooperation, JBIC Review, No. 1 (2000) p.20; JBIC Review, No.6 (2002) p.43; JBIC Review No.7 (2003) p.63; JBIC Review No.9 (2004) p.50, JBIC Review No.13 (2005) p.77, JBIC FY2007 Survey: Outlook for Japanese Foreign Direct Investment (2007) p.13.

Although the largest number of production bases is located respectively in the ASEAN-4 countries, China, North America, NIES, the EU, and other Asian countries[1], Brazil received special attention from the Japanese companies as a promising destination for overseas business operation over the medium term (next three years). The country has been in the top ten ranking in 1997-1999, 2002, and 2005-2006. As shown in Table 7, over the medium term, most of the promising destination countries are concentrated in the Asian region, except for the U.S. and U.K. (developed countries), recently Russia, and Brazil. The last three periods, Brazil has entered the top ranking, moving from the sixteenth (2003) and thirteenth (2004) places to become the seventh (2006 and 2007) most promising host country for Japanese business investments on next three years. The reasons for Brazil being viewed as a promising investment destination for Japan are due to the future growth of local market, inexpensive source of labor, supply base for automobile assemblers, base of export to third countries, and current size of local market (JBIC, 2007).

When taking into consideration the ranking of promising destinations for overseas business operations over the long term, which is the prospect for the ten years and so on, once again Brazil received special attention from Japanese investors (Table 8). Over the long term, Brazil ranks in the top ten countries for all years during the period 1997-2007, followed by China, the U.S., Russia, and some Asian countries. The ranking in Table 8 clearly show that since year 2002, the so-called BRICs economies have increasing its importance as a promising market for Japanese companies in the long term strategy. This also reinforces the attractiveness of the Brazilian market for future destination of Japanese investment. Brazil ranks the fifth place in 2007 and for the fist time, the country is considered in a better position than the U.S. and Thailand, which are usually listed as traditional attractive destinations for Japanese business.

Table 9. Ten Major Japanese Investment Destinations (Manufacturing Industries)

Rank	2001	2002	2003
1	U.S.	U.S.	U.S.
2	Netherlands	France	Netherlands
3	U.K.	China	China
4	China	Belgium	Thailand
5	**Brazil**	U.K.	Indonesia
6	Philippines	Indonesia	Germany
7	Thailand	Thailand	Belgium
8	Singapore	**Brazil**	**Brazil**
9	Belgium	Taiwan	France
10	Indonesia	India	Australia

Source: Japan Bank for International Cooperation, JBIC Review No.11 (2004) p.77.

[1] Classification of main regions used in JBIC survey:
- ASEAN4: Thailand, Indonesia, Malaysia, the Philippines
- NIES: South Korea, Taiwan, Singapore, Hong Kong
- North America: U.S. and Canada
- EU: U.K., Germany, France, Italy, Netherlands, Belgium, Greece, Luxemburg, Denmark, Spain, Portugal, Austria, Finland, Sweden, Ireland
- Other Asian countries: including India and Vietnam

In addition, another result which includes the major Japanese FDI destinations in the manufacturing industries showed Brazil in the top ten ranking (Table 9). In 2001, Brazil ranks the fifth, followed the U.S., two Europeans countries (Netherlands and U.K.), and China. In 2002 and 2003, Brazil ranks the eighth, after the U.S., some European countries, China, and two ASEAN4 countries. Brazil is the only developing country outside the Asian region that was ranked in all years in this list, which emphasizes an important role that Brazil is playing as a host country for Japanese manufacturing industries.

Finally, according to JBIC survey, the three main purposes for Japanese companies making FDI in Brazil are related to the following factors: (1) stability of local currency; (2) local political and social situation; (3) availability of local financing. This implies that the policy implemented by the Brazilian government since 1994, which focused on the economic and political stability, clearly demonstrated as an important factor for attracting Japanese foreign investments. There are, however, some issues faced in Brazil by Japanese companies including security and social instability, intensive competition with others companies, as well as sense of instability regarding currency and costs (JBIC, 2007).

Nevertheless, the results of JBIC survey showed the growing interest of Japanese companies in emerging countries such as Brazil, which is the only developing country outside the Asian region ranked as the most promising Japanese FDI destinations over the medium and long term.

Conclusion

The background of the evolution of Japanese FDI in Brazil was first presented in this chapter by examining the initial process in the 1930s, two waves of investments during the 1950s and the 1970s, the current situation of Japanese FDI in the country including a discussion of the third wave of investments, and finally the view of Brazil as a potential host country for Japanese business operation.

In overall terms, the Japanese FDI in Brazil presented two main points. First, several ventures established in the country focused on investments in raw material sectors, including iron, steel, and nonferrous metals such as aluminum. These investments aim at securing a supply to the Japanese market. Although a large number of investments were associated with the joint projects during the 1970s, Japanese FDI in resource-related projects still continued in later periods. Recently, a number of investments are linked with the renewable sources of energy, particularly bioethanol.

Second, Japanese companies established subsidiaries in the manufacturing sector primarily directed at the Brazilian market with its enormous growth potential. Nevertheless, due to the Brazilian debt crisis and economic instability during the 1980s and the beginning of 1990s, almost for two decades the bilateral trade and investment relations between Brazil and Japan were marked by low dynamism. The level of FDI flows from Japan to Brazil was discreet to such an extent that the total stock of Japanese investments in the country during this period still reflects the level of decades prior to the 1980s. From the middle 1990s, Brazil experienced a dynamic transformation in its economy and industries, with macroeconomic stability, success in controlling inflation, privatization of telecommunications, transportation, and power services. Although Brazil still requires continuous improvement of the economic, political and structural environment, the country is driving continued FDI attractiveness.

In recent years, an increasing amount of Japanese investments in Brazil is occurring once again. Although the country is considered an important market for Japan as showed by the survey of promising destination of Japanese overseas investments conducted by JBIC, it remains far behind Asia. Despite the Asian financial crisis in 1997, Asia is still the strongest economic network for Japanese investments. At this time, however, Brazil is not viewed as a sole growth potential market, but also a platform to access a wider regional market including Mercosur, South and North America, Europe, and Africa. In this era of economic globalization, it is important to diversify its investments and Brazil may well represent an alternative for Japanese FDI rather than a mere continuation of old patterns. From the perspective that Brazil became an attractive destination of world FDI and a hub of the regional networks of production in South America, Japanese companies are definitely expected to make further commitments and advances in Brazil. It is still unclear, however, whether or not the recent investments will become in fact the "third wave" of Japanese FDI in Brazil, as pointed out by Yuji Watanabe, the president of JETRO-Brazil. Only after some years this question will be definitely answered.

References

Ajinomoto (2004) Steadily achieving goals – Annual Report 2004. *Ajinomoto Co., Inc.* Retrieved from http://www.ajinomoto.com/mx_03/ar/i_r/pdf/20040712_ar.pdf

Alencar, K. (2008, March 9) Toshiba abandona projeto de semicondutor no Brasil. *Folha de S. Paulo.* Retrieved from http://www1.folha.uol.com.br/folha/colunas/brasiliaonline/ult2307u379998.shtml

Amorim, W.D. (1991) Contraste e contato: Aspectos de relacionamento econômico entre Brasil e Japão. (Master thesis, Instituto de Relações Internacionais, Universidade of Brasília).

Asahi Shimbun (2004, September 4) Toyota targets BRICs. *The Asahi Shimbun.* Retrieved from Factiva database (Document ASAH000020040903e0940000c)

A.T. Kearney (2004) *FDI Confidence Index: Global Business Policy Council* Volume 7. Vienna: A.T. Kearney Inc.

A.T. Kearney (2005) *FDI Confidence Index: Global Business Policy Council Volume* **8**. Alexandria: A.T. Kearney Inc.

A.T. Kearney (2007) *New concerns in an uncertainty world: The 2007 A.T. Kearney foreign direct investment confidence index.* Vienna: A.T. Kearney Inc.

BACEN (2008) Séries temporais: Investimento estrangeiro direto. *Banco Central do Brasil.* Retrieved from http://www.bcb.gov.br/?INVED

CNI & Nippon Keidanren (2007) Declaração conjunta sobre o fortalecimento das relações econômicas Brasil-Japão. *XII Reunião do Comitê Brasil-Japão, CNI-Nippon Keidanren.* Retrieved from http://box129.bluehost.com/~camarado/pt/images/M_images/a-07-03-06-declaracao-pot.pdf

Delanghe, H. (1999) Japanese imports of Brazilian raw cotton in the second half of the 1930s: The beginning of significant Japanese-Brazilian trade and investment relations. *História Econômica & História de Empresas,* **2**(2), 83-101.

Exame (1999, January 27) A nova tendência dos investimentos japoneses no Brasil. *Revista Exame,* **669**.

Gusmão, L. (2008, January 17) TV digital e álcool abrem nova relação econômica entre Brasil e Japão. *Folha de S. Paulo*. Retrieved from http://www1.folha.uol.com.br/folha/dinheiro/ult91u364433.shtml

Handa, T. (1976) *Burajiru Nihon Iminshi Nenbyô* (Chronology of the history of Japanese migrants in Brazil). São Paulo: Centro de Estudos Nipo-Brasileiros.

Hollerman, L. (1988) *Japan's economic strategy in Brazil: Challenges for the United States*. Lexington: Lexington Books.

Horisaka, K. (1997) Alvorada das relações econômicas nipo-brasileiras. In P. Yokota (Ed.), *Fragmentos sobre as relaçoes nipo-brasileiras no pós-guerra* (pp.33-78). Rio de Janeiro. Topbooks.

IMF (2007) World economic and financial surveys - World economic outlook database. October 2007 Edition. *International Monetary Fund*. Retried from http://www.imf.org/external/pubs/ft/weo/2007/02/weodata/index.aspx

Japan Times (2007a, March 29) Sumitomo Metal, Vallourec target Brazil, China. *The Japan Times Online*. Retrieved from http://search.japantimes.co.jp/cgi-bin/nb20070329a6.html

Japan Times (2007b, August 27) Brazil priming ethanol initiative to supply fuel-thirsty Japan. *The Japan Times Online*. Retrieved from http://search.japantimes.co.jp/cgi-bin/nb20070822a3.html

Japan Times (2008, March 15) Mitsui, Petrobras ink bioethanol deal. *The Japan Times Online*. Retrieved from http://search.japantimes.co.jp/cgi-bin/nb20080315a6.html

JBIC (2007) Survey report on overseas business operations by Japanese manufacturing companies - Results of JBIC FY2007 Survey: Outlook for Japanese Foreign Direct Investment (19th Annual Survey). *Japan Bank for International Cooperation*. Retrieved from http://www.jbic.go.jp/autocontents/english/news/2007/000150/index.htm

JETRO (2001) *JETRO White paper on Foreign Direct Investment 2001: Accelerated corporate realignment through mergers and acquisitions*. Tokyo: Japan External Trade Organization.

Manzini, G. (2008, February 22) Brazil e Japão cunham moedas pelo centenário da imigração japonesa. *Folha de S. Paulo*. Retrieved from http://www1.folha.uol.com.br/folha/cotidiano/ult95u374900.shtml

Marubeni (2007) Establishment of production/distribution company for bio-diesel fuel in Brazil. *Marubeni Corporation News Release*. Retrieved from http://www.marubeni.com/news/2007/070222e.html

MHI (2004, November 15) MHI to establish 4 new overseas subsidiaries: Boosting presence in Brazil, India, Singapore and Korea. *Mitsubishi Heavy Industries News Release*. Retrieved from http://www.mhi.co.jp/en/news/sec1/200411151029.html

MOF (1983) Taigai chokusetsu toushi [Foreign direct investment]. *Zaisei kinyuu toukei geppou 356 [Financial Statistics of Japan, Monthly Report 356]*. Ministry of Finance of Japan. Retrieved from http://www.mof.go.jp/kankou/hyou/g356/356_b.pdf

MOF (1991) Toukei Taigai chokusetsu toushi [Statistics on Foreign direct investment]. *Zaisei kinyuu toukei geppou 476 [Financial Statistics of Japan, Monthly Report 476]*. Ministry of Finance of Japan. Retrieved from http://www.mof.go.jp/kankou/hyou/g476/476_03_01.xls

MOFA (2008) Japan-Brazil relations. *The Ministry of Foreign Affairs of Japan*. Retrieved from http://www.mofa.go.jp/region/latin/brazil/

Nakasumi, T., & Yamashiro, J. (1992) Fim da imigração e consolidação da nova colônia nikkei. In Comissão de Elaboração da História dos 80 Anos da Imigração Japonesa no Brasil (Eds.) *Uma Epopéia Moderna: 80 Anos da Imigração Japonesa no Brasil* (pp.381-458). São Paulo: Hucitec/Sociedade Brasileira de Cultura Japonesa.

Nikkei (2008, March 25) Nippon Steel to build Y500bn-plus furnace complex in Brazil. *Nikkei Net Interactive.* Retrieved from http://www.nni.nikkei.co.jp/AC/TNKS/Nni20080324D24JFF06.htm

Nippon Keidanren & CNI (2000) Brazil-Japan "Alliance for the 21st century". Retrieved from www.keidanren.or.jp/english/policy/2000/053.html

Nippon Keidanren (2004) Request for early start of intergovernmental study of the Japan-Brazil economic partnership agreement (EPA) – Report on the Japan-Brazil EPA. Retrieved from http://www.keidanren.or.jp/english/policy/2004/044.html

Nunes, P.H.F. (2006) As relações Brasil-Japão e seus reflexos no processo de ocupação do território brasileiro. *Caminhos de Geografia*, **6**(19), 90-101.

Okubaro, J. (2007, July 17) Investimentos, a terceira onde de cooperação. *O Estado de S. Paulo.* Retrieved from http://www.estadao.com.br/ext/especiais/2007/07/imigracaojaponesa/14.htm

Otta, L.A. (2007, July 17) Brasil-Japão: a parceria do século 21. *O Estado de S.Paulo.* Retrieved from http://www.estadao.com.br/ext/especiais/2007/07/imigracaojaponesa/18.htm

Ozawa, T., Pluciennik, M., & Rao K.N. (1976) Japanese direct investment in Brazil. *The Columbia Journal of World Business,* **11**(3), 107-116.

Segalla, A. (2006, June 7) Os japoneses estão de volta. *Revista Exame*, **869**.

Siqueira, J. (2003) Japanese political culture under the realist perspective with reference to the Nipo-Brazilian relations. *Sincronía Verano*, **2**. Retrieved from http://sincronia.cucsh.udg.mx/nipobraz.htm

Shiffer, S.R. (2002) Sao Paulo: Articulating a cross-border region. In S. Sassen (Ed.), *Global Network: Linked cities* (pp.209-236). New York: Routledge.

Suzuki, N. (1995) Nihon Ijû To Nichi-Haku Keizai Kankei [Japanese emigration and Japanese-Brazilian economic relations]. In Nihon Burajiru Chûô Kyôkai (Eds.) *Nihon Burajiru Kôryûshi. Nichi-Haku Kankei 100nen No Kaiko To Tenbô* [History of the Japanese-Brazilian exchange. Recollection and prospect of 100 Years of Japanese-Brazilian relations] (pp.149-164). Tokyo: Nihon Burajiru Chûô Kyôkai.

Tonooka, E. (1998) Investimento direto japonês direto na década de 80: Uma análise dos seus determinantes no Brasil e no mundo (Doctoral dissertation, Faculdade de Economia, Administração e Contabilidade, Universidade de São Paulo).

Toyo Keizai (2006) *Kaigai Shinshutsu Kigyou Souran: Kuni Betsu* [Japanese overseas investments: By country]. Tokyo: Toyo Keizai Inc.

Uehara, A.R. (1999) Brazil and Japan: Bringing the antipodes closer together? *Asia-América Latina*, **7**(1). Retrieved from http://www.eurosur.org/FLACSO/asiamer/ing199.htm

Uehara, A.R. (2006) O crescimento econômico e os investimentos diretos japoneses no Brasil. *Revista Eletrônica Ponto de Encontro de Ex-Fellow, Fundação Japão,* **2**. Retrieved from www.fjsp.org.br/estudos/ed%2002/crescimento_economico.doc

UNCTAD (2005) *Prospects for foreign direct investment and the strategies of transnational corporations, 2005-2008*. New York & Geneva: United Nations Publication.

Wilson, D., & Purushothaman, R. (2003) Dreaming with BRICs: The path to 2050. *Goldman Sachs Global Economics Paper,* **99**, 1-23.

Yokota, P. (1998) *Fragmentos sobre as relações nipo-brasileiras no pós-guerra*. Rio de Janeiro: Topbooks

In: Foreign Direct Investment
Editor: Harrison G. Blaine, pp. 21-43
ISBN: 978-1-60456-921-6
© 2009 Nova Science Publishers, Inc.

Chapter 2

Labour Market Flexibility as a Key Determinant of Foreign Direct Investment: Evidence from the UK

Philip B. Whyman[1] and Mark Baimbridge[2]
[1]University of Central Lancashire, UK
[2]University of Bradford, UK

Abstract

There are many determinants of FDI, including factors related to market access and demand, risk factors including (though not exclusively) political and legal stability, the desire to gain access to natural resources and policy-related variables. For policy-makers, the ability to influence inward investment flows may extend to all of these areas, for example, in relation to deregulating market access, promoting a high growth strategy (to extend market size) and liberalising access to raw materials. Alternatively, government potentially has a more direct influence over variables such as exchange rate policy, environmental protection, infrastructure, taxation, together with human resource quality and availability. Hence, it is not surprising that a strategic approach toward the attraction of FDI might focus upon these factors.

This chapter concentrates upon labour market flexibility as a key determinant of FDI, both in terms of its relative importance vis-à-vis other attractors of inward investment, but also in terms of the significance of the constituent characteristics of this aggregate variable. The UK economy is a good case study for an evaluation of this type, as it embodies both a relatively flexible labour market, certainly in terms of its regulatory framework, and is consistently one of the leading recipients of FDI.

Drawing upon a primary dataset, generated through a government-funded study, the chapter examines the drivers for FDI, disaggregated according to sector, business strategy type and technological risk. It additionally examines the potential for policy conflict and misdirection, due to a lack of targeting upon those specific characteristics most attractive to inward investors.

Introduction

This chapter seeks to investigate the interaction between Foreign Direct Investment (FDI) and labour market flexibility, in terms of its importance as a key determinant of inward investment flows. The ability to attract FDI depends upon many different factors, including the relative development of physical and informational infrastructure, wealth and growth rates of national (and/or regional) markets, factor endowments, skill levels and quality of training, political stability and possession of raw materials, in addition to policy measures favouring business development. Such policy factors include relative tax rates, levels of regulation, provision of location incentives and the existence of labour market rigidities.

It is, however, upon the issue of such rigidities that this chapter concentrates. This is due in large part to the identification of labour market flexibility as facilitating superior financial performance and higher levels of productivity at firm level (Kling, 1995; Ichniowski *et al*, 1996; Becker and Huselid, 1998). Moreover, the degree of flexibility in the labour market is associated with the achievement of favourable macroeconomic benefits including lower levels of unemployment and reducing inflationary bottlenecks, thereby reducing the economy's Non-Accelerating Inflation Rate of Unemployment (NAIRU) (OECD 1994a and 1994b; Nickell and Layard, 1999). These conclusions are not, however, universally shared as other studies have found no significant impact arising from labour market deregulation (OECD, 1999:88; Blanchard and Wolfers, 2000; Arestis and Sawyer, 2004:93). Nevertheless, the UK government's position is that 'flexible and dynamic markets' are considered to be 'a precondition for economic strength' (HM Treasury, 2003:239).

The United Kingdom (UK) has been selected as the focus of this chapter because it is a good case study for an evaluation of this type, as the economy embodies both a relatively flexible labour market and is consistently one of the leading recipients of FDI. Indeed, in 2006, the UK ranked second only to the USA in terms of inward FDI flows (UNCTAD, 2006). The evidence presented in this chapter is drawn from a study undertaken for the UK government, and utilises primary data, generated from a sample drawn from a questionnaire distributed to 1800 Trans-National Corporations (TNCs), all of whom possess existing production facilities in the UK. The study sought to identify drivers influencing the location of investment flows selected by leading decision-makers in TNCs. Factors were disaggregated according to sector, the type of business strategy pursued by the investor organisations and the degree of technological risk involved in the production process or service delivery. The results were used to comment upon the potential for policy conflict and misdirection, caused in part by a lack of targeting upon those specific characteristics most attractive to inward investors.

Implications of FDI Inflows

There are a number of general benefits of FDI, all of which contribute to higher economic growth through its impact upon domestic saving, foreign exchange, investment, employment, trade, tax, income distribution, technology transfer, human capital, competition, enterprise development and the environment. In particular, an inflow of FDI contributes to the home country's development by helping to reduce the shortage of domestic savings and by increasing the supply of foreign exchange (Meier, 1968). Moreover, FDI increases the level of investment in the home country and the level of employment (OECD, 1987). In addition, FDI may integrate the home economy more closely into the world economy in a process likely to include higher imports as well as exports (OECD, 2002). Furthermore, profits generated by FDI contribute to corporate tax revenues in the home country (Loungani and Razin, 2001). FDI may make income distribution in host developing countries less unequal, since the accumulation of human capital has an equalizing impact on income distribution (UNCTAD, 1999).

Technology transfer is perhaps the most important channel through which foreign companies may produce positive externalities in the host country, whereby TNCs are the developed world's most important source of corporate research and development (R&D) activity, whereby they generally possess a higher level of technology than is available in developing countries, so they have the potential to generate considerable technological spillovers (OECD, 2002). Consequently, domestic firms may become more productive by imitating the more advanced technologies. Whilst in the absence of FDI, acquiring the necessary information for adopting new technologies is too costly for local firms. Thus, FDI lowers the cost of technology adoption and may expand the set of technologies available to local firms (Lensink and Morrissey, 2001).

Additionally, FDI can enhance human capital in the host country, whereby foreign investors may provide working training which can not be replicated in domestic firms or purchased from abroad, such as managerial skills. Furthermore, technology diffusion may occur through labour turnover as domestic employees move from foreign to domestic firms (Meier and Rauch, 2005). Additionally, by purchasing raw materials or intermediate goods a strong buyer-seller relationship may develop that gives rise to technical assistance or training from the foreign firm to the domestic firm (Lensink and Morrissey, 2001).

A further potential benefit is that FDI may make domestic companies more competitive whereby the entry of foreign companies may provoke local companies to protect their profits, and hence increase productivity. An increase in productivity may occur as existing technology and resources are more efficiently exploited, by the use of new and more efficient technology, or through the copying of technology used by foreign companies (Soreide, 2001). Consequently, FDI has the potential to spur enterprise development in host countries through the achievement of synergies within the acquiring TNC, efforts to raise efficiency and reduce costs in the targeted enterprise, and the development of new activities. In addition, efficiency gains may occur in unrelated enterprises through demonstration effects and other spillovers akin to those that lead to technology and human capital spillovers (OECD, 2002).

Finally, FDI has the potential to bring social and environmental benefits to host economies through the dissemination of good practices and technologies within TNCs and through their subsequent spillovers to domestic enterprises. (OECD, 2002). There are, however, a number of potential costs to FDI that may be detrimental to the host country's development in relation to government expenditure, domestic saving, terms of trade, balance of payments, overinvestment, resource allocation, competition, adjustment costs, and environment.

To attract foreign capital, the government of the host country may have to provide special facilities, extend financial assistance or subsidize inputs to the foreign enterprise. These have an opportunity cost in absorbing governmental resources that could be used elsewhere. In encouraging foreign investment, there is thus a fiscal cost through increased government expenditure of forgone revenue. FDI may reduce domestic saving in the home country if the foreign investment competes with home investment and reduces profits in domestic industries. Moreover, the terms of trade may worsen when there is a return flow of capital from the borrowing country, then the net gain from foreign capital will be diminished. In addition, when a country is not currently earning sufficient foreign exchange to cover the external servicing of the foreign investment, the adverse effects of measures designed to re-equilibrate the balance of payments will entail indirect costs of foreign investment (Meier, 1968).

Secondly, there may be the problem of overinvestment whereby through FDI, foreign investors gain crucial inside information about the productivity of the firms under their control. This gives them an informational advantage over 'uninformed' domestic savers, whose buying of shares in domestic firms does not entail control. Taking advantage of this superior information, foreign direct investors will tend to retain high-productivity firms under their ownership and control and sell low-productivity firms to the uninformed savers. As with other so-called adverse-selection problems of this kind, this process may lead to overinvestment by foreign direct investors (Loungani and Razin, 2001).

When FDI is geared toward serving domestic markets that are protected by high-tariff or non-tariff barriers, it may become a political-economy lobbying facility to perpetuate the misallocation of resources. There could also be a loss of domestic competition that can arise when foreign acquisitions lead to a consolidation in the number of domestic producers, either through takeovers or corporate failures. (Loungani and Razin, 2001).

While the overall impact of FDI on enterprise development and productivity is almost always positive, it generally also brings distributional changes and a need for industrial restructuring in the host country. Changes give rise to adjustment costs and are resisted by social groups that do not expect to be among the beneficiaries. Structural rigidities in the host economy exacerbate such costs, not least where labour markets are too slow to provide new opportunities for individuals touched by restructuring (OECD, 2002). Finally, there may be some potential harmful environmental impacts especially in the extractive and heavy industries (OECD, 2002).

Trends in FDI Flows

FDI flows tend to follow a business cycle fluctuation, albeit on a rising trend across different cycles. This can be seen in the following two diagrams. Thus, Figure 1 illustrates that global FDI inflows decreased between 1990 and 1991, whilst from 1991 onwards they increased substantially and rose to a peak level in 2000. According to UNCTAD (2006), inflow trends are driven by cross-border mergers and acquisitions (M&A) especially in developed countries. However, from an all-time high level in 2000, world FDI inflows fell by more than 40 percent in 2001, returning it to the inflow level previously occurring in 1998.

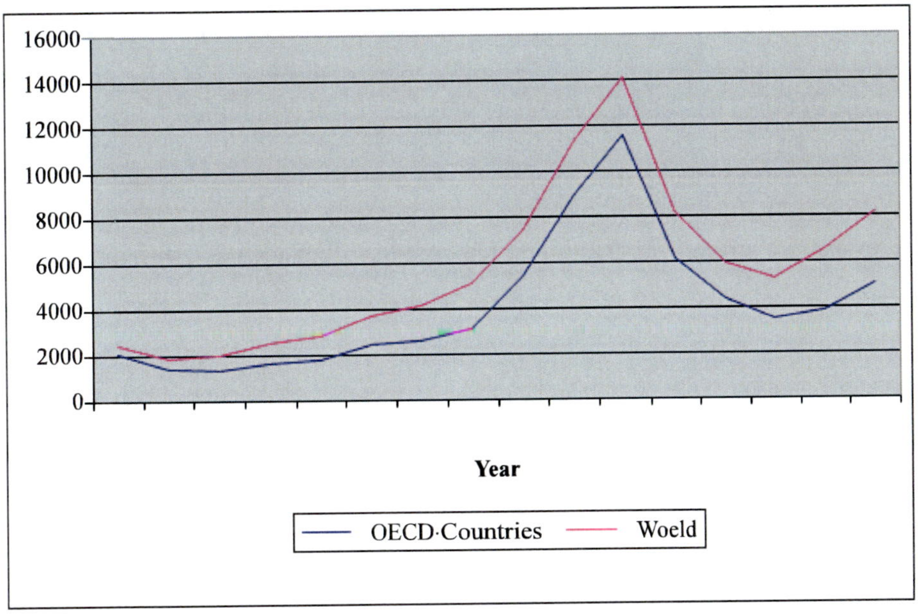

Data source: UNCTAD (2006).

Figure 1. Global and OECD FDI inflows 1990-2005 ($m constant).

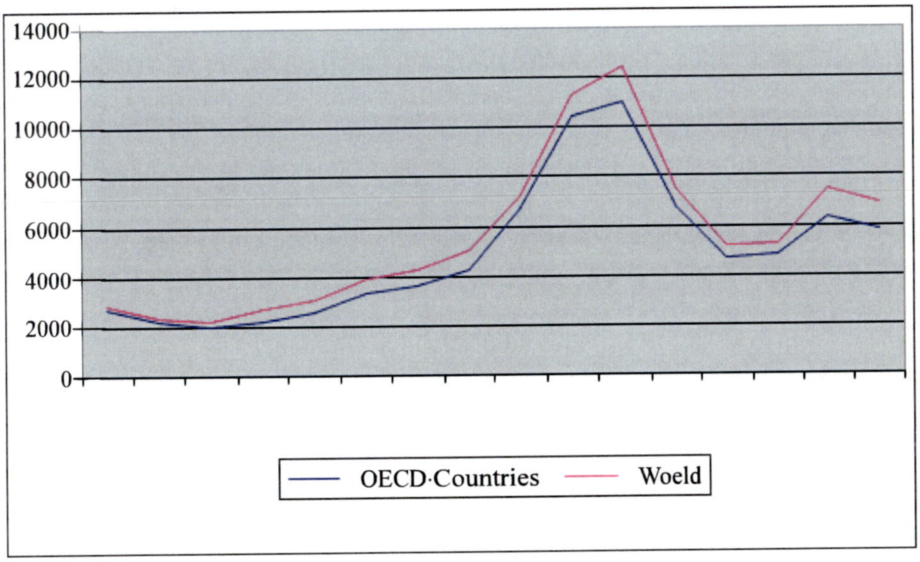

Data source: UNCTAD (2006).

Figure 2. Global and OECD FDI outflows 1990-2005 ($m constant).

This reversal, after steady growth since 1991 and very large rises in 1999 and 2000, reflects two factors. Firstly, the slowing of economic activity in major industrial economies and a sharp decrease in their stock market activity, which combined to slow down new international investment, particularly the cross-border M&As that have driven FDI. Secondly, the slowdown in FDI in reflects that in the world economy, whereby more than a dozen countries, including the world's three largest economies fell into recession in 2001. Additionally, the events of 11 September 2001 probably exacerbated the slowdown and may also have contributed to the further decline in FDI in 2002 and 2003 (UNCTAD, 2002). However, by 2004, cross-border M&As started to pick up following three years of decline (UNCTAD, 2005). The pattern of OECD countries is very similar to the global pattern, suggesting that OECD countries account for a significant proportion of world inflows and therefore tend to drive global FDI patterns.

In terms of FDI outflows, figure 2 illustrates that global FDI outflows followed a similar pattern to that for inflows, whereby they fell between 1990 and 1992 and rose rapidly until 2000.

From 2000, we again see the decline for the next 3 years. However, the recovery is short lived as there is a further peak decline in 2004-05. This is in contrast to the rising trend of inflows illustrated in Figure 1. Once again the pattern of OECD countries is very similar to global trends with an even greater proximity between the lines. Consequently, when considering global FDI flows, it is apparent that the OECD countries encompass the significant proportion and FDI inflows are between OECD countries.

Determinants of FDI

FDI may be defined as capital invested for the purpose of acquiring a lasting interest in an enterprise, whilst simultaneously exerting a degree of influence on its operations. It is this combination of ownership and control that distinguishes FDI from other forms of trans-national investment and/or production, such as portfolio investment (i.e. ownership of financial assets without the same degree of direct control) and franchising (i.e. control over production technology and process but without ownership) (Dunning, 1979).

The international business literature proposes that firms tend to consider FDI once they have developed certain competitive advantages that they feel they can more effectively exploit by engaging in a strategic location of production abroad rather than export goods and services, whilst maintaining direct control over the process to minimise transaction costs, technological and other elements of the production process, together with organisation knowledge (Morgan, 1997). Assuming rational action, firms must be responding to, firstly, incentives to locate production abroad, rather than export from their existing home base, and secondly, a separate set of incentives to internalise the production process. The latter may centre upon the perceived risk inherent within the principal-agent problem, whereby the reliance upon an agent to fulfil objectives established by the principal might lead to sub-optimal solutions, due to differences in self-interest, and may require costly solutions, involving the provision of additional incentives for the agent or otherwise intensive monitoring of their activities. Risk of this nature may include the threat of theft of technological knowledge, or, less dramatically, the provision of greater opportunities for the diffusion of technological knowledge, and hence erosion of competitive advantage, together with possible loss of reputation and goodwill due to the operations of low quality franchise operations.

There are many inter-related determinants of FDI and the ultimate decision for a TNC to invest in a particular country depends upon a composite of these various variables. The United Nations World Investment Report (UNCTAD, 1998) argued that FDI arises due to a combination of, firstly, host country (or locational) determinants, based upon the social and economic factors together with the attractiveness of government policy framework for the attraction of FDI, and secondly, the strategic motives of TNCs. This is illustrated in Figure 3.

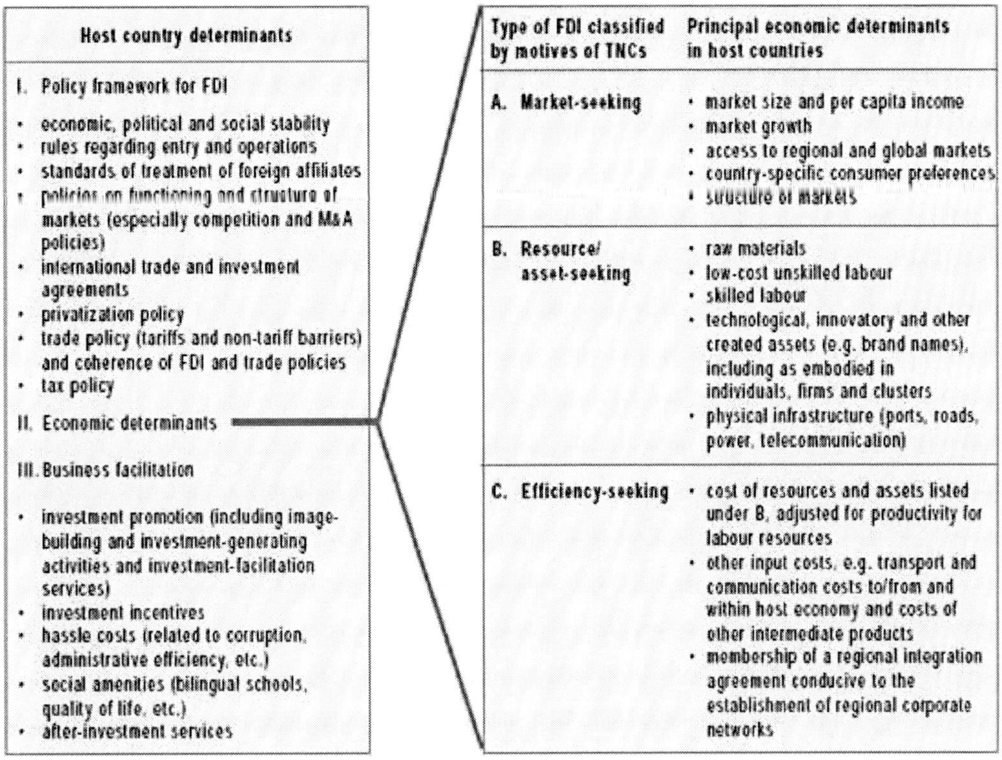

Source: UNCTAD (1998:91).

Figure 3. Host Country Determinants of FDI.

Subsequently, this representation of the determinants of FDI can be categorised in terms of risk, cost and demand:

Minimising Risk

TNCs prefer to minimise the risk associated with their investments, and therefore they favour the combination of a stable political climate together with a dependable macroeconomic framework (Wheeler and Mody, 1992). Hence, in terms of macroeconomic effects, high rates of inflation, budget deficits and government debt (associated with future inflationary pressures), together with unpredictable fluctuations in exchange rates, threaten to erode the financial value of the assets purchased or developed by the inward investor, and thereby increase the risk premium of FDI in that particular nation. Risk is further minimised through investor preference for a secure and transparent legal framework, designed to protect their property and security of their business contracts. Additional attractive policy-related factors include the maintenance of a reasonable rate of economic growth, low costs of borrowing (via a low rate of interest), low levels of taxation and/or the provision of specific investment incentives intended to lower the cost of inward investment. Furthermore, the potential offered by privatisation, through potential undervaluing of former state assets and/or the opportunity provided to purchase strategically valuable assets, has further encouraged increases in FDI throughout the past two decades.

Demand Factors

The size and growth rate of the national and/or regional market is of great significance, since it is primarily to serve this market by localised production, rather than export from the home nation (or region), that FDI occurs (Culem, 1988). However, to the extent that goods or services (or components) are traded, the evidence tends to suggest that investors prefer nations with relatively liberal trade regimes, perhaps some type of regional supra-national trade arrangement, such as the European Union single market, NAFTA, ASEAN and so forth.

National-Specific Factors

These may relate to the existence of a natural resource, technology or production method protected by legal patent, to which the TNC wishes to gain access (Neven and Siotis, 1996).

Cost Factors

FDI is influenced by the relative cost of production and distribution within potential host nations, which is in turn affected by the quality and reliability of physical and communications infrastructure, relative unit costs, the cost and ease of access to raw materials and the cost of capital. Government policy can influence these variables, through infrastructure investment, monetary policy maintaining a relatively low rate of interest, deregulation of financial markets and the promotion of a labour market characterised by a flexible supply and use of human resources. It is this aspect of FDI that the paper now examines in greater detail.

Characteristics of Labour Market Flexibility

Labour market flexibility derives from the degree to which labour market outcomes are determined by the operation of market forces free from rigidities and/or restrictions imposed by powerful actors such as monopsony employers, trade unions and government. A perfectly flexible labour market would imply the absence of all hindrances to the free operation of market forces. This not only includes examples of labour market regulation (e.g. job protection legislation) and institutional arrangements (e.g. systems of sectoral wage bargaining), but also unorganised forms of market imperfection (e.g. resulting from insider-outsider power imbalances and/or irrational employment practices arising from labour market segmentation or discrimination). Furthermore, there is a sizeable literature pointing to the existence of labour market inflexibility due to various factors, including implicit contracts, efficiency wages, transaction costs in the renegotiation of contracts and incentives provided due to the principle-agent problem (Bosworth *et al*, 1996). Finally, certain types of labour market inflexibility are more easily subject to corrective government policy reforms, whilst others appear more intractable.

The literature on labour market flexibility denotes a range of different factors that, in aggregate, determine the extent to which the labour market is comparatively more or less flexible. At any one moment, it is possible that a number of these characteristics of flexibility are moving towards greater flexibilisation whereas others are indicating increasing rigidities. This can explain why labour markets that are generally considered as exhibiting a high degree of flexibility nevertheless contain features that depart significantly from this norm. For example, the fact that US and UK labour markets have a relatively low incidence of temporary workers as a proportion of the total workforce does not necessarily imply labour market rigidity, but rather reflects the fact that employers are relatively unencumbered by labour market regulation and are therefore more able to hire and fire core workers without having to resort to other forms of non-standard employment contract to avoid regulation and pursue the flexibility agenda through a core-periphery split (Robinson, 2000:36).

Additionally, there are a number of different typologies that run throughout the literature. One emphasises the fact that labour market flexibility is concerned with both *micro* and *macro* issues. For example, whereas the pay structure for an individual firm would have considerable significance for micro-flexibility, it would have little influence upon the macro-flexibility of the economy as a whole; the latter being concerned with matters such as national wage bargaining institutions and the resultant real wage flexibility. Similarly, micro-flexibility would focus upon the impact of increasing self-employment and growth in temporary employment at firm level, whereas macro-flexibility would be concerned with deregulation of the regulation of working time, together with various labour market programmes (Beatson, 1995).

Flexibility characteristics can be further identified with the concepts of numerical and functional flexibility (Weiss 2001), whereby the former concerns the capacity to adapt the quantity of labour inputs to changing demand patterns. This could relate to a shift in the numbers of potential workers willing to work at the going wage rate (perhaps due to a reduction in reservation wages), changes in the value or duration of social benefit entitlements, active labour market policies, a shift in relative trade union bargaining power, and/or changing employment regulations which impinge upon the cost of hiring and firing workers (and hence firm demand for new labour). It might similarly involve temporal flexibility (namely the capacity to introduce variability in working time whether through changes in holidays), the length of the working week, shift working patterns and overtime working. Alternatively, numerical flexibility might be enhanced through shifts towards non-standard employment, through an increase in part-time working, temporary employment contracts, sub-contracting job tasks outside the core organisation, home-working, and consultancy.

In contrast, functional flexibility embraces work reorganisation initiatives in the attempt to increase efficiency and/or adapt to changing patterns of product demand. Examples include the introduction of multi-skilling (or multi-tasking) and reduction in job demarcation, the enhancement of employee participation within the workplace and 'teamworking', together with measures to sub-contract elements of production to external actors. Inspired by the philosophies of 'lean production', 'just-in-time-production' and 'total quality management' (Hackman and Wageman, 1995), functional flexibility may encompass initiatives designed to flatten organisational hierarchies and thereby reduce bureaucratic overheads (Hudson, 2002:44).

Subsequently, this conceptual framework was extended by Monastiriotis (2003), through the addition of a third category, namely labour costs (i.e. flexibility in pay and non-wage costs). Hence, wage flexibility is perceived to be a central element in achieving labour market flexibility through its adjustment to maintain the balance between demand for, and supply of, labour. Consequently, such developments can explain the initiative introduced by the UK government to promote regional variations in those areas of the public sector currently utilising national pay bargaining (HM Treasury, 2003:244-7). Moreover, wage flexibility can be affected by the development of industrial relations legislation and government action as employer relating to promotion or restriction of trade union activity (Carruth and Disney, 1988).

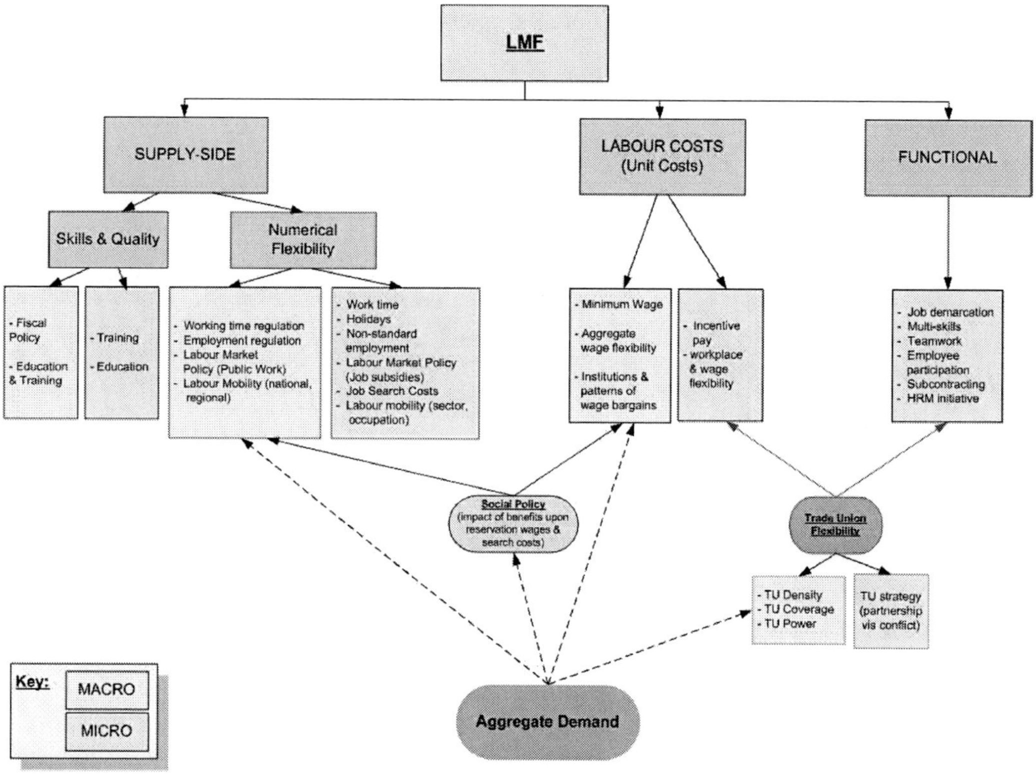

Figure 4. Labour Market Flexibility.

The synthesis of the literature, illustrated in Figure 4, highlights the multi-faceted nature of labour market flexibility, together with the potential for conflict between the different types of flexibility, thereby potentially partially offsetting reform objectives. For example, deregulating employee training regimes to workplace level might improve firm flexibility and hence micro-flexibility, but if the result is a decline in aggregate training, as competitive pressures squeeze individual training budgets, then aggregate macro-flexibility may be reduced over time (ILO, 2004:191-220). Similarly, the decentralisation of wage formation may facilitate pay structures best suited to the incentive structures sought by individual managers, yet the rise in pay diversity in the labour market as a whole, together with the removal of the moderating effect of peak level bargaining partners, might provoke increased industrial unrest and hence damage macro-flexibility.

A second issue relates to the *means* by which flexibilisation is pursued. Research indicates that work intensification, downsizing, flattening hierarchies and giving employees greater responsibility, are all associated with heightened feelings of anxiety and stress, which, in turn, may result in demoralisation and demotivation of concerned employees, thereby impairing productivity (Wichert, 2002). Similarly, the OCED acknowledged potential costs associated with an expansion in 'non-regular' forms of employment, including potential conflict between certain forms of greater flexibility of working hours and family life responsibilities. Thus, if initiatives are incorrectly designed, the extraction of functional, numerical and labour-cost flexibility may be secured at the expense of attitudinal and/or behavioural inflexibility, thereby reducing the net value of potential gains (Mankelow, 2002:137).

A third, distinctive feature of this synthesis concerns the theoretical limitations demonstrated by much of the existing literature relating to the assumption that employment is determined by supply-side factors in the labour market and is not therefore influenced by aggregate demand. This is questionable given that it is well established that the level of demand impacts upon many of the other variables outlined in this chapter. For example, research indicates that the level of aggregate demand has a significant impact upon trade union activity and the optimality of wage bargaining institutions and patterns of bargaining (Calmfors and Driffill, 1988). Furthermore, aggregate demand is closely related to the degree of capacity pertaining in an economy at any given time and this, in turn, is associated with encouraging industrial investment, enhancing productivity and acting as a significant determinant of the level of unemployment (Rowthorn, 1995; Arestis and Mariscal, 2000:487). Demand factors therefore influence the labour supply curve, thereby affecting numerical flexibility, whilst the buoyancy of the economy may influence the replacement ratio, degree of wage flexibility and willingness of employees to accept certain types of non-standard employment.

Labour Market Flexibility as a Key Determinant of FDI?

The evidence of the impact of labour costs on FDI is mixed, but tends to indicate a negative association (OECD, 2000; Floyd, 2003). Nevertheless, it remains the case that four-fifths of the world stock of FDI is located in the high-wage and relatively high-tax nations, primarily the USA, UK, Germany and Canada, where this proportion has *increased* by 12 per cent over two decades (Weiss, 1998:186). Indeed, alternative evidence suggests that labour costs are not ranked very highly amongst other determinants of FDI (Traxler and Woitech, 2000), such that a majority of UK-owned TNCs do not collect data on overall labour costs and labour productivity (Marginson *et al*, 1996), and that sizeable (and growing) differences in unit labour costs, amongst EU nations during the 1980s, failed to result in significant differences in FDI (Erickson and Kuruvilla, 1994). Moreover, absolute figures for labour costs may mis-specify the indicator as a determinant of FDI due to the higher level of capital (both physical and human) investment in developed nations resulting in higher rates of productivity, whereby their unit labour costs may actually be lower than in low-wage, less developed nations. Therefore, unit labour costs may be a more preferable indicator to inward investors than the level of wages and/or non-wage costs per se.

A further potential labour market influence upon FDI relates to the issue of regulation which is generally perceived to be a disadvantage for a nation seeking to attract FDI, and particularly so for those industries subject to a greater than average risk of failure, whereby exit costs from a particular market become increasingly important. Thus, many studies indicate that flexible labour markets characterised by low closure costs are significant attractors for FDI (Bentolila and Bertola, 1990). Similarly, Dewit *et al.* (2003) found that differences in employment protection between nation states is a significant determinant of FDI location, and that this effect increases the higher the cost associated with FDI; although this is partially tempered by the fact that domestic levels of employment protection discourages outward flows of FDI.

However, not all studies have discovered a statistically significant link between labour market regulation and job creation (Leonard and Schettkat, 1991), rather it is a stylistic fact that FDI tends to be higher in countries with stronger employment rights. In response to this Kucera (2002:63) suggests that this contradiction with the 'conventional wisdom' might derive from the fact that the non-wage advantages associated with these nations outweigh the dissuasive impact of higher labour costs. An alternative rationalisation focuses upon the differential risk of failure facing 'traditional' and 'innovative' firms, with the former more interested in entry costs and structural features of potential markets, whereas the latter may be more interested in exit costs due to their higher exposure to the risk of failure. Moreover, fact that the theoretical predictions that labour market rigidities impose resource costs is based upon the assumption of competitive markets, and therefore the recognition of the existence of market imperfections implies that certain forms of labour market regulation may have beneficial effects upon human capital investment and productivity (Addison and Teixeira, 2001:2-3).

Finally in relation to regulatory issues, employment protection measures may, under certain circumstances, reinforce commitment and loyalty to the employing firm, whereby the subsequent reduction in labour turnover costs, together with the maintenance of a trained workforce, may offset the perceived disadvantages related to labour market rigidities. Indeed, whilst labour market flexibility is an advantage in attracting FDI in markets with no strategic interaction between firms, this is not necessarily the case where strategic interaction occurs (Dewit *et al.*, cited in Haaland and Wooton, 2003).

In terms of industrial relations factors acting as potential determinants of FDI, the presence of trade unions tends to have an inconclusive impact, even though the relative weakness in trade union power is claimed to be amongst the UK's attractive features when seeking to attract FDI (Floyd, 2003). Similarly, the literature indicates that the institutional framework relating to wage formation significantly influences a nation's ability to attract FDI. Consequently, firm- or workplace-level wage determination enables remuneration packages to be tailored to the specific characteristics of the firm and its competitive environment, such that a high-risk TNC would pay correspondingly lower wages due to this risk factor. This would suggest that decentralisation facilitates labour market flexibility and would enhance the attractiveness of a host economy to potential inward investors. However, the literature is not so clear cut in its conclusions.

Haaland and Wooton (2003:19), for example, argue that a similar effect could be secured through an increase in labour market flexibility, and particularly through a reduction in employment protection, thereby lowering potential redundancy costs for the high-risk firm. Consequently, employment regulation and wage formation may be perceived as substitutes, as well as complements, and therefore the existence of firm-level wage determination implies that the relative flexibility of the national labour market no longer remains a significant determinant for inward investment.

In addition, the sizeable corporatist literature raises the possibility that *macro*, as opposed to *micro*, flexibility can be secured through co-ordinated, centralised wage bargaining, which thereby has the potential to secure a slower rate of growth in aggregate real wages, reduce labour turnover (with associated reduction in recruitment costs and possible productivity impact) and industrial conflict (Bruno and Sachs, 1985). Furthermore, through negotiation of wages independently of productivity in individual workplaces, centralised wage bargaining may promote structural change, as high productivity plants are able to create jobs due to a lower wage rate than the marginal productivity of labour, whilst a low productivity plant will shed labour for the opposite reason (Salvanes, 1997).

UK Labour Market Flexibility and FDI

The evidence presented here regarding FDI and labour market flexibility in the UK is derived from primary data collection, utilising a sample drawn from a questionnaire which was circulated to 1,800 TNCs with existing production operations located in the UK. The questionnaire utilised a combination of open and closed questions in order to combine standardised with less easily quantifiable data, in order to provide elucidation and greater emphasis upon those factors considered by the respondent to be particularly significant. From the questionnaires submitted, an error rate of 80 occurred associated with data imperfections in the database, together with a number of companies stating their policy to refrain from responding to any format requesting information, limited the effective sample. This has implications for the analysis and interpretation of this first tranche of data, together with the potential policy recommendations. However, given that the study was an exercise in primary data collection, together with the wide ranging nature of the survey which explored determinants of investment within the UK and associated labour market factors, the information gathered provides a unique insight into the underlying thought and decision-making process of large UK- and foreign-owned companies currently operating within the UK.

Employer surveys, although considered to be more subjective than data drawn from secondary sources, nevertheless contain information provided by business people who, presumably, are in the ideal position to denote those aspects of labour market flexibility that impact upon the location of FDI. Previous studies have tended to reply upon indexes derived from comparative surveys of employer attitudes relating to a variety of issues, including, for example, estimates of business competitiveness incorporated within annual *Global Competitiveness Report* (Porter *et al.*, 2004).

In relation to labour market factors, 61.4 per cent of all respondents identified labour market flexibility as a "very important" or "vitally important" determinant of FDI, although responses followed the earlier pattern of identifying this as a second-level factor, with twice as many individuals preferring the lesser characterisation of importance. Nevertheless, 30.5 per cent of respondents stated that labour market regulation imposed a large cost upon their business, with 62.7 per cent indicating a more moderate impact. Attempting to quantify the reduction in costs that could be secured via a more flexible labour market, respondents suggested an average of 15.4 per cent of variable, and 12.7 per cent of total, costs. Consequently, irrespective of whether labour market issues are second-level in terms of relative importance, their *perceived* potential absolute benefit to the companies concerned is most significant.

Disaggregating the constituent elements related to labour market flexibility, respondents assigned the greatest weight towards the availability of a highly skilled and educated labour force, functional flexibility, numerical flexibility (in terms of both time and non standard employment) and low levels of employment regulation. This is illustrated in Table 1. Wage-cost and industrial relations factors were considered to be less significant factors, whether relating to wage flexibility, the ease of introduction of pay incentives, form of wage formation, ease of operating HRM policies, the balance of labour relations laws benefiting employees and the potential to develop a favourable relationship with trade unions.

Table 1. Top 5 features of labour market flexibility for FDI

	Frequency (%)						
	1	2	3	4	5	Mean	SD
Availability of highly skilled / educated workforce	1.8	16.1	17.9	26.8	37.5	3.82	1.16
Flexibility in work context	1.8	5.5	23.6	49.1	20.0	3.80	0.89
Flexible use of work time	3.7	5.6	29.6	35.2	25.9	3.74	1.03
Low levels of employment regulation	7.4	7.4	25.9	24.1	35.2	3.72	1.23
Ease of use of non-standard employment	1.9	13.0	29.6	25.9	29.6	3.69	1.10

The weakest elements of a flexible labour market in terms of attracting FDI, relate to the creation of work incentives for the unemployed, whether through 'pull' factors such as provided through intensified job search services, improved pay via tax credits and a minimum wage, or 'push' factors related to the shortening of the duration of benefits, reduction of the replacement ratio and intensification of requirements placed upon unemployed individuals to actively seek work. This is perhaps not particularly surprising since TNCs place the importance of a skilled labour force at the top of their list of requirements and equate their own production strategy more closely with the type of differentiated-focus strategy, which relies upon skilled, multi-tasking employees, than low cost strategies that may employ traditional 'Fordist' techniques of employing unskilled and semi-skilled operatives. However, this finding tends to raise questions relating to whether the attraction of FDI is particularly appropriate for regional development in so far as directly tackling stubborn, long term unemployment, rather than playing an indirect role through attracting new, highly paid jobs to an area. An influx of FDI may facilitate the rise in regional aggregate demand, pulling additional jobs into the area, many of which may be more suitable for the skills base of the long term unemployed which tends to be lower than in the employed population as a whole.

When asked to prioritise labour market factors in terms of their significance in attracting FDI, respondent selections reinforced the earlier results. The importance of a highly trained, skilled labour force emerged as the most significant factor, which reinforced the findings from a number of supplementary questions in the survey. Indeed, fully 42 per cent of respondents selected this factor as their prime labour market attractor for FDI. One aspect of numerical flexibility, namely the flexible use of working time, was ranked the second most significant determinants of FDI, and yet, intriguingly, other aspects of numerical flexibility, including labour mobility and the ease of use of non-standard employment, were considered to be of relatively little importance. Third ranked elements of labour market flexibility were identified as functional flexibility, via facilitation of multi-skilling and reduction of demarcation in the workplace, together with a greater flexibility in terms of employment protection regulation.

In terms of the remaining factors, wage flexibility is ascribed more significance in this question in the survey to elsewhere, but this is pretty consistently in terms of individual respondents ranking it outside of their top three selections. Consequently, there does appear to be a consistent pattern arising from responses to the survey, where a more functionally and numerically flexible, highly skilled labour force is deemed to be more significant for a majority of inward investors than the degree of wage flexibility, state of industrial relations, form of wage formation, use of incentive pay and other aspects of wage-cost flexibility. Once again, government policy to provide incentives for the unemployed to seek work might be considered to be significant in terms of creating overall labour market flexibility, but it has little value as an attractor for FDI.

Table 2. Features of labour market flexibility (risk in technology)

		Level of risk in technology		
	Total sample	**High**	**Moderate**	**Low**
First-level				
Availability of highly skilled / educated workforce	3.82	4.89	3.73	3.38
Second-level				
Flexibility in work context	3.80	3.88	3.79	3.85
Flexible use of work time	3.74	3.38	3.88	3.67
Low levels of employment regulation	3.72	3.63	3.79	3.75
Ease of use of non-standard employment	3.69	3.88	3.76	3.50
Third-level				
High degree of labour mobility		3.50	3.00	
Relatively easy to operate HRM policies		3.50	3.00	2.91
Wage flexibility		3.25	3.33	3.17
Relatively easy to introduce incentive pay		3.25	3.21	3.23
Low non-wage costs		3.00	3.45	3.25
Favourable relationship with trade unions			3.00	
Balance of industrial relations laws beneficial to employers				3.42

A further disaggregating is undertaken in accordance to the level / type of technology utilised by companies, which is classified as being: (a) high risk, cutting edge technology, (b) moderate risk, established technology and (c) low risk, older (very established) technology. We assume, *a priori*, that each of these different types of technology require differing levels of FDI and will be triggered by different factors. In relation to the level of risk in technology, high-risk firms appear to be disproportionately favourable towards the availability of a skilled workforce, together with a high degree of labour mobility. They additionally display a greater preference for decentralised or individual wage bargaining than other company types, favour the ease of operations of HRM policies, numerical flexibility through the utilisation of non-standard employment, and flexible allocation of working time (Table 2).

Medium risk firms tend to favour labour market deregulation, numerical flexibility through the use of work time, low non-wage costs and the establishment of a favourable relationship with trade unions. Low risk companies have little enthusiasm for skills although they do profess an atypical interest in functional flexibility through the introduction of multiskilling in the workplace, but prefer the deregulation of the labour market, the establishment of industrial relations laws that favour employers together with wage flexibility.

Adding consideration of company strategies, low-cost firms tended to prefer labour market deregulation, numerical (working time) and functional flexibility, together with registering an interest in working with 'partnership' forms of trade unionism (Table 3). Differentiation-niche firms, by contrast, tend to prioritise the quality of a skilled labour market above all other factors, although they are predisposed towards preferring numerical flexible through labour mobility and the exercising the potential for individual pay setting.

Table 3. Features of labour market flexibility (cost strategy)

		Base of competitive strategy	
	Total sample	**Low**	**Niche/high**
First-level			
Highly trained labour force	4.34	5.91	3.73
Second-level			
Flexible use of working time	4.59	3.91	4.64
Flexible employment protection regulation	5.88	5.64	5.97
Ease of introducing multi-skilling in the workplace	5.88	4.73	6.00
Wage flexibility	6.46	6.50	6.29
Third-level			
Flexible dismissal protection regulation		**6.45**	6.69
Ease of use of incentive pay		7.40	
Ease of use of non-standard employment		8.00	
Low non-wage costs		8.36	7.78
'Partnership' forms of trade unionism		8.63	
Ability to set individual pay – without bargaining with a trade union			**6.08**
Decentralised wage bargaining – at firm or workplace level			7.11
Labour mobility – within the economy			7.54

Disaggregating the data by company characteristics of operating sector, however, reveals little difference from the overall prioritising in relation to labour market factors. For manufacturing companies there is only a marginal reordering of the relative degree of importance, with no single factor emerging with greater strength than the sample as a whole. In contrast, for service sector firms the presence of flexible dismissal protection regulation was ranked within their top 5 factors regarding labour market flexibility, whilst the issue of introducing multi-skilling in the workplace was outside their top 5 drivers.

Furthermore, 72 per cent respondents identify the level of entry costs to be more important as a determinant of FDI than exit costs. However, no correlation is apparent between the probability of expressing this preference and the self-identified level of technological risk inherent within the company concerned.

To examine the issue of human resource practices within their own companies, respondents were asked to identify significant areas of non-standard employment. Table Four illustrates the proportion of firms and the average percentage of employees within various categories. This combined analysis permits the examination of numerical flexibility, whereby it is possible to identify both the breadth and depth of the adoption of non-standard contracts.

Table 4. Human resource practices

		% of employees	
	% of firms	**Mean**	**SD**
Part-time	68	8.01	13.07
Temporary contracts	47	4.28	4.59
Agency workers	48	4.97	4.88
Short, fixed-term contracts	35	3.76	5.26
Franchising	10	0.33	0.82
Variable (or zero) hours contracts	15	11.11	19.45
Sub-contracting	22	8.19	13.25
Consultants	22	2.30	2.84
Freelance	13	2.38	2.56
Outworkers, Home workers	15	3.56	4.13
Teleworking	12	1.50	2.40
Seasonal working	22	4.81	6.08

Firstly, in terms of the utilisation by companies of non-standard employment practices, the more established formats of part-time, agency workers, temporary contracts and short/fixed-term contracts are predominate with at least one-third of respondents citing them. However, the two largest types of non-standard employment are variable hours contacts and sub-contracting, although these are only adopted by 15 per cent and 22 per cent of firms respectively.

A second point arising from Table 4 relates to the relatively low levels of part-time working and other forms of non-standard contracts declared by respondents relative to the higher rates found in the Labour Force Survey. One reason for this result may relate to the fact that, typically, TNCs demonstrate less interest than domestic UK firms in utilising non-standard working arrangements to deliver internal labour force flexibility (Morley *et al.*, 1995).

Respondents were relatively split over their categorisation of utilising the 'flexible firm' model to describe their companies' organisation. According to this approach, a firm is characterised as 'flexible' if the workforce is split into 'core' and 'peripheral' employees, with the former receiving permanent contracts and being treated as almost fixed costs, whereas the latter tend to receive non-standard contracts (i.e. part-time, casual, zero-hours, agency employees, consultants) and who provide most of the flexibility required in terms of the labour time, cost and length of employment. Thus, 44.6 per cent of respondents identified their companies with the 'flexible firm' model. However, when asked to identify the proportions of 'core' and 'peripheral' workers, respondents suggested an 82.3 per cent against 18.6 per cent split. This evidence, together with the data generated elsewhere in the survey, implies that, whilst numerical flexibility is deemed to be important for half of the respondent companies, the potential gains are concentrated to a relatively small number of employees.

Fully 90.9 per cent of respondents claimed to utilise incentive pay in their organisation, with these companies split two-to-one in favour of all employees receiving an element of incentive award, rather than restricting such schemes to management grades. In terms of its significance, 56 per cent of companies claimed that incentive payments accounted for in excess of 5 per cent of total wages, with 22.8 per cent stating that such schemes represented more than 10 per cent of their total wage bill. These results are interesting since the relative ease of introducing incentive schemes for employees was identified as being of only moderate or average importance.

In terms of wage formation, 68.5 per cent of respondents stated that their firm preferred to establish a reward structure according to internal requirements to incentivise employees and support HRM strategy, rather than setting pay according to national labour market objectives to pay the 'going rate', secure sectoral industrial peace, promote national competitiveness and macroeconomic goals including low inflation. Moreover, 48.2 per cent of respondents stated that their firm preferred setting wages based upon task or position irrespective of the country in which the employee found themselves, as opposed to 33.9 per cent who accounted for national variations in the cost of living and paid according to the "rate for the job", whilst the remaining 17.9 per cent preferred to prioritise the minimisation of wage costs.

The micro-flexibility created by decentralised (firm or plant-level) wage bargaining is preferred by an overwhelming proportion (93 per cent) of respondents to more co-ordinated wage bargaining, even if the latter delivered more moderate wage growth. This answer is perhaps not surprising, but due to the disagreement in the literature relating to whether co-ordinated or decentralised wage formation delivers superior macroeconomic outcomes, this warrants further investigation to discern whether this may be a case where micro-flexibility conflicts in some manner with macro-flexibility.

The relative insignificance of wage flexibility as a human resource policy pursued by respondent companies is demonstrated by 42.4 per cent prioritising utilising quality training programmes to increase productivity and thereby lower unit costs, with 26.3 per cent and 23.7 per cent preferring numerical and functional flexibility respectively, to lower unit costs, and only a residual 8.8 per cent advocating the reduction of unit costs through lowering of labour costs directly, either through downsizing or reductions in remunerations. Indeed, when asked to make a straight choice between lowering labour costs and lowering unit costs through raising productivity, 96.6 per cent of respondents selected the latter option as identifying the current practice of their firm.

Conclusion and Policy Recommendations

This chapter has generated primary data, direct from senior executives of TNCs that have invested in the UK, which indicates that the primary determinants of FDI flows relate more strongly to market-seeking factors, followed by resource- and asset-seeking labour market variables. Although not the most important attractor for inward investment, labour market flexibility was nevertheless identified as representing moderate or high degrees of importance by 59.7 per cent of respondents.

Disaggregating the data and testing for association with various company characteristics identifies a number of interesting features of the data. Firstly, small but notable differences in emphasis appear to exist between companies utilising high risk technology upon the quality of national labour force skills base and physical infrastructure, together with the significance of location near a large international market, compared to moderate and lower cost firms who tend to demonstrate a relative predisposition towards primarily national factors, such as size of national market, policy-related variables, including deregulation, tax rates, and the maintenance of a low cost of capital. The similarity between high risk firms and those companies utilising a differentiated-niche strategy is close, although incomplete, as most respondents identified their enterprises having a moderate level of risk whilst the majority also adopted differentiation-niche strategies, therefore necessitating a substantial over-lap between categories. Thus, it would appear useful for government policy to seek to identify the preferred profile for those firms considering investing in the UK, before determining which factor will prove the most attractive to the potential investor.

Examining those characteristics that form the basis for labour market flexibility, this paper has found that respondents identified the existence of a highly trained, skilled labour force as the primary labour market attractor for FDI, followed by elements of numerical flexibility, namely the flexible use of working time and labour mobility, functional flexibility, via the facilitation of multi-skilling and reduction of demarcation in the workplace, together with employment protection regulation and wage flexibility. Thus, these are the elements of labour market flexibility that governments should concentrate their resources upon to maximise the inward flow of FDI. The promotion of a high skilled workforce benefits all companies, but disproportionately favours high risk, differentiation-niche firms, whereas the benefits arising from numerical and functional flexibility are more evenly spread throughout the various clusters of companies analysed in this chapter.

A number of features arise from the analysis, however, relating to government policy. Firstly, it is important for policymakers to keep in mind the fact that labour market flexibility is not a single phenomenon, but rather is an agglomeration of multiple individual characteristics, many of which have the potential to conflict with each other in practice. Moreover, respondents have indicated that it is only with certain of these characteristics that they are primarily concerned. Thus, there exists a clear potential for a degree of misdirection inherent within policy reforms intended to promote FDI by strengthening the less significant aspects of labour market flexibilisation. For example, whilst the introduction of 'push' and 'pull' initiatives to incentivise the unemployed to seek work may be justified on the grounds that this may facilitate a reduction in unemployment and thereby is warranted as part of an overall flexible labour market strategy, it is of little significance in terms of attracting FDI. Similarly, factors including the cost of labour, wage flexibility, utilisation of incentive pay, industrial relations restrictions upon trade union activity and the decentralisation of wage bargaining act as relatively weak attractors for FDI.

This conclusion is reinforced by the data concerning how the investing companies treat labour market issues once they have located in the UK economy, through their overwhelming prioritisation of competition via lowering unit costs through training and productivity gains, rather than forcing down costs and wages per se. Numerical and functional flexibility, according to this analysis, are of intermediate significance.

In relation to alternative forms of non-standard employment adopted by the firms, our survey indicated that these remain confined to orthodox measures, whilst the average proportion of employees rarely rises above 5 per cent. Hence there appears little evidence of a wide spread utilisation of numerical flexibility beyond established formats.

It would therefore appear that inward investors behave in a relatively consistent manner to their expressed preferences relating to those factors in the UK labour market that first attracted them to locate in the country, and which they themselves pursue in practice. Firms are typically concerned about the quality of their employees, the ability to pursue functional and numerical flexibility, where necessary, and prioritise internal pay setting over national labour market interests.

Two additional points to arise out of the survey that have some utility for policymakers include, firstly, the fact that only 13.3 per cent of the respondents acknowledge use of indexes, produced by the ILO and OECD, comparing the relative competitiveness of national economies and/or the relative flexibility of national labour markets. Thus, although the provision of one source of information for policymakers, a movement in the 'league table' will not directly influence FDI flows, but only as a reflection of economic fundamentals and as an *indirect* influence upon the perceptions of leading business executives involved in determining the investment patterns in their company.

Secondly, when asked their perceptions of the UK's labour market, 69.8 per cent of respondents stated that it is characterised by a lower level of employment regulation than other EU economies, however a similar number (67.3 per cent) believe there to have been a deterioration in the degree of labour market flexibility since 1997, with only 21.2 per cent suggesting that circumstances have improved over this period. This is clearly not an objective measure, and many other indexes may suggest that little or no deterioration has in fact occurred. However, the expectations and perceptions of businesspeople are significant determinants of the future development of investment flows and economic success in general. Therefore, policymakers should embrace this as a challenge to focus upon the most productive elements of labour market flexibility to facilitate enhanced future inward investment flows.

Finally, in relation to avenues of further study, this unique primary data analysis has provided a number of insights relating to the thought and decision-making process of TNCs, with existing production facilities located within the UK. From both the overall sample and the sub-samples based on company characteristics, it indicates those drivers that act as significant attractors to FDI. In relation to the previous literature, it suggests that there are a relatively small number of central factors that strongly determine investment undertakings, whilst a large number of hypothesised variables appear to possess little influence. Hence, it raises as many questions as it answers, for example, to determine more precisely what type of skill and education firms prefer, namely whether this relates to in-house training, state education and/or government sponsored college-based generic training programmes.

Similarly, interest in the quality of infrastructure could be more precisely delineated in terms of physical transport links or communications networks. Moreover, due to the fact that the nature of the research design has necessarily produced a cross sectional, time-specific snapshot of drivers for FDI location, it would be helpful to supplement these findings by replicating this initiative over time, thereby creating a panel data set capable of insulating findings from potential bias due to factors such as the position within the business cycle.

References

Addison, J.T. & Teixeira, P. (2001). 'The Economics of Employment Protection'. *IZA Discussion Paper* No. **381**, October, Institute for the Study of Labour (IZA), Bonn, Germany.

Arestis, P. & Mariscal, I. (2000). 'Capital Stock, Unemployment and Wages in the UK and Germany'. *Scottish Journal of Political Economy*, **47** (5): 487-503.

Arestis, P. & Sawyer, M. (2003). 'Aggregate Demand, Conflict and Capacity in the Inflationary Process'. *Levy Economics Institute Working Paper* No. **391**, The Levy Economics Institute, Bard College, Annandale-on-Hudson, New York.

Beatson, M. (1995). 'Labour Market Flexibility'. *Department of Employment Research Series* No. **48,** Sheffield: Department of Employment.

Becker, B.E. & Huselid, M.A. (1998). 'High Performance Work Systems and Firm Performance: A Synthesis of Research and Managerial Implications'. *Research in Personnel and Human Resource Management*, **16**, 53-101.

Bentolila, S. & Bertola, G. (1990). 'Firing Costs and Labour Demand: How Bad is Eurosclerosis?'. *Review of Economic Studies*, **57**, 381-402.

Blanchard, O. & Wolfers, J. (2000). 'The Role of Shocks and Institutions in the Rise of European Unemployment: The Aggregate Evidence'. *The Economic Journal*, **110** (462): c1-c33.

Bosworth, D., Dawkins, P. & Stromback, T. (1996). *The Economics of the Labour Market.* Harlow: Addison Wesley Longman.

Bruno, M. & Sachs, J. (1985). *Economics of Worldwide Stagflation.* Boston: Harvard University Press.

Calmfors, L. & Driffill, J. (1988). 'Bargaining Structure, Corporatism and Macroeconomic Performance'. *Economic Policy*, **6** (April): 13-62.

Carruth, A.A. & Disney, R. (1988). 'Where Have Two Million Trade Union Members Gone?'. *Economica*. **55**, 1-20.

Culem, C.G. (1988). 'The Locational Determinants of Direct Investments Among Industrialised Countries'. *European Economic Review*, **32** (4): 885-904.

Dunning, J.H. (1979). 'Explaining Patterns of International Production: In Defence of the Eclectic Theory'. *Oxford Bulletin of Economics and Statistics*, **41**, 269-295.

Erickson, C.L. & Kuruvilla, S. (1994). 'Labor Costs and the Social Dumping Debate in the European Union'. *Industrial and Labor Relations Review*, **48**, 28-47.

Floyd, D. (2003). 'How Can a Flexible Labour market Influence the Amount of Foreign Direct Investment Atracted by a Host Nation? The Case of the UK'. *European Business Review*, **15** (5): 334-339.

Haaland, J.I. & Wooton, I. (2003). 'Domestic Labour Markets and Foreign Direct Investment'. *CEPR Working Paper*, No. **3989**, July, CEPR, London.

Hackman, J.R. & Wageman, R. (1995). 'Total Quality Management: Empirical, Conceptual and Practical Issues'. *Administrative Science Quarterly*, June, 309-342.

HM Treasury (2003). Pre-Budget Report: Appendix C – Flexibility in the UK Economy. London: HM Treasury.

Hudson, (2002). 'Flexibility and the Reorganisation of Work'. In Burchell, B., Ladipo, D. & Wilkinson, F. (Eds.), *Job Insecurity and Work Intensification*. London: Routledge, 39-60.

Ichniowski, C., Kochan, T.A., Levine, D., Olson, C. & Strauss, G. (1996). 'What Works at Work: Overview and Assessment'. *Industrial Relations*, **35** (3): 299-333.

ILO (2004). Economic Security for a Better World. Geneva: ILO.

Kling, J. (1995). 'High Performance Work Systems and Firm Performance'. *Monthly Labor Review*, **118** (5): 29-36.

Kucera, D. (2002). 'Core Labour Standards and Foreign Direct Investment'. *International Labour Review*, **141** (1-2): 31-69.

Lensink, R. & Morrissey, O. (2001). Foreign direct investment: flows, volatility and growth in developing countries. *Credit Research Paper* No. **01/06**, Centre for Research in Economic Development and International Trade, University of Nottingham.

Leonard, J. & Schettkat, R. (1991). 'A Comparison of Job Stability in Germany and the US'. *Labour*, **5** (2): 143-157.

Loungani, P. & Razin, A. (2001). 'How beneficial is foreign direct investment for developing countries?'. *Finance & Development*, **38**, 6-9.

Mankelow, R. (2002). 'The Organisational Costs of Job Insecurity and Work Intensification'. In Burchell, B., Ladipo, D. & Wilkinson, F. (Eds.), *Job Insecurity and Work Intensification*. London: Routledge, 137-153.

Marginson, P., Armstrong, P., Edwards, P. & Purcell, J. (1996). 'Facing the Multinational Challenge'. In Leisink, P., Van Leemput, J. and Vilrokx, J. (Eds.), *The Challenges to Trade Unions in Europ*e. Cheltenham: Edward Elgar, 187-204.

Meier, G. M. & Rauch, J. E. (2005). *Leading issues in economic development*, Oxford: Oxford University Press.

Meier, G.M. (1968). Private foreign investment. in Dunning, J.H. (Ed.) *International investment: selected readings*, London: Penguin.

Monastiriotis, V. (2003). 'A Panel of Regional Indicators of Labour Market Flexibility: the UK, 1979-1998'. *New Directions in Labour Market Flexibility Research*, DTI, London, 26th November.

Morgan, K. (1997). 'The Learning Region: Institutions, Innovation and Regional Renewal'. *Regional Studies*, **31**, 491-503.

Morley, M., Gunnigle, P. & Haraty, N. (1995). 'Developments in Flexible Working Practices in the Republic of Ireland'. *International Journal of Manpower*, **16** (8): 38-58.

Neven, D. & Siotis, G. (1996). 'Technology Sourcing and FDI in the EC: An Empirical Evaluation'. *International Journal of Industrial Organisation*, **14**, 543-560.

Nickell., S. & Layard, R. (1999). 'Labour Market Indtitutions and Economic Performance'. In Ashenfelter, O. & Card, D. (Eds.), *Handbook of Labor Eco*nomics Vol. 3. Amsterdam: North Holland.

OECD (1987). International investment and multinational enterprises: recent trends in international direct investment. Paris: OECD.

OECD (1994a). Jobs Study, Evidence and Explanations – Parts 1 and 2. Paris: OECD.

OECD (1994b). Jobs Study, Taxation, Employment and Unemployment. Paris: OECD.

OECD (1999). Employment Outlook. Paris: OECD.

OECD (2000). International Trade and Core Labour Standards. Paris: OECD.

OECD (2002). Foreign direct investment for development: maximising benefits and minimising costs. Paris: OECD.

Porter, M.E., Schwab, K., Sala-i-Martin, X. & Lopez-Claros, A. (2004). Global Competitiveness Report 2004-2005. London: Palgrave.

Robinson, P. (2000). 'Insecurity and the Flexibly Workforce: Measuring the Ill-Defined'. In Heery, A. & Salmon, J. (Eds.), The Insecure Workforce. London: Routledge.

Rowthorn, R. (1995). 'Capital Formation and Unemployment'. *Oxford Review of Economic Policy*, **11** (1): 26-39.

Salvanes, K.G. (1997). 'Market Rigidities and Labour Market Flexibility: An International Comparison'. *Scandinavian Journal of Economics*, **99** (2): 315-333.

Soreide, T. (2001). 'FDI and industrialisation: why technology transfer and new industrial structures may accelerate economic development'. *Chr. Michelsen Institute (CMI) working papers*. CMI: Norway.

Traxler, F. & Woitech, B. (2000). 'Transnational Investment and National Labour Market Regimes: A Case of "Regime Shopping"?'. *European Journal of Industrial Relations*, **6** (2): 141-159.

UNCTAD (1998). *World Investment Report 1998*. New York: United Nations.

UNCTAD (1999). *Foreign direct investment and development*, UNCTAD series on issues in international investment agreements. New York: United Nations.

UNCTAD (2002), *World Investment Report 2002*. New York: United Nations.

UNCTAD (2005), *World Investment Report 2005*. New York: United Nations.

UNCTAD (2006). *World Investment Report 2006*. New York: United Nations.

UNESCO. *Statistical Yearbook*, several years.

Weiss, C. (2001). 'On Flexibility'. *Journal of Economic Behaviour and Organisation*, **46** (3): 347-356.

Weiss, L. (1998). *The Myth of the Powerless State: Governing the Economy in a Global Era*. Cambridge: Polity Press.

Wheeler, D. & Mody, A. (1992). 'International Investment Location Decisions: The Case of US Firms'. *Journal of International Economics*, **33** (1-2): 57-76.

Wichert, I. (2002). 'Job Insecurity and Work Intensification: The Effects on Health and Well-Being'. In Burchell, B., Ladipo, D. & Wilkinson, F. (Eds.), *Job Insecurity and Work Intensification*. London: Routledge, 92-111.

In: Foreign Direct Investment
Editor: Harrison G. Blaine, pp. 45-56

ISBN: 978-1-60456-921-6
© 2009 Nova Science Publishers, Inc.

Chapter 3

INTELLECTUAL PROPERTY RIGHTS AND FOREIGN DIRECT INVESTMENT: THE IMPLICATIONS OF LABOR UNION

Arijit Mukherjee*

School of Economics, University of Nottingham,
UK and GEP, University of Nottingham

Abstract

An important aspect of the current WTO regime is to standardize patent systems across countries, thus strengthening patent protection in the developing countries. In a North-South trade model, we analyze the effect of a stronger Southern patent protection on the Northern firm's incentive for foreign direct investment (FDI), when the Southern labor market is unionized. If there are firm-specific unions in the South, the incentive for inward FDI is higher under weak patent protection than under strong patent protection if the Southern firm is sufficiently cost inefficient. However, if there is an industry-wide union in the South, the incentive for inward FDI is always higher under strong patent protection in the South. The unionization structure plays an important role in determining the effect of patent protection on inward FDI.

Key Words: Foreign direct investment; Labor union; Patent protection

JEL Classifications: D43; F12; J51

1. Introduction

A fascinating development in recent decades is the dominance of foreign direct investment (FDI) over international trade (UNCTAD, 2006), which has generated a vast theoretical and

* E-mail address: arijit.mukherjee@nottingham.ac.uk. Fax: +44-115-951 4159. Correspondence to: Arijit Mukherjee, School of Economics, University of Nottingham, University Park, Nottingham, NG7 2RD, UK.

empirical literature on FDI.[1] A factor which is often considered to be an important determinant of FDI is the protection of intellectual property rights. Since the developed-country firms make use of their intellectual property related assets under FDI, a common concern of these firms is about the patent protection in the developing countries. Since the inception of the Uruguay round of the General Agreement on Tariffs and Trade, developing countries are increasingly urged to strengthen their patent systems in order to standardize the patent regime across the world, thus trying to protect the intellectual properties of the developed-country firms.

The evidence is mixed on patent protection and FDI. While the empirical studies by Lee and Mansfield (1996) and Maskus (1998) provide support for the positive relationship between patent protection and FDI, other works show that there is either a negative (Yang and Maskus, 2001, Pfister and Deffains, 2005) or an insignificant (see, Seyoum, 1996 and Fosfuri, 2004) relationship between these two. Nunnenkump and Spatz (2004) show that industry as well as the host-country characteristics play important roles in determining the relationship between FDI and patent.

While the empirical literature has paid some attention to uncover the relationship between patent protection and FDI, the theoretical literature did not pay much attention to this issue. However, in this era of globalization, it is certainly important to see the effects of intellectual property rights on the incentives for FDI.

In this paper, we develop a simple North-South trade model and show that the unionization structure in the host-country labor market may play an important role in determining the effect of host-country patent protection on inward FDI. To the best of our knowledge, this is the first paper which shows the implications of labor union in determining the effect of patent protection on inward FDI. We show that if there are firm-specific unions in the host-country, the incentive for inward FDI is higher under weak patent protection than under strong patent protection if the host-country firm is sufficiently cost inefficient. However, if there is an industry-wide union in the host-country, the incentive for inward FDI is always higher under strong patent protection in the host-country.

There is a theoretical literature which shows the effects of patent system in the North-South trading environment (see, e.g., Chin and Grossman, 1990, Segerstrom *et al.*, 1990, Diwan and Rodrik, 1991, Grossman and Helpman, 1991, Deardorff, 1992, Taylor, 1994, Vishwasrao, 1994, Fosfuri, 2000, Markusen, 2001 and Sinha, 2006). However, this literature does not focus on FDI.

There are few theoretical works, which, in a North-South model, analyze the effects of the patent system on the incentive for FDI (Helpman, 1993, Lai, 1998, Glass and Saggi, 2002 and Mathew and Mukherjee, 2008). However, unlike the present paper, neither of those works considers unionized labor market. As a result, those works do not capture the implications of unionization structure in determining the effect of patent protection on inward FDI.

The remainder of the paper is organized as follows. Section 2 describes the model and shows the results. Section 3 concludes.

[1] See, Saggi (2002) for a recent survey on FDI.

2. The Model and the Results

Consider two countries, called North and South. Assume that there is a firm in the North, called firm N, and there is a potential entrant in the South, called firm S. Assume that firm 1 has a technology to produce a product, Q, and wants to sell its product in the South. Firm N can sell its product in the South either through export or through FDI. We assume that firm 1 needs to incur a per-unit transportation cost t under export, while it requires a fixed investment, F, under FDI.

We assume that production requires labor and firm 1 requires 1 labor to produce one unit of output. We further assume that the labor market in the North is perfectly competitive, while that is in the South is unionized. However, the reservation wage rates in both the countries are assumed to be zero, for simplicity. Therefore, the marginal cost of firm N is t under export, while it is w_n under FDI, where w_n is the wage rate charged by the Southern labor union to firm N.

Let us now consider the patent systems of these countries. We assume that the patent regime in the North is perfect and makes firm N as a monopolist producer in the North. However, the patent systems in the South can be either weak and or strong.

Under weak patent protection in the South, if firm N undertakes FDI, firm S can imitate and produce the product Q. We assume that firm S requires 1 labor to produce one unit of output, and also needs a cost c per-unit of output. Hence, under FDI by firm N, the marginal cost of firm S is $c + w_s$, where w_s is the wage rate charged by the labor union to firm S. The cost c is a proxy for the difficulty in imitation, which may arise due to the technical complexity or because of the strength of the weak patent system. A higher technical complexity or a relatively higher strength of the weak patent protection implies a higher value of c.

If there is weak patent protection in the South and firm N exports, we assume that imitation is not feasible, and firm N produces like a monopolist. It is indicated in Helpman (1993) that the foreign investors are likely to be exposed to a greater threat of imitation than the exporters, which can justify our assumption of no imitation under export. In general, one can think that the parameter c will be higher under export than under FDI. However, no imitation under export simplifies our analysis without loosing useful insights.

In the case of strong patent protection in the South, we assume that there is no threat of imitation in the South, irrespective of export or FDI firm N. Hence, firm N produces like a monopolist under strong patent protection.

Note that if there is weak patent protection in the South and firm N undertakes FDI, there are two producers in the Southern country, and each of them needs to hire workers from the labor union in the Southern country. In the following analysis, we will consider two types of labor unions in the Southern country: (i) the case of firm-specific labor union, and (ii) the case of an industry-wide labor union.

As for the objectives of the labor unions, we assume that the labor unions determine the wage rates to maximize the union rents, and the firms determine the number of workers according to their need. Hence, we consider a right-to-manage-model of labor union, as in

Bughin and Vannini (1995), López and Naylor (2004) and Mukherjee (2007), to name a few.[2] Therefore, in the case of firm-specific union, each union determines the respective wage rate to maximize the respective union rent. In the case of an industry-wide union, the union determines the wage rates to maximize the total union rent. The case of an industry-wide union can also be viewed as the situation where different unions cooperate and determine the wage rates to maximize total union rents.

We assume that the inverse market demand function in the South is

$$P = a - q \tag{1}$$

where P is price, q is total output and $a > 0$.

2.1. The Benchmark Case of Perfectly Competitive Labor Markets

Before doing our analysis with unionized labor market in the South, let us first consider the benchmark case where the labor markets are perfectly competitive in both the countries. In this situation, the wage rates are zero in both the countries.

We consider the following game in the benchmark model. At stage 1, firm N determines whether to export or to undertake FDI. At stage 2, the outputs are determined and the profits are realized. If firm N undertakes FDI and there are two producers in the South, the output decisions are taken like Cournot duopolists. We solve the game through backward induction.

Let us first consider export by firm N. Since there is no imitation under export, irrespective of the patent system in the South, given the demand and the cost conditions, the equilibrium output of firm N can be found as $q_n^x = \frac{a-t}{2}$, and it is positive for $a > t$. Hence, the profit of firm N can be found as

$$\pi_n^x = \frac{(a-t)^2}{4} \tag{2}$$

Let us now consider FDI by firm N. Under FDI, imitation is possible only under weak patent protection in the South.

If there is strong patent protection in the South, the equilibrium output of firm N under FDI can be found as $q_n^{f,sp} = \frac{a}{2} > 0$. Hence, the profit of firm N under FDI in the presence of strong Southern patent protection is

$$\pi_n^{f,sp} = \frac{a^2}{4} - F \tag{3}$$

[2] The 'efficient bargaining' model, which stipulates that the firms and unions bargain over wages and employment, is an alternative to the right-to-manage model. See, Layard et al. (1991) for arguments in favor of right-to-manage models.

Therefore, under strong patent protection in the South, firm N undertakes FDI if

$$F < \frac{a^2}{4} - \frac{(a-t)^2}{4} \equiv \hat{F}^{sp} \tag{4}$$

However, there is imitation under FDI if there is weak patent protection in the South. If there is weak patent protection in the South, the equilibrium outputs of firms N and S under FDI can be found as $q_n^{f,wp} = \frac{a+c}{3} > 0$ and $q_s^{f,wp} = \frac{a-2c}{3}$. The output of firm S is positive if $c < \frac{a}{2}$, which is assumed to hold. Otherwise, the threat of imitation is empty in our analysis.

The profit of firm N under FDI in the presence of weak Southern patent protection is

$$\pi_n^{f,wp} = \frac{(a+c)^2}{9} - F \tag{5}$$

Therefore, under weak patent protection in the South, firm N undertakes FDI if

$$F < \frac{(a+c)^2}{9} - \frac{(a-t)^2}{4} \equiv \hat{F}^{wp} \tag{6}$$

Proposition 1

If the labor markets are perfectly competitive in both North and South, firm N's incentive for FDI is always higher under strong patent protection in the South.

Proof

We get that $\hat{F}^{sp} > \hat{F}^{wp}$ if $c < \frac{a}{2}$, which always holds due to the requirement for positive outputs of the firms. Q.E.D.

2.2. The Implications of Unionized Labor Market in the Host-Country

Let us now assume that the labor market is unionized in the host-country, i.e., in the South.

We consider the following game. At stage 1, firm N decides whether to export or to undertake FDI. At stage 2, the labor union in the Southern country determines the wage rate. Note that, stage 2 is relevant provided there is FDI by firm N. At stage 3, the output decisions are taken and the profits are realized. If firm N undertakes FDI and there are two producers in the South, the output decisions are taken like Cournot duopolists. We solve the game through backward induction.

2.2.1. Export

Let us first consider the situation under export by firm N. Since there is no labor union in the North and there is no imitation under export, the equilibrium output of firm N can be found as $q_n^x = \frac{a-t}{2}$, and it is positive for $a > t$. The profit of firm N is given by (2).

2.2.2. FDI

Let us now consider the situation under FDI. Since imitation is possible under FDI, we need to consider the case of weak and strong Southern patent protections separately.

2.2.2.1. Strong Patent Protection in the South

If there is strong patent protection in the South, firm N produces like a monopolist under FDI and its equilibrium output can be found as

$$q_n^{f,sp} = \frac{a-w_n}{2} \tag{7}$$

The Southern labor union maximizes the following expression to determine w_n:

$$\underset{w_n}{Max} \frac{w_n(a-w_n)}{2} \tag{8}$$

The equilibrium wage rate is $w_n = \frac{a}{2}$. Hence, if there is strong patent protection in the South, the equilibrium output of firm N under FDI is $q_n^{f,sp} = \frac{a}{4} > 0$. Hence, the profit of firm N is

$$\pi_n^{f,sp} = \frac{a^2}{16} - F \tag{9}$$

The comparison of (2) and (9) gives the following result immediately.

Lemma 1

If there is strong patent protection in the South, firm N undertakes FDI if $F < \frac{a^2}{16} - \frac{(a-t)^2}{4} \equiv \overline{F}^{sp}$.

2.2.2.2. Weak Patent Protection in the South

Let us now consider the case of weak patent protection in the South. In this situation, under FDI, firm N faces competition from firm S. Given the cost and the demand conditions, the equilibrium outputs of firms N and S can be found as

$$q_n^{f,wp} = \frac{a - 2w_n + c + w_s}{3} \quad \text{and} \quad q_s^{f,wp} = \frac{a - 2w_s - 2c + w_n}{3} \tag{10}$$

If there are firm-specific unions in the South, the ith union maximizes the following expression to determine the wage rates:

$$\underset{w_i}{Max} \frac{w_i(a - 2w_i + c + w_j)}{3} \tag{11}$$

where $i, j, = n, s$ and $i \neq j$.

The equilibrium wage rates can be found as

$$w_n = \frac{5a + 2c}{15} \quad \text{and} \quad w_s = \frac{5a - 7c}{15} \tag{12}$$

We assume that $c < \frac{5a}{7}$, which ensures non-negative wage rates in the South.

If there is weak patent protection, firm N undertakes FDI and there are firm-specific unions in the South, the equilibrium outputs of firms N and S are respectively $q_n^{f,wp,fu} = \frac{10a + 4c}{45} > 0$ and $q_s^{f,wp,fu} = \frac{10a - 14c}{45}$. The output of firm S is positive if $c < \frac{5a}{7}$, which is assumed to hold.

If there are firm-specific unions, and firm N undertakes FDI, the profit of firm N is

$$\pi_n^{f,wp,fu} = \frac{(10a + 4c)^2}{2025} - F \tag{13}$$

The comparison of (2) and (13) gives the following result immediately.

Lemma 2

If there are firm-specific unions in the South, firm N undertakes FDI under weak patent protection in the South if

$$F < \frac{(10a+4c)^2}{2025} - \frac{(a-t)^2}{4} \equiv \overline{F}^{wp,fu}.$$

Now, we are in position to see the effects of patent protection on the incentive for FDI in the presence of firm-specific unions in the South.

Proposition 2

If there are firm-specific unions in the South, firm N has higher incentive for FDI under weak patent protection if $c \in (\frac{5a}{16}, \frac{5a}{7})$.

Proof

We get that $\overline{F}^{wp,fu} > \overline{F}^{sp}$ if

$$\frac{(10a+4c)^2}{2025} > \frac{a^2}{16} \quad \text{or} \quad c > \frac{5a}{16} \tag{14}$$

Given our assumption of $c < \frac{5a}{7}$, which ensures positive outputs of the firms, we get that, if there are firm-specific unions in the South, the incentive for FDI by firm N is higher under weak patent protection if $c \in (\frac{5a}{16}, \frac{5a}{7})$.Q.E.D.

The above result is in contrast to Proposition 1, which considers perfectly competitive labor markets in both countries. Hence, in the presence of host-country labor union, the incentive for inward FDI may be higher under weak host-country patent protection. An implication of the above result is that, in the presence of firm-specific host-country labor union, there may be fixed cost of FDI such that FDI occurs only under weak patent protection.

The intuition for Proposition 2 is as follows. If there is weak patent protection in the South, it creates competition in the Southern market, which tends to reduce firm N's incentive for incentive. However, competition in the Southern country helps to reduce the Southern wage rate faced by firm N. Note that the wage rate faced by firm N in the South is $w_n = \frac{5a+2c}{15}$ under weak patent protection, and it is lower than the wage rate faced by firm N under strong patent protection in the South, which is $w_n = \frac{a}{2}$, since $c < \frac{5a}{7}$. If c is sufficiently large, the competition effect under weak patent protection is not very strong, while competition under weak patent helps firm N to get the positive wage effect. As a result, firm N's incentive for FDI is higher under weak patent protection in the South if c is sufficiently large. However, if c is small, the negative competition effect dominates the positive wage effect, thus creating lower incentive for FDI by firm N under weak patent protection.

Let us now consider the case of an industry-wide union in the South. Given the outputs of firms N and S, shown in (10), the industry-wide union maximizes the following expression to determine the wage rates:

$$\underset{w_n, w_s}{Max} \frac{w_n(a - 2w_n + c + w_s) + w_s(a - 2c - 2w_s + w_n)}{3} \tag{15}$$

The equilibrium wage rates can be found as

$$w_n = \frac{a}{2} \quad \text{and} \quad w_s = \frac{a - c}{2} \tag{16}$$

It follows from (16) that the wage rates are non-negative in the South as long as $a > c$.

If there is weak patent protection in the South, firm N undertakes FDI and there is an industry-wide union in the South, the equilibrium output of firms N and S are respectively $q_n^{f,wp,iu} = \frac{a+c}{6} > 0$ and $q_s^{f,wp,iu} = \frac{a-2c}{c}$. The output of firm S is positive if $c < \frac{a}{2}$, which is assumed to hold.

If there is an industry-wide union and firm N undertakes FDI, the profit of firm N is

$$\pi_n^{f,wp,iu} = \frac{(a+c)^2}{36} - F \tag{17}$$

The comparison of (2) and (17) gives the following result immediately.

Lemma 3

If there is an industry-wide union in the South, firm N undertakes FDI under weak patent protection in the South if

$$F < \frac{(a+c)^2}{36} - \frac{(a-t)^2}{4} \equiv \overline{F}^{wp,iu}.$$

Now, we are in position to see the effects of patent protection on the incentive for FDI in the presence of an industry-wide union in the South.

Proposition 3

If there is an industry-wide union in the South, firm N always has higher incentive for FDI under strong patent protection.

Proof

We get that $\overline{F}^{sp} > \overline{F}^{wp,iu}$ if

$$\frac{a^2}{16} > \frac{(a+c)^2}{36} \quad \text{or} \quad c < \frac{a}{2} \tag{18}$$

which is always satisfied due to requirement for positive outputs of the firms. Q.E.D.

The intuition for Proposition 3 is as follow. If there is an industry-wide labor union in the South, it internalizes competition between the unions, and the wage rates for firm N is the same under weak and patent protections. However, weak patent protection in the South creates higher product market competition. Hence, unlike the firm-specific unions, we do not get the positive wage effect under weak patent protection when there is an industry-wide labor union, while the negative competition effect prevails. Hence, in the case of industry-wide labor union, the negative competition effect under weak patent protection always reduces firm N's incentive for FDI under weak patent protection in the South.

The absence of positive wage effect under the industry-wide labor union creates the difference between Propositions 2 and 3. Hence, the unionization structure plays an important role in determining the effect of the Southern patent system on inward FDI.

3. Conclusion

It is believed that patent protection in the host-country has significant effect on inward FDI, though the exact effect in controversial. We show that the unionization structure plays an important role in determining the effect of the host-country patent system on inward FDI.

If there are firm-specific unions in the host-country, the incentive for inward FDI is higher under weak patent protection than under strong patent protection if the host-country firm is sufficiently cost inefficient. However, if there is an industry-wide union in the host-country, the incentive for inward FDI is always higher under strong patent protection in the host-country.

To show our results in the simplest way, we have considered monopoly labor union, which has full bargaining power in determining the wage rate. However, it must be clear that if we consider the other extreme situation, where the firms have full bargaining powers in the determining the wage rates, the equilibrium wage rates in the South will be equal to the reservation wage rates of the workers. In this situation, the analysis will be similar to our benchmark case of perfectly competitive labor markets in both countries, and the incentive for inward FDI will always be higher under strong patent protection in the South. Hence, weak patent protection can increase the incentive for inward FDI in the presence of firm-specific Southern labor unions if the bargaining powers of the unions are not very small.

References

Bughin, J., and S. Vannini, 1995, 'Strategic direct investment under unionised oligopoly', *International Journal of Industrial Organisation*, **13**: 127-45.

Chin, J. C. and G. M. Grossman, 1990, 'Intellectual property rights and North-South trade', in: Jones R. W., Krueger, A. O. (Eds.), *The Political Economy of International Trade*, Essays in honor of R. E. Baldwin, Cambridge: Mass. Basil Blackwell, pp. 90-107.

Deardorff, A. V. 1992, 'Welfare effects of global patent protection', *Economica*, **59**: 35-51.

Diwan, I. and D. Rodrik, 1991, 'Patents, appropriate technology and North-South trade', *Journal of International Economics*, **30**: 27-47.

Fosfuri, A. 2000, 'Patent protection, imitation and the mode of technology transfer', *International Journal of Industrial Organization*, **18**: 1129-49.

Fosfuri, A. 2004, 'Determinants of international activity: evidence from the chemical processing', *Research Policy*, **33**: 1599-1614.

Glass, A. and K. Saggi, 2002, 'Intellectual property rights and foreign direct Investment', *Journal of International Economics*, **56**: 387-410.

Grossman, G. M. and E. Helpman, 1991, 'Endogenous product cycles', *Economic Journal*, **101**: 1214-29.

Helpman, E. 1993, 'Innovation, imitation and intellectual property rights', *Econometrica*, **61**: 1247-80.

Lai, E. L.C. 1998, 'International intellectual property rights protection and the rate of product innovation', *Journal of Development Economics*, **55**: 133-153.

Layard, R., S. Nickell and R. Jackman, 1991, *Unemployment, macroeconomic performance and the labour market*, Oxford University Press, Oxford.

Lee, J. and E. Mansfield, 1996, 'Intellectual property protection and US foreign direct investment', *Review of Economics and Statistics*, **78**: 181-86.

López, M. C. and R. A. Naylor, 2004, 'The Cournot-Bertrand profit differential: a reversal result in a differentiated duopoly with wage bargaining', *European Economic Review*, **48**: 681-96.

Markusen, J. R., 2001, 'Contracts, intellectual property rights and multinational investment in developing countries', *Journal of International Economics*, **53** : 189-204.

Maskus, K. E., 1998, 'The role of intellectual property rights in encouraging FDI and technology transfer', *Duke Journal of Comparative and International Law*, **9**: 109-39.

Mathew, A. J. and A. Mukherjee, 2008, 'Intellectual property rights, southern innovation and foreign direct investment', *Mimeo*, School of Economics, University of Nottingham.

Mukherjee, A., 2007, 'Unionised labour market and strategic production decision of a multinational', *The Economic Journal*, Forthcoming.

Muniagurria, M. E. and N. Singh, 1997, 'Foreign technology, spillovers, and R&D policy', *International Economic Review*, **38**: 405-30.

Nunnenkamp, P. and J. Spatz, 2004, 'Intellectual property rights and foreign direct investment: a disaggregated analysis', *Review of World Economics*, **140**: 393-414.

Pfister, E. and B. Deffains, 2005, 'Patent protection, strategic FDI and location choices: empirical evidence from French subsidiaries' location choices in emerging economies', *International Journal of the Economics of Business*, **12**: 329-46.

Saggi, K., 2002, 'Trade, foreign direct investment, and international technology transfer: A survey', *World Bank Research Observer*, **17**: 191-235.

Segerstrom, P., T. C. A. Anant and E. Dinopoulos, 1990, 'A Schumpeterian model of the product life cycle', *American Economic Review*, **80**: 1077-91.

Seyoum, B. 1996, 'The impact of intellectual property rights on foreign direct investment', *Columbia Journal of World Business*, **31**: 51-9.

Sinha, U. B., 2006, 'Patent enforcement, innovation and welfare', *Journal of Economics (Zeitschrift für Nationalokonomie)*, **8**: 211-41.

Taylor, M. S. 1994, 'TRIPS, trade and growth', *International Economic Review*, **35**: 361-81.

UNCTAD (2006) *World Investment Report: FDI from developing and transition economies: implications for development*, United Nations, New York and Geneva.

Vishwasrao, S. 1994, 'Intellectual property rights and the mode of technology transfer', *Journal of Development Economics*, **44**: 381-402.

Yang, G. and K. E. Maskus, 2001, 'Intellectual property rights and licensing: an econometric investigation', *Review of World Economics*, **137**: 58-79.

In: Foreign Direct Investment
Editor: Harrison G. Blaine, pp. 57-84
ISBN: 978-1-60456-921-6
© 2009 Nova Science Publishers, Inc.

Chapter 4

CORE LABOR STANDARDS AND FOREIGN DIRECT INVESTMENT IN LATIN AMERICA AND THE CARIBBEAN: DOES LAX ENFORCEMENT OF LABOR STANDARDS ATTRACT INVESTORS?

Christian Daude and Jacqueline Mazza
OECD Development Centre
Andrew Morrison
World Bank

Abstract

This paper studies the impact of core labor standards on foreign direct investment in Latin America and the Caribbean. One of the potentially key attractions developing countries hold for foreign investment is their lower average wage costs. In particular, we study if lax enforcement of labor standards is a criterion that really counts for investors in deciding whether and where to invest? This thorny issue has been at the center of much of the debates on north-south free trade agreements (like NAFTA and more recently CAFTA). Clearly, foreign investors care about much more than labor costs. Capital costs matter as well, as do current demand conditions for the firm's output and expectations of future profitability. Even if the argument is refined to a ceteris paribus argument that – other things equal – investors prefer to invest in where labor costs are lower, there is an important debate about whether stricter observance of labor standards will in fact lead to higher labor costs. In addition to its specific focus on Latin America and the Caribbean, this paper departs from previous studies on foreign direct investment and core labor standards in a number of ways. Rather than examine foreign direct investment in the aggregate, it examines, to the extent possible with available current data, a sectoral breakdown of FDI. The purpose of disaggregating FDI flows is to determine whether broad economic sectors (manufacturing/non-manufacturing) are more sensitive to the enforcement of core labor standards than others. Also, we do not use ratification of ILO core labor conventions as a variable or proxy for enforcement of these standards. While widely used in other models, this study argues that ratification is likely to have little or no link with enforcement efforts in the case of Latin America and the Caribbean.

Therefore, in contrast to previous studies that have used mainly measures of ratification, we show that enforcement and labor market conditions demonstrate to be more important for the region. We also analyze whether some core labor standards are more important than others in influencing foreign investment decisions. In particular, the paper examines whether indicators of collective bargaining, unionization and civil rights seem to be more relevant to investment patterns than child labor, for example. This contrasts with the majority of studies that either examine the impact of only one core standard or – in the case in which the impacts of multiple standards are examined –treat the standards one-by-one.

I. Introduction

The majority of Latin American and Caribbean countries have ratified key conventions of the International Labor Organization (ILO), committing to uphold four core labor standards. These core standards – prohibition against child labor, forced labor, the right of free association and collective bargaining, and freedom from discrimination – have become synonymous with fundamental labor protections and rights worldwide.[1] But ratifying an ILO convention and fully enforcing it in a proactive manner is another matter: violations of core labor standards can be seen in nearly every country in the world, including the most developed nations.

There is no doubt that enforcement of these four core labor standards is less systematic and more uncertain in developing countries. In addition, one of the potentially key attractions developing countries hold for foreign investment is their lower average wage costs. Thus, a particularly important question is if the lax enforcement of labor standards are perceived to keep labor costs down. Are Latin American and Caribbean countries then compelled to compete, not by improving labor conditions and productivity, but by removing labor protections in an attempt to lower wages? The economics literature has characterized this type of competition as "the race to the bottom."[2] This issue has been of particular importance in the public debate (both, in the north and the south) about the effects of free trade and investment agreements between developed and developing countries. The "race to the bottom" argument rests upon two assumptions: that lower labor standards lead to lower labor costs, and that foreign investors prefer to invest where labor costs are lower (Kucera, 2002).

Neither of these two assumptions has gone unchallenged. The first line of attack is that foreign investors care about much more than labor costs. Capital costs matter as well, as do current demand conditions for the firm's output and expectations of future profitability. Even if the argument is refined to a *ceteris paribus* argument that—other things equal—investors prefer to invest in where labor costs are lower, there is an important debate about whether stricter observance of labor standards will in fact lead to higher labor costs.

Some have argued, for example, that stricter observance of core labor standards may in fact increase the efficiency with which labor markets operate and raise the productivity of workers. This might be the case because greater equality is associated with more rapid economic growth, because reduction of child labor leads to greater accumulation of human capital and hence faster rates of future growth, or because freedom of association and

[1] Annex I describes these eight separate ILO conventions, two which apply to each of the four core labor standards.

[2] The "race to the bottom" stands in stark contrast to the long-held belief that foreign direct investment is welfare-improving because foreign investment potentially generates increased employment, wages and labor productivity, leading to sustained increases in personal and national income.

collective bargaining remove the ability of employers to engage in anti-competitive employment practices and provide workers greater job security. This, in turn, creates the conditions under which workers will have sufficient incentives to acquire firm-specific human capital and contribute productivity-enhancing innovations to firms (Kucera, 2002; Maskus, 1997, Piore 2000).

The proof, as the cliché goes, is in the pudding—or in this case, in empirical studies of the relationship between the enforcement of core labor standards and foreign direct investment (FDI).[3] Surprisingly, there have been relatively few such studies, and none have paid special attention to Latin America and the Caribbean. This paper estimates the impact of the enforcement of core labor standards on FDI in the region. Section II below begins by surveying the literature on the determinants of FDI: theoretical models, empirical estimation of the determinants of FDI, and the few studies that have examined specifically the links between core labor standards and FDI. Section III describes the data used in this study and explains our decision to use sectorally-disaggregated bilateral flows of FDI from the U.S. and Japan as our dependent variable. Section IV details the methodology used in the estimations, while Section V presents the results. Finally, Section VI presents our conclusions.

In addition to its specific focus on Latin America and the Caribbean, this paper departs from previous studies on FDI and core labor standards in a number of important ways:

- Rather than examine FDI in the aggregate, it examines, to the extent possible with available current data, a sectoral breakdown of FDI. The purpose of disaggregating FDI flows is to determine whether broad economic sectors (manufacturing/non-manufacturing) are more sensitive to the enforcement of core labor standards than others.
- It does not use ratification of ILO core labor conventions as a variable or proxy for enforcement of these standards. While widely used in other empirical studies, this study argues that ratification is likely to have little or no link with enforcement efforts in the case of Latin America and the Caribbean. In contrast to previous studies that have combined measures of ratification, enforcement and labor conditions, this study then tests whether enforcement and labor market conditions demonstrate to be more important for the region.
- The present paper also tries to determine whether some core labor standards are more important than others in influencing foreign investment decisions. In particular, it examines whether indicators of collective bargaining, unionization and civil rights seem to be more relevant to investment patterns than child labor, for example. This contrasts with the majority of studies that either examine the impact of only one core standard or – in the case in which the impacts of multiple standards are examined – treat the standards one-by-one.

---

[3] It is important at the outset to make the distinction between ratification of the ILO conventions on core labor standards and effective enforcement of these standards. We would expect that enforcement of conventions might impact FDI (in one direction or another), but that ratification per se would have little impact. Unfortunately, ratification is much easier to measure than enforcement—a topic that is discussed in more detail in the data section.

II. Literature Review

This section summarizes the theoretical and empirical literature on the determinants of FDI and more specifically on the relationship between foreign direct investment and core labor standards. The first sub-section describes the theory on FDI and reviews some key findings of the empirical literature on the topic related to the present paper. The second subsection narrows the scope to the limited number of studies that have examined the relationship between FDI and core labor standards, thus setting the stage for the new empirical work presented in this paper.

A. Determinants of FDI: Theoretical and Empirical Models

This subsection briefly reviews four broad explanatory models of FDI and some of the associated empirical literature, looking in particular at their interrelationships.

OLI Model

For many years, the dominant paradigm in the modeling of FDI has been that proposed by John Dunning (1977, 1981). Over time, Dunning has integrated a number of theories into a general paradigm explaining international production. Rather than looking at foreign investment as principally a financial (portofolio) flow, he models FDI from the standpoint of investor decision-making. The basic premise of the Dunning OLI model is that FDI is undertaken if three conditions are met *simultaneously*: ownership advantages (O), locational advantages (L), and internalization incentives (I), hence OLI.

Ownership advantage refers to a firm's tangible and intangible assets which provide a foreign firm some advantage over its domestic competitors. Intangible assets include such factors as human resource management approaches and marketing skills. Tangible assets are often associated with size – factors such as economies of scale or scope, distribution chains and access to international credit markets (Cooke and Noble, 1998: 589-90).

Locational advantage hypothesizes that the location of international production (i.e., where FDI is situated) is determined by production costs and the attractiveness of local markets. Early examinations of locational advantage focused on low factor costs and high trade barriers as incentives for FDI. In part because empirical work documenting labor costs and trade barriers provided incomplete explanations for the location of FDI and in part because of advances in modeling, more attention has been focused on the attractiveness of local markets (Meyer, 1998: 65-6).

These two concepts of locational and ownership advantage can be thought of as the lens through which multinational firms view potential locations for FDI. Different potential locations are assessed for their locational advantages, and the firm examines its own ownership advantages vis-à-vis competing firms in potential locations for FDI. For any given firm, the result of the application of this model might be zero foreign investment (i.e., either remain a domestic firm rather than becoming a multinational enterprise or refrain from investing additional resources to expand the stock of foreign assets already owned), or it might be flows of FDI to one or more locations.

Internalization, the third of the simultaneous conditions, asks the more basic question: why does a firm undertake FDI at all, rather than simply using existing international markets to buy goods and services from external suppliers? In other words, why does a firm choose to internalize their foreign operations by pursuing FDI? The choice whether or not to internalize hinges on the relative transaction costs associated with each option.[4] Simply put, a firm compares the transaction costs associated with using international markets for goods and services with those of pursuing FDI to achieve the same objective.[5] FDI, according to this model, occurs when transactions costs associated with FDI are lower than those associated with purchases of products and services from external foreign firms.

Within the OLI paradigm, there has been empirical research on all three factors whose impact on FDI must be examined: ownership advantages, locational advantages, and internalization incentives. By far the largest amount of research has been on locational advantages. The reason is straightforward: since locational advantage focuses on country-specific factors – unlike the other two types, which have both country-specific and firm-specific factors in varying degrees – it lends itself far more easily to empirical testing. Data to test for the existence of ownership advantages and internalization incentives, available only from firm-specific data sets, are much more difficult to obtain.[6]

The most frequently tested explanatory variables are thus production costs and attractiveness of local markets. Production costs are particularly important to locational decisions when transportation costs are low. Key among production costs is the productivity-adjusted cost of labor; thus, factors influencing productivity can influence FDI. Such factors include transportation and communications infrastructure, as well as the quality of human capital.

The literature has called attention to market-related advantages as replacing factor costs for prime determinants of FDI in more modern times. Market-related advantages include: protectionism (FDI as a way around protected markets), transportation costs, availability of local producers of needed inputs, distribution channels (Solvell, 1987), production, sales and other services, and access to localized knowledge (Cantwell, 1989).

Industrial Relations Systems and Institutional Analysis

Several other theoretical models of FDI have emerged to compete with or complement Dunning's OLI model. One of the most prominent is know alternatively as "industrial relations systems" (Cooke and Noble, 1998) or "institutional analysis" (Meyer, 1998). Cooke and Noble's industrial relations systems (henceforth, IRS) model uses Dunning's OLI model as a jumping-off point. Cooke and Noble develop a typology of IRS on the basis of labor force attributes and management's ability to set terms and conditions of employment in a given country. Countries are categorized on the basis of worker's skill levels (educational levels serving as a proxy for skill level), compensation costs, and constraints on management

[4] Transaction costs in this context are defined as the unobservable costs of using the price mechanism. In the case of engaging in market transactions, transaction costs would include costs of negotiation and contracting, costs of information gathering on prices and quality, as well as opportunity costs associated with delays in delivery of products or services (Meyer, 1998: 88). Of course, there are transaction costs associated with FDI as well.

[5] Meyer (1998: 88-90) provides a simple but elegant mathematical formulation of this decision.

[6] There has been some interesting empirical research undertaken on ownership advantage, though despite the fact that specific ownership advantages may vary significantly by home country of the FDI and by economic sector.

imposed by government and/or collective bargaining structures.[7] They conclude for their 33 country/9 industry sample that the type of IRS significantly influences US FDI abroad. For example, education is negatively related to FDI across low skill-low wage countries, but positively related across high skill and high wage countries.

The empirical work on IRS and institutional analysis takes account of the social, legal, institutional and general policy environment. Typical explanatory variables include measures of: workers' education and skill levels; compensation costs and productivity; the presence of labor legislation such as restrictions on layoffs, provisions for severance pay, or the ratification of key ILO conventions; market size and growth rates; tax policy; incentives for FDI; political risk; and distance from source country for the FDI. For Meyer (1998: 68-9), the institutional framework includes the social, legal, institutional and general policy environment. An important element of the institutional framework is political risk, as reflected in potential changes in the legal framework, political violence or revolutions, as well as changes in the structure of taxes, tariffs or the regulatory environment.

Results using this framework suggest that the general policy environment of the host country is a more important determinant of FDI than are fiscal measures designed to attract such investment. At most, fiscal and tax incentives may shape the location of FDI within a destination country or region (Guisinger, 1985; Hill, 1990; Safarian, 1993, cited in Meyer, 1998). Trade openness of the economy is one key policy factor (Li and Guisinger 1992) along with the regulatory environment. Source country policies matter in exceptional cases of such as Japan in the 1970s (Ozawa 1979) and Sweden (Blomstrom and Kokko 1995).

Economic Geography

Krugman (1991) uses economic geography as an explanation of the regional concentration of economic activity. He focuses on external economies of scale in labor and input markets to explain the cumulative process of geographic concentration. Examples could include: local institutions/workforces adapted to foreign investment (e.g. speak foreign languages) attracting more concentrated investment and suppliers of intermediate goods (e.g., automobile parts) following their customers. Once a critical mass of capital and industry-specific infrastructure is reached, locational patterns can change very suddenly, with investment moving to new centers by historical accident or temporary protectionism (Krugman 1991). Economic geography has made an important contribution to the theoretical literature on the determinants of the location of FDI, focusing on the importance of agglomeration economies in firms' decision calculus. Agglomeration economies can arise from a number of sources, including the geographic concentration of labor markets for specialized skills, information flows and telecommunications infrastructure, and the presence of specialized suppliers of non-labor inputs to production (Krugman, 1991 and 1992). There are, to date, no direct empirical tests of the economic geography approach concerning agglomeration, although the empirical FDI literature that borrows from the trade "gravity" model includes some variables related to this approach (see

[7] Six categories are specified: i) high skill-high wage-high constraint systems; ii) high skill-high wage-low constraint systems; iii) low skill-high wage-high constraint systems; iv) low skill-low wage-low constraint systems; v) low skill-low wage-moderate constraint systems; and vi) mixed systems, with varying levels of skill, compensation costs and constraints. The authors then proceed to estimate a model of the determinants of FDI, including variables that reflect Dunning's OLI model, as well as variables that capture skills, wages and constraints.

Daude and Stein, 2007; Stein and Daude, 2007). The empirical research that has been done has used simulations of the impact of agglomeration economies on FDI (Meyer, 1998).

Conceptualizing the Theoretical Approaches to FDI

One way to conceptualize these different theoretical approaches is in terms of their focus on either country-specific or firm-specific factors; some approaches bridge the gap and focus on both country- and firm-specific considerations. Figure 1 presents this conceptualization.

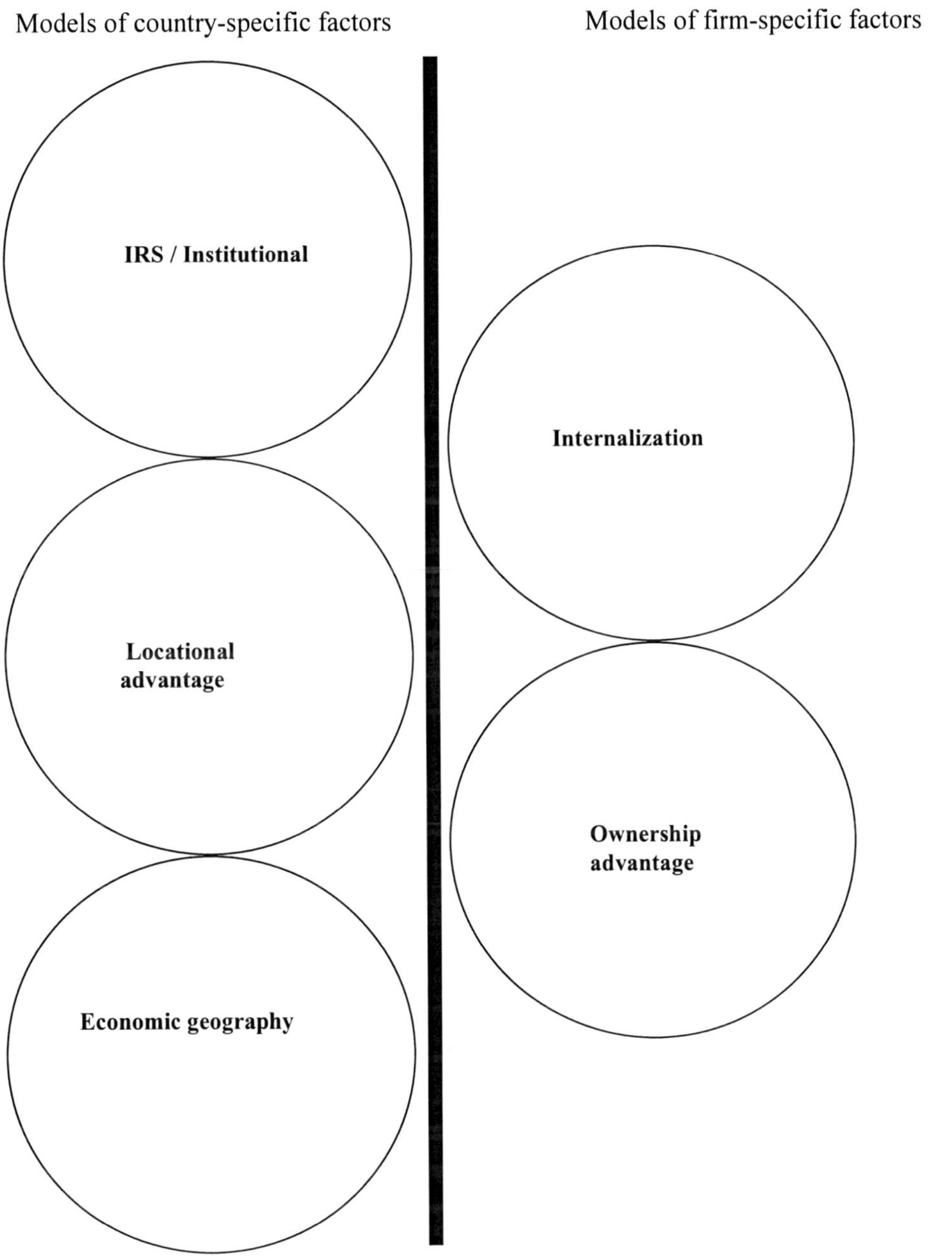

Figure 1. Models of country-specific and firm-specific determinants of FDI.

Institutional analysis/industrial relations systems, locational advantage and economic geography all focus exclusively on conditions in potential destinations of FDI; thus, they are located to the left of the line separating country-specific from firm specific determinants. The fact that locational advantage overlaps with IRS/Institutional models indicates that the two explanations share common elements, as do locational advantage and economic geography to a lesser degree. Internalization and ownership advantage, on the other hand, include both country- and firm-specific factors.

Heterodox Models

Heterodox models are characterized by not being clearly identified with any one theoretical approach; rather, they are reduced form equations with a set of explanatory variables, which may vary significantly from author to author. Table 1 summarizes the explanatory variables used in two such heterodox studies of the determinants of FDI, by Harrison (1996) and Billington (1999). The table is useful for two reasons. First, it indicates that there frequently

Table 1. Explanatory variables used in heterodox studies[8]

Variable	Concept measured	Harrison (1996)[9]	Billington (1999)
GDP	Size of market	N/A	
Sales in sector as percentage of total manufacturing sales	Size of market	+ (C,V)	N/A
GDP growth rate	Market potential	N/A	+
Expenditures on transport and communications	Infrastructure	N/A	
Energy consumption	Infrastructure	N/A	
Hourly manufacturing wages in destination country	Labor cost	N/A	
Sectoral manufacturing wages in source country	Labor cost		N/A
Unemployment rate	Availability of labor	N/A	+
% of government revenue from taxes on international trade and transactions	Openness	N/A	
Import penetration	Openness	(M) + (V)	N/A
Corporate tax rate	"friendliness" to FDI	N/A	-[10]
Severity of regulatory restrictions on FDI	Friendliness to FDI		N/A
Nominal interest rate	Cost of capital raised domestically	N/A	+
Herfindahl index	Market concentration	- (C,M,V)	N/A
Labor-capital ratio	Capital intensivity in sector	+,- (C) - (V)	N/A
Costs of pollution abatement	Migration of "brown" industries to developing countries	+ (C,M)	N/A

[8] Positive or negative signs indicate statistically significant coefficients and the sign of these coefficients. A blank cell indicates that the coefficient was not statistically significant. N/A indicates that the variable was not included in the regression equation.

[9] Harrison ran separate regressions for Cote d'Ivoire, Morocco and Venezuela. Positive or negative signs are included if the coefficient in question was significant in any of the three countries, and the letters in parentheses indicate for which countries the coefficients were statistically significant.

[10] the square of the corporate tax rate.

is significant overlap in types of variables that are typically included: measures of market size, labor cost, friendliness to FDI, and economic openness. Second, it shows that studies also diverge in terms of the types of explanatory variables included. There is no one standard, accepted heterodox model.

By presenting these different types of empirical models, the reader may be left with the impression that they generate quite distinct sets of explanatory variables. This is only partially the case; the different approaches frequently share key explanatory variables. One clear example of this is the variables that operationalize locational advantage and those that capture industrial relations systems. Since locational advantage is determined by production costs and attractiveness of local markets, factors such as wage levels and worker productivity certainly should be included in any test of this model. But they also belong in any test of the industrial relations system. Heterodox models, as their name implies, include explanatory variables from that emerge from different theoretical models. This "sharing of variables" across different models means that it is very difficult to arrive at one best or dominant model of FDI.

B. Core Labor Standards and FDI: Empirical Studies

Relatively few studies have examined empirically the links between core labor standards and FDI. The methodologies and conclusions of these studies have varied, particularly in how to identify and measure enforcement of core labor standards. All studies (including this one) suffer from weak or incomplete measures of the enforcement of labor standards. Generally, studies to-date have found little evidence that foreign direct investment is correlated with lower enforcement of core labor standards (Rodrik 1996, Kucera 2001, OECD 1996, 2000). Interestingly, though, a number of studies (Rodrik 1996, Kucera 2001) have found that higher child labor standards are positively correlated with investment, that is, investors are more attracted to countries where child labor is less prevalent or standards are better enforced. Kucera, however, cautions that greater specificity is needed before drawing conclusions, particularly in examining child labor in traded vs. non-traded sectors, and for wage vs. non-wage labor.

To advance on the common challenges on how to measure labor standards enforcement, some studies (e.g. Kucera, 2001, Rama and Artecona 2002) have combined indicators on the number and type of ILO labor standards ratified with other indicators that these conventions are or are not being observed (e.g. rates of child labor, gender pay gaps).

The first study to combine data on ratification with measures of enforcement on a broad basis was undertaken by the OECD in 1996, and focused on the relationship of free association and collective bargaining (FACB) to FDI.[11] The OECD study examined the impact on FDI between 1995 and 1998 of a composite index that reflects both violations of FACB standards and government efforts to enforce compliance with FACB standards. Regarding violations, the OECD study developed an index of violations that ranked 24 OECD countries and 50 others on a 1-5 scale from "most severe violations" (ranking 5) to "least severe restriction (rank 1). The OECD drew on U.S. State Department Annual Human Rights reports (Section 6, Labor Rights), the ICFTU's annual survey, and ILO reports. These sources identify specific instances of violations of national laws, harassment of workers and

[11] The study was updated in 2000.

union members, and efforts to prevent union activity and formation. These reports were also used to construct a rating of government compliance/enforcement from "no efforts" to comply with ILO standards to government compliance "with satisfaction." The composite index represents the most comprehensive measure to-date of free association and collective bargaining rights. The OECD study found a small but positive correlation (rho = 0.20) between FDI and FACB. This evidence suggests that FDI levels tend to be somewhat greater in countries with better labor rights scores; the study, however, did not control for other determinants of FDI.

Rodrik (1996) examined FDI from the U.S. in 40 countries, and found no relationship between U.S. manufacturing FDI and the number of ILO conventions ratified, when using ratification of ILO conventions as a proxy for enforcement. Of course, there are significant limitations to the use of ratifications as a proxy for enforcement (see data section below). When Rodrik used other measures of the enforcement of labor standards, he found a significant correlation. His model found FDI greater in countries with stronger workers rights as measured by the Freedom House indicators (e.g. civil liberties, democracy, and political rights). He also found a significant negative correlation between investment levels and lack of enforcement of child labor prohibitions, as reported by the U.S. Department of Labor.[12] One limitation of Rodrik's model is that it does not control for labor costs.

Cook and Noble (1998) also examine the link between U.S. FDI and the ratification of ILO labor conventions, as well as other indicators of labor market conditions within their IRS (industrial relations systems) model. In contrast to Rodrik, Cook and Noble find U.S. FDI significantly greater in countries with more ratifications and with more works council policies. Cook and Noble find, however, that union penetration, centralized negotiation structures and government restrictions on layoffs are negatively related to US FDI. As the study includes only five, relatively higher-income Latin American countries, the broader applicability of the findings to the region is unknown.[13]

Flanagan (2002) offers a twist on the measurement of core labor standards ratified by comparing ratifications of a wider range of labor standards to that of the four core labor standards. His regression analysis finds no influence of international labor standards on labor costs, exports, or foreign investment. His results prompt him to conclude that these standards are more symbolic and have little effect on workers.

Of all studies to date, Kucera (2001) includes the most extensive set of country-level indicators of labor rights. He tests their relationship to foreign direct investment and wage costs (manufacturing wages) for 127 countries worldwide. Kucera's conclusions are consistent with prior studies. He finds no solid evidence of a race to the bottom; on the contrary, he shows that investment is attracted to more stable environments with higher labor standards. He suggests that the effects of worker rights may be transmitted not only through labor costs and productivity, but also through enhanced political and social stability and higher levels of human capital accumulation that attract investors. The study does not employ panel data for the 127 countries in the sample, but rather cross sectional data for one a point in time. While a path-breaking study in many respects, it has one serious weakness: in the econometric specification, the core labor standards variables are never introduced

[12] Countries were coded on a scale from 1 – 3 based on reported problems/inadequacies of legislation or enforcement of child labor prohibitions.

[13] These countries are Mexico, Venezuela, Brazil, Colombia, and Argentina.

simultaneously, but rather are considered in isolation from one another.[14] This approach, unfortunately, is likely to lead to biased estimates of the marginal impact of each standard, since the regressions will suffer from omitted variable bias.

There are a range of associated studies that look at the correlation of enforcement of core labor standards with other key economic variables such as exports, trade and growth. Rama and Ravallion (2001) examine whether labor market indicators explain any of the "unexplained" variation in income inequality across countries. Their results show "most labor market indicators, including in particular the ratification of the ILO conventions associated with "core" labor standards were basically irrelevant (Rama and Artecona, 2002: 16). In a series of works, Palley (2002, 2000) demonstrates the importance of core labor standards to developing country growth, income distribution, and improved governance.

III. Data

The data for this study covers the years 1989 -2000. To capture flows of foreign direct investment overtime and smooth out some year-to-year reporting discrepancies, period averages were used for 1989-92, 1993-96 and 1997-2000. In this section, we provide an overview of the nature and limitations of the data used for foreign investment, macroeconomic conditions, core labor standards and related labor market and political conditions. We also briefly discuss the choice of these indicators.

A. Data on Foreign Investment and Macroeconomic and Labor Conditions

This study uses bilateral FDI flows rather than total inflows to the host country. Bilateral data on investment flows have several advantages vis-à-vis data on total flows by host country. The first advantage is that bilateral flows allow one to control for characteristics in the source country, as well as for characteristics that capture the relationship between the source and host countries. A number of theories on the determinants of FDI focus on host country characteristics. Most of these characteristics, though, should be considered in relation to the source country. These characteristics might also depend on the nature of FDI flows. For example, a narrow interpretation of locational advantage might consider only the size of the internal market of the host country.[15] If the dependent variable is gross investment flows, however, size of the source economy clearly also matters. Production costs are another area where source country characteristics are important: in the decision whether to locate some stage of its production process abroad in order to take advantage of factor price differences, a firm will take into consideration not the absolute factor prices in the potential host country, but rather host country prices relative to source country prices. Furthermore, because vertical

---

[14] In other words, Kucera first estimates a baseline model of the determinants of FDI, with all explanatory variables except enforcement of core labor standards. Then he adds to this baseline specification a measure of enforcement of one of the core labor standards (e.g., child labor). A second regression will examine enforcement of a second core standard (e.g., freedom of association), but will not contain an explanatory variable for the first core standard (child labor). Clearly, Kucera adopts this approach to conserve degrees of freedom.

[15] This could be especially relevant for FDI in non-tradable goods, where the host country is the only destination market.

FDI is complementary to trade flows, other variables, e.g. the distance to the source country's market or the size of the source country's market, become relevant to foreign investors. Daude, Levy-Yeyati and Stein (2004) find that vertical FDI patterns seem to especially relevant in Latin America and the Caribbean, so that it is important to account for bilateral characteristics and source country characteristics.

The second advantage of using bilateral data is that some bilateral flow data contains sectoral breakdowns of FDI that are not available in total flows data. This sectoral breakdown is essential in order to test whether a "race to the bottom" is occurring. The argument of lower standards leading to lower labor costs would seem more important for the sectors that were more intensive in unskilled labor and produce tradable goods; the use of aggregate FDI data may not allow distinguishing very different level of sensitiveness to labor standard enforcement across sectors.

Recent trends underscore further the importance of analyzing the effects of labor standards on a sectoral level and over time. According to the IDB (2002), in 1988 around of 65 percent of FDI towards Latin America and the Caribbean was in manufacturing, 10 percent in natural resources and 25 percent in services. However, in 1999 due to processes of privatization and deregulation the composition has changed significantly. The share of manufacturing has declined to 37.5 percent, while services increased to around 55 percent and natural resources to 12.5 percent.

Of the available bilateral flow data, only U.S. and Japanese FDI offer a sectoral breakdown that is both sufficiently detailed and comparable enough by sector to be used in this study. Clearly our preference would have been to incorporate a wider range of source countries, but such data are not currently available.

In the case of U.S. FDI flows we used data reported by the *Bureau of Economic Analysis* of the Department of Commerce. The data on FDI flows are reported by country and sector of destination with a breakdown of 13 sectors.[16] The Latin American countries included are: Argentina, Brazil, Chile, Colombia, Costa Rica, Ecuador, Guatemala, Honduras, Mexico, Panama, Peru, and Venezuela.

There are two major shortcomings to this data set. First, due to confidentiality requirements investment in several sectors is not reported for several countries.[17] These missing observations do not allow us to use a detailed breakdown since we would lose observations and may induce important sample selection biases by systematically excluding smaller economies and sectors from the sample. We overcome this problem by aggregating over manufacturing and non-manufacturing sectors. Second, the breakdown does not include particular sectors that *a priori* would be of interest, such as agriculture or textiles. In this case, our solution is to test the relevance of labor standards on FDI in these sectors using only the Japanese data (see below).

In the case of Japan we used outflows from Japan to countries in Latin America and the Caribbean at a two-digit ISIC breakdown reported by the *International Finance Division* of the Ministry of Finance of Japan between 1989 and 2000. We aggregated the data into

[16] The sectors are: petroleum, food and kindred products, chemicals and allied products, primary and fabricated metals, industrial machinery and equipment, electronic and other equipment, transportation equipment, other manufacturing, wholesale trade, depositary institutions, finance Insurance and real estate, services, other industries.

[17] Basically, data are not reported if the number of companies investing in a given sector and a given country is so small that firm-specific information could be deduced from the sectoral data.

compatible groups with the U.S. data and converted them to dollars using the average exchange rate reported in the *International Finance Statistics* of the IMF. Finally, before aggregating the data over the periods 1989-1992, 1993-1996 and 1997-2000, we expressed all FDI data in constant prices of 1995 prices using the U.S. GDP Deflator. The Japanese database contains investment figures for 21 countries in the region. These countries are: Argentina, Bahamas, Belize, Brazil, Barbados, Chile, Colombia, Costa Rica, Dominican Republic, Ecuador, Guatemala, Honduras, Jamaica, Mexico, Panama, Peru, Paraguay, El Salvador, Trinidad and Tobago, Uruguay, and Venezuela.

We use average GDP at 1995 constant prices from the *World Development Indicators (WDI)* database to capture the effect of the host country's market size. We use this variable as well to take into account the difference in the size of the economy of the source country. As discussed previously, in the case of vertical FDI transportation and trade costs might be relevant in the location of FDI. In order to address these issues, we use the distance between both countries and trade openness. As is standard in the gravity trade literature, we calculate the distance as the great circle distance between Chicago or Tokyo with respect to host country's capital in miles.[18]

The investment climate may also be affected by the quality and consistency of macroeconomic policies in the host country. Greater stability may induce higher predictability of the overall economic environment the firm is placed and reduce uncertainty. We deal with this issue by incorporating the average inflation rate in the host country from the *WDI* database.

As investment decisions may be based on the availability of factors and their prices, we incorporated the average illiteracy rate from the *WDI* database to capture the availability of skilled versus unskilled labor. Additionally, in order to control for labor productivity and labor costs jointly, as Kucera (2001), we use the average ratio of wages to value added in the manufacturing sector from UNIDO.[19]

B. Data on Core Labor Standards and Related Labor Market and Political Conditions

Data on ratification of the eight ILO conventions related to the four core labor standards by Latin American and Caribbean countries was examined initially for possible use in the econometric work. Several things stand out from a cursory inspection of these data. First, the majority of Latin American and Caribbean countries (14 out of 26) have ratified all eight conventions. All countries have ratified convention 105 on forced labor, and only one country, Suriname, has not ratified the two conventions regarding discrimination.

Second, the pattern of non-ratification does not, on the surface, appear to be correlated with strength of enforcement efforts particularly when we examine Latin America and the Caribbean. Compared to other developing regions such as Asia, Latin America and the Caribbean have much greater coverage of ILO conventions, and when ratification has not happened, there are often more plausible explanations for non-ratification than non-

[18] See Frankel (1997) for a discussion of the trade literature and the gravity model.

[19] This variable is only used in the regressions for the manufacturing sector, since this measure of productivity is likely to be quite sector-specific.

enforcement. Moreover, non-ratification does not necessarily seem to capture the countries perceived to have lower standards. Bolivia, Colombia, Haiti, Jamaica, Suriname and Venezuela have not yet ratified Convention 182 (Convention regarding the Prohibition and Immediate Action for the Elimination of the Worst Forms of Child Labor), the most recent of the conventions related to the core labor standards. While these may well be countries where child labor enforcement is especially lax, weak institutions and legislative delays may be better explanations of non-ratification. Bolivia is the only country that did not ratify Convention 29 on forced labor, but it was Belize, Haiti, and the Dominican Republic that were recently named by the U.S. State Department as tier three countries, associated with the worst violations of forced labor standards, and these three countries ratified both forced labor conventions. Brazil is the only country in the region not to ratify Convention 87 on freedom of association, because its legislation does not allow more than one union to represent the same occupational or economic group (Raynaud and Vidal, 1998: 53). Others have reported (Sussekind, 1984) that it would be incorrect to use this national context to argue that there is low enforcement of freedom of association in Brazil. Suriname may be the only country that did not ratify the two anti-discrimination conventions, but neither did the United States – again raising questions about just what non-ratification measures. In sum, particularly for Latin America and the Caribbean the indicator of ratification of a convention does not appear to be a good predictor of enforcement of the corresponding core labor standard.[20]

By jettisoning the traditional indicator of non-enforcement – non-ratification of ILO conventions – a much more complex and difficult problem arises: namely, how to find consistent indicators on a time-series basis of enforcement of labor standards in each of the four areas.

To measure enforcement of the child labor conventions, this study uses labor force participation rates of children ages 10-14 and non-enrollment rates in secondary education. Higher rates are indicative, in both cases, of lower observance of child labor conventions.

There are no specific direct indicators of discrimination that cover a wide range of Latin American and Caribbean countries. Disaggregation of the workforce on a time series basis when it is available, covers only gender differences (male/female), and not race, ethnicity (indigenous peoples or afrodescendents) or other distinguishing labor market characteristics (e.g. persons with disabilities). Gender pay differences were first explored as a proxy variable for labor market discrimination but the data sample set was too sparse to be used. As a result, differentials in illiteracy rates (male/female) were used. This requires an important *caveat* as illiteracy rates would reflect pre-labor market conditions, not actual discrimination levels in the workforce. The working assumption is that labor market and pre-labor market discrimination would occur in roughly similar proportions, although it is recognized that a labor market indicator would clearly be superior.

Freedom of association and collective bargaining has frequently been measured by rates of unionization and numbers of workers covered by collective bargaining arrangements. These measures were considered for this study, but substantial gaps in data availability for regional countries, together with instability of the data within countries over time, raised questions of how significant were these indicators for the region and their utility in the model.

[20] While this conclusion regarding ratification contrasts with Chau and Kanbur (2001), it is based on a review of LAC countries' ratification, rather than a more comprehensive global review.

Thus, these indicators were jettisoned in favor of a broader indicator of labor and political rights as described below.

No data source could be found to consistently measure the number of forced laborers in a given Latin American or Caribbean economy overtime (as an indicator of non-enforcement). Available qualitative information indicates that conditions of forced labor exist in Latin America, predominantly in the agricultural sector and in often illicit sectors such as prostitution. Rankings of slavery and human trafficking compiled by Bales (Bales, 2002) contain information on only 10 Latin American and Caribbean nations.[21] With the exception of agriculture, it is not likely that lax enforcement of forced labor laws would be reflected in any significant way in foreign investment statistics. For this reason and because of the limited country coverage of Bales' data, we have chosen to have no specific forced labor indicator, but interpret conditions permitting forced labor to occur as being reflected more broadly in political and civil conditions.

As broad indicators of national conditions permitting the exercise of civil, political and labor rights, the study uses two indicators: one of civil liberties/rights, the other of political rights developed by *Freedom House*[22] that are available on an annual basis for the overwhelming majority of Latin American and Caribbean countries. While admittedly not a specialized indicator on labor rights, the Freedom House indicators can be useful as broad indicators of the political environment for labor rights drawn from diverse sources (e.g. document review, fact-finding missions, and interviews). The civil liberties index in particular contains references to freedom of association and collective bargaining. The political rights index that we also use is more broadly indicative of business climate in terms of stable, participatory democracy. All three Freedom House indicators were used in the Kucera model (2001) (civil rights, political rights, and a democracy index which is a composite of the previous two), while Rodrik (1996) used the composite indicator that reflects both civil liberties and political rights.

Finally, we also employ data from the ILO on the number of workers on strike in a given year. This indicator must be interpreted with caution, given its complex relationship to collective bargaining and free association. On the one hand, a large number of strikes may reflect a poor environment for collective bargaining in which workers are left no option but to strike in order to press collective grievances. On the other hand, a large number of strikes is a priori evidence that workers are in fact organized and the right to free association is respected. It may also reflect a non-repressive political environment in which the right to strike is respected rather than repressed. Perhaps it is best to interpret this indicator as broadly indicative of a potentially negative climate for investors, both foreign and domestic, since strikes interrupt production and introduce uncertainty over future profit f lows.

The reader will note that this study does not contain variables that measure the enforcement of core labor standards as evaluated in qualitative reports published by the U.S. State Department and others. Work using these variables (by Kucera (2001) and the OECD (1994, 2000) is a valuable contribution to CLS research, but these variables are currently available on a cross-sectional basis and are not disaggregated by economic sector or over

[21] These countries are: Argentina, Barbados, Brazil, Colombia, Costa Rica, Dominican Republic, Haiti, Mexico and Peru with the largest aggregate numbers reported for Brazil and Haiti.

[22] Freedom House. Freedom in the World. New York. An explanation of each of these indicators can be found at http://www.freedomhouse.org/research/freeworld/.

time. Since our study covers FDI in three time periods and uses sectorally disaggregated FDI flows – and because resource and time constraints precluded us developing such measures for all the time periods covered in this study – such measures are not employed here.

IV. Empirical Methodology

The methodological approach used to measure the impact of core labor standards on FDI is to first estimate a "baseline model" of the determinants of FDI without including measures of the enforcement of core labor standards. The measures of core labor standards are then introduced. Dummies for the sub-regions of Latin America and the Caribbean are subsequently introduced to determine whether the results vary significantly by sub-region.

The base line specification employed is:

$$\ln(1 + FDI_{ijt}) = \alpha + x'_{jt}\beta + \gamma \ln(GDP_{it}) + \varphi \ln(\text{Dist}_{ijt}) + \varepsilon_{ijt},$$

where FDI_{ijt} is foreign direct investment flows from country i to country j in period t, x_{jt} is a vector that contains the following host country characteristics: GDP in logs, inflation rate, trade openness, and illiteracy rate, GDP_{it} is the GDP of the source country i in period t, and *Dist* is the distance between either Chicago or Tokyo (depending on the source country) and the host country's capital city.

The dependent variable is defined as the natural log of 1 + the gross flow of foreign direct investment from country i to j. The log transformation has been used extensively in the gravity model of trade (see Frankel, 1997). It has sound theoretical foundations in trade, somewhat ad-hoc in FDI, but also often used in empirical studies of FDI. In order to keep the zero observations, we add a one as Eichengreen and Irvine (1995, 1997) in the case of trade do, and more recently Daude, Levy-Yeyati and Stein (2004), and Daude and Stein (2007) for FDI.[23]

We pool the data for U.S. and Japanese FDI flows, taking care to use consistent definitions of sectors across the two data sources. The use of source country GDP as an explanatory variable will limit problems in the heteroskedasticity of error terms brought about by the pooling of the data. We also test for the appropriateness of fixed effects versus a random effects specification; a Hausman test indicates that the random effects specification is appropriate. Thus, we report both OLS regressions with White consistent heteroscedastic standard errors and random effects regressions.

[23] The use of the log transformations means that observations for which the gross flow of FDI is negative cannot be used. Gross flows can be negative if: equity capital flows are negative (i.e., a U.S. parent firm reduces its equity interest in an existing foreign affiliate); a foreign affiliate repays a loan to a U.S. parent firm or extends a loan to its U.S. parent; or when a foreign affiliates earnings are negative or a U.S. parent receives dividends in excess of its claim on current earnings (see Bureau of Economic Analysis, 1995 for more details). In our data set, we lose 16 observations because of negative gross flows. This option is deemed preferable to using a non-log specification, both because the log specification gives less weight to outliers in the data set and because the fit of the equation is much better with a log specification.

V. Econmetric Results

A. Baseline Regressions

The results of the baseline specification are reported in Table 2. Six different regressions are reported: for total FDI, for the manufacturing sector, and for non-manufacturing. In each case both standard OLS and random effects results are reported.

Table 2. Determinants of FDI, *excluding* core labor standards, for total FDI, manufacturing FDI and non-manufacturing FDI.

	(1)	(2)	(3)	(4)	(5)	(6)
	Total OLS	Total Random Effects	Manufac-turing OLS	Manufac-turing Random Effects	Non Manufacturing OLS	Non Manufacturing Random Effects
Host Country GDP (log)	1.467	0.89	1.516	1.431	0.951	0.509
	[5.42]**	[2.89]**	[7.56]**	[5.70]**	[2.69]**	[1.55]
Source Country GDP (log)	4.017	3.693	3.419	2.009	5.487	4.938
	[3.27]**	[2.48]*	[2.37]**	[1.29]	[3.50]**	[3.02]**
Distance (log)	-0.987	-1.097	-1.028	-1.294	-0.718	-0.914
	[2.56]*	[1.98]*	[2.68]*	[3.16]**	[1.64]	[1.48]
Inflation (log[1+inflation])	-0.063	0.015	0.065	0.065	-0.032	-0.045
	[0.55]	[0.17]	[0.44]	[0.45]	[0.29]	[0.45]
Openness (Trade/GDP)	0.028	0.013	0.028	0.027	0.015	0.006
	[2.80]**	[1.12]	[2.54]*	[2.37]*	[1.32]	[0.46]
Illiteracy Rate	-0.052	-0.066	0.029	0.020	-0.056	-0.047
	[2.83]**	[1.86]#	[1.09]	[0.70]	[2.23]*	[1.19]
Wages/Added Value	-	-	1.183	0.502	-	-
	-	-	[0.60]	[0.22]	-	-
Political rights	0.357	0.307	0.20	0.221	0.246	0.256
	[2.13]*	[2.17]*	[0.85]	[1.35]	[1.31]	[1.68]+
Number of strikes (log)	-0.295	0.059	-0.138	-0.098	-0.330	0.129
	[1.36]	[0.41]	[1.09]	[0.68]	[1.12]	[0.81]

Table 2. Continued

	(1)	(2)	(3)	(4)	(5)	(6)
	Total OLS	Total Random Effects	Manufac-turing OLS	Manufac-turing Random Effects	Non Manufacturing OLS	Non Manufacturing Random Effects
Constant	-142.19	-118.07	-127.95	-82.116	-174.27	-147.32
	[3.75]**	[2.73]**	[2.90]**	[1.77]#	[3.55]**	[3.09]**
Observations	82	82	57	57	68	68
R-squared	0.7	0.66	0.82	0.82	0.64	0.59
R-squared within	-	0.40	-	0.11	-	0.44
R-squared between	-	0.67	-	0.81	-	0.59
Number of pair	-	30	-	26	-	28

Robust t statistics in brackets

significant at 10%;* significant at 5%; ** significant at 1%

The first thing to note is that this model explains a significant proportion of the total variability of FDI flows in our sample – between 57 and 82 percent, depending on the specification and the sector. While the significance and magnitude of particular coefficients vary somewhat among regression specifications, there are some results that are quite consistent across specifications. As predicted in a gravity model of FDI, host country GDP is positive and significant in almost all specifications, as is source country GDP. Similarly, distance separating source and destination countries is negative and significant in every case except for the non-manufacturing sector.[24] The fit produced by inclusion of the three gravity variables – host country GDP, source country GDP and distance – is quite good. If only these three variables are included, almost 60% of the total variation in FDI flows is explained in the regression for total FDI flows.

The remaining explanatory variables in the baseline specification explain a much smaller share of the variation in investment flows. Openness, measured as the share of trade in GDP, has a positive and significant effect on total FDI (in the OLS specification) and on FDI in manufacturing (in both OLS and random effects specifications). Openness, on the other hand, is not relevant for the non-manufacturing sector, perhaps due to the importance of non-tradables in the non-manufacturing sector. The illiteracy rate, a proxy for the skill level of the labor force, is negative and significant in several specifications (in both specifications for total FDI and in the OLS specification for the non-manufacturing sector); it does not have any impact on FDI in the manufacturing sector. The wage-to-value-added ratio in manufacturing is included as an explanatory variable only for the manufacturing sector, but it does not achieve statistical significance.

[24] Note that while for the manufacturing sector this can be interpreted as confirmation of the importance of transportation costs (relevant for re-export to the source country), it does not have such an easy interpretation in non- manufacturing, which includes both tradable and non tradable goods. For the non-manufacturing sector, it can be interpreted as a proxy for transportation costs in the case of tradable goods, but in the case of non-tradable goods it must be capturing some other effect, such as information asymmetries (see Daude and Fratzscher, 2008).

Two additional variables are included as measures of the general investment climate for foreign investment: the log of the number of strikes and the Freedom House score for respect for political rights.[25] The strikes variable is never a statistically significant determinant of FDI. The coefficient on the political rights variable has an unexpected sign in all regressions, indicating that greater respect for political rights is associated with lower levels of FDI; it is statistically significant in the total FDI regressions and in the random effects specification for the non-manufacturing sector.[26]

Since this is a pooled regression with bilateral flows from both the U.S. and Japan, we tested whether the coefficients on the explanatory variables vary significantly for U.S. vis-à-vis Japanese FDI. We tested this hypothesis by interacting a dummy for U.S. flows with all the explanatory variables. For the variables GDP, distance, inflation and illiteracy, there are no differences between U.S. and Japanese flows. Only for openness is there a small difference: increased openness in the host country will attract more U.S. than Japanese FDI.[27]

B. Core Labor Standards and FDI: the Overall Picture for the Region

The baseline regressions reported in the previous section are perhaps not of great interest in and of themselves; rather, they are the building blocks upon which a more complete model of the determinants of FDI is built – a model that includes measures of the enforcement of core labor standards.

As described in Section II.B on data availability, we are able to construct variables that capture enforcement of three of the four core labor standards: prohibition against child labor, the right of free association and collective bargaining, and freedom from discrimination. Unfortunately, we have no measure of freedom from forced labor.

Table 3 reports the results from the regressions that include measures of enforcement of core labor standards. The first thing to note in this table is the coefficients of some of the variables present in the baseline regressions maintain their significance levels and magnitudes; this is the case for host country GDP, source country GDP, distance, and, for most specifications, openness. The inflation rate continues to be an insignificant determinant of FDI. A small number of coefficients on variables in the baseline regressions are affected by the introduction of the labor standards variables. The number of strikes becomes statistically significant in several specifications (total FDI and manufacturing FDI); an increase in the number of strikes is associated with a decrease in FDI. The illiteracy variable loses its negative impact on total FDI flows, becoming statistically insignificant. In the case of manufacturing FDI, illiteracy becomes statistically significant and has a surprising positive relationship with FDI.[28] Political rights generally lose their statistical significance (and the surprising negative impact on FDI).

---

[25] As detailed in section II.B, number of strikes is difficult to interpret as an indicator of observance of the core labor standards of freedom of association and collective bargaining. Thus, we include it only as a general indicator of investment climate.

[26] The Freedom house variables (both civil and political rights) are defined such that fewer rights are reflected in higher values of the indicator. Thus, a positive coefficient on political rights means that lower political rights is associated with more FDI.

[27] Somewhat surprisingly, the intercept for the two countries is also the same; i.e., flows of U.S. FDI do not tend to be larger than Japanese FDI, despite the larger size of the U.S. economy.

[28] This is at least partially due to the relatively high correlation between illiteracy and child labor rates (rho=0.70).

Table 3. Determinants of FDI, *including* core labor standards, for total FDI, manufacturing FDI and non-manufacturing FDI.

	(1)	(2)	(3)	(4)	(5)	(6)
	Total OLS	Total Random Effects	Manufac-turing OLS	Manufac-turing Random Effects	Non Manufacturing OLS	Non Manufacturing Random Effects
Host Country GDP (log)	1.651	0.947	2.265	2.265	0.729	0.646
	[4.89]**	[2.52]*	[6.94]**	[6.94]**	[2.09]*	[1.70]+
Source Country GDP (log)	4.120	4.015	2.474	2.474	4.624	1.79
	[2.77]**	[2.07]*	[2.10]*	[2.10]*	[2.40]*	[0.83]
Distance (log)	-1.024	-1.173	-1.286	-1.286	-1.190	-1.988
	[2.12]*	[1.73]+	[4.14]**	[4.14]**	[2.30]*	[2.54]*
Inflation (log[1+inflation])	0.059	0.091	-0.008	-0.008	0.075	-0.064
	[0.49]	[0.82]	[0.06]	[0.06]	[0.65]	[0.46]
Openness (Trade/GDP)	-0.002	0.004	0.027	0.027	-0.020	-0.003
	[0.15]	[0.30]	[2.02]+	[2.02]+	[1.21]	[0.22]
Illiteracy Rate	0.023	-0.059	0.199	0.199	-0.044	-0.035
	[0.44]	[0.93]	[2.88]**	[2.88]**	[0.92]	[0.48]
Wages/Added Value	-	-	-3.822	-3.822	-	-
	-	-	[1.84]+	[1.84]+	-	-
Political rights	0.561	0.627	0.262	0.262	0.475	0.232
	[1.49]	[2.67]**	[0.85]	[0.85]	[1.10]	[0.96]
Number of strikes (log)	-0.537	0.025	-0.513	-0.513	-0.363	0.085
	[2.01]*	[0.14]	[2.84]**	[2.84]**	[1.28]	[0.47]
Constant	-143.30	-125.33	-112.63	-112.63	-134.20	-46.61
	[3.06]**	[2.17]*	[3.03]**	[3.03]**	[2.15]*	[0.72]
Child labor	-0.149	-0.015	-0.089	-0.089	-0.076	-0.041
	[1.62]	[0.16]	[1.26]	[1.26]	[1.02]	[0.38]
Civil liberties	-0.586	-0.618	-1.013	-1.013	-0.399	-0.147
	[1.36]	[2.02]*	[3.12]**	[3.12]**	[0.77]	[0.48]

Table 3. Continued

	(1)	(2)	(3)	(4)	(5)	(6)
	Total OLS	Total Random Effects	Manufac-turing OLS	Manufac-turing Random Effects	Non Manufacturing OLS	Non Manufacturing Random Effects
Illiteracy ratio	-1.407	-0.754	-0.006	-0.006	-1.462	-0.71
	[3.35]**	[1.06]	[0.01]	[0.01]	[3.20]**	[0.89]
Observations	74	74	47	47	60	60
R-squared	0.75	0.69	0.91	0.91	0.70	0.63
R-squared within	-	0.28	-	0.19	-	0.13
R-squared between	-	0.73	-	0.95	-	0.67
Number of pair	-	29	-	23	-	27

Robust t statistics in brackets

significant at 10%;* significant at 5%; ** significant at 1%

Of course, the variables of interest are those reflecting core labor standards. As seen in Table 3, several of these variables are statistically significant determinants of FDI, but none in the direction suggested by the "race to the bottom" hypothesis. Civil liberties – a proxy for freedom of association and collective bargaining – is statistically significant in several specifications (total FDI using random effects and manufacturing FDI using both OLS and random effects); more civil liberties are associated with more, not less, FDI. The female-to-male illiteracy ratio is negative and significant in two specifications (total FDI and non-manufacturing FDI, both using OLS), implying that more discrimination in labor markets against women is associated with less, not more, FDI. Finally, the point estimate for the coefficient on labor force participation of 10 to 14 year olds is never statistically significant, although its coefficient sign suggests that higher rates of child labor are associated with less, not more, FDI.

The overall fit of the regression is quite good, explaining between 63 and 91 percent of the variance in the FDI flows. It is important to note, however, that the R^2 of these regressions is only modestly higher than those of the baseline regressions. For total FDI, the addition of the core labor standards variables explains an additional 3% to 5% of the variation in FDI, for manufacturing an additional 9% of the variation is explained, and in the non-manufacturing sector an additional 4% to 6% is explained. In sum, the core labor standards variables explain only a small percentage of the variation in FDI flows.[29]

[29] It is important to note that while the core labor standard variables do not add significantly to the explanatory power of the baseline regressions and in some cases their coefficients are not statistically significant, this does not mean that they do not have some impact on FDI and the overall performance of the economy. The regression results indicate is that there is no direct linkage – e.g., between child labor and FDI. Since a reduction in child labor, however, can lead to higher school attendance and therefore lower illiteracy rates, there are potentially important indirect and positive effects of the observance of core labor standards.

Table 4. Elasticities of FDI with respect to key variables.

Explanatory variable	Elasticity		
	Total FDI	Mfg. FDI	Non-mfg. FDI
Host country GDP	1.47	1.52	0.95
Source country GDP	4.02	3.42	5.49
Distance	-1.02	-1.29	-1.19
Openness	—	1.62	—
Illiteracy rate	—	2.64	—
Strikes	-0.54	-0.51	—
Wages/Added Value	—	-1.05	—
Child labor	—	—	—
Civil liberties	—	-2.94	—
Illiteracy ratio (female/male)	-1.84	—	-1.96

A relevant and important question is the relative impact of changes in core labor standard enforcement vis-à-vis changes in the other determinants of FDI. One way to make this comparison is by computing the elasticity of FDI with respect to the proxies for core labor standard enforcement and with respect to the other variables in the regression that can be influenced by policy interventions. As can be seen in Table 4, the highest elasticity of FDI flows is with respect to exogenous economic conditions in the source country. Some variables that can be influenced by policy in the host country exert a considerable impact on FDI. In the case of trade openness a one percent increase in this variable would lead to an increase in FDI of about 1.6 percent in the manufacturing sector. Improving the level of education of the labor force would have a positive impact on FDI as well: a one percent decline in the illiteracy rate results in an increase in FDI of approximately 2.6 percent. Considering the core labor standards indicators, FDI is quite responsive to increased respect for civil liberties. A one percent increase in the Freedom House score (in the direction of increased respect) will lead to an almost 3 percent increase in FDI in manufacturing. A decrease in labor market discrimination against women, as measured by the illiteracy ratio, will increase total and non-manufacturing FDI by 1.8 and 2.0 percent, respectively.[30]

[30] These elasticities are computed on the basis of the coefficients reported in Table 3.

In summary, for the region as a whole, our baseline regressions provide a quite good fit. The core labor standards variables add only a small amount of explanatory power, but there is absolutely no support for the "race to the bottom" hypothesis; on the contrary, when the coefficients on these variables achieve statistical significance, they seem to indicate that stronger enforcement of core labor standards is associated with more, not less, FDI.

C. Core Labor Standards and FDI: The Sub-regional Picture

In order to detect whether the impact of core labor standard enforcement on FDI flows varies by sub-region, we ran a series of regressions in which the labor standard variables were interacted with regional dummies for Central America (Costa Rica, Dominican Republic, El Salvador, Guatemala, Honduras, Nicaragua and Panama), the Andean Region (Bolivia, Ecuador, Colombia, Peru and Venezuela), and the Southern Cone (Brazil, Chile, Paraguay and Uruguay).[31]

In the case of total FDI, the presence of child labor (as measured by the labor force participation rate of 10 to 14 year olds) had an even stronger negative effect on FDI in Central America than in the regional regressions as a whole. The interaction term in the Andean region and the Southern Cone is positive and significant and larger in absolute value than the child labor coefficient itself – indicating that in these regions the presence of child labor attracts FDI.

In all three sub-regions, the interaction term with the illiteracy ratio is positive and significant, and larger in absolute value than the negative coefficient in the illiteracy ratio by itself. This result indicates that FDI to these two regions is attracted by the presence of low-skilled female workers, perhaps because of *maquila* production. Finally, the coefficient on the interaction term with strikes is negative and significant in Central America and the Andean region, indicating that the effect of strikes in these two regions is especially prejudicial to FDI. In the Southern Cone, this coefficient is not statistically significant.

In general terms, the results for the non-manufacturing sector are quite similar to those reported above for total FDI, while no interaction terms are significant for the manufacturing sector.

VI. Conclusion

To examine the potential relationship between foreign direct investment and the enforcement of key core labor standards for the Latin America and the Caribbean region, this study developed an econometric model built on panel data for a wide range of Latin American and Caribbean countries. It is the first study to examine the link between FDI and core labor standards specifically for the Latin American region, and it is the first study that we know of that uses panel data for any region of the world. The most important conclusion reached is that results from the Latin American region seem to be broadly consistent with those cross sectional studies with a more global focus: we find no evidence of a "race to the bottom" in

[31] Because of the limited degrees of freedom available, the interaction dummies were introduced one region at a time; i.e., the base case for all the regional dummies was "rest of Latin America". Due to space constraints, the results from these regressions are not reported in table form.

Latin America. As previous studies typically had data for only a smaller range of Latin American countries, the broadening of this conclusion to a more diverse range of countries and a longer time frame solidifies this finding.

Also in consonance with other studies, we find that the observance of some core labor standards leads to higher levels of FDI. This is the case, for example, with free association and collective bargaining and for labor market discrimination. We must interpret these results with caution, however, since the proxy variables used to measure the enforcement of these standards are far from perfect. Unlike some other studies, we did not find evidence that enforcement of child labor standards attracts more FDI. Nor did we find that more political rights lead to higher levels of foreign investment, as has been documented for a wider cross section of countries (Kucera 2001, Rodrik 1996, OECD 1994, 2000).

The study also documented that the more traditional determinants of foreign direct such as market size and distance between source and destination country are more important than the observance of core labor standards for determining the location of FDI, at least in terms of explaining observed flows. At the same time, our work has documented that, counter to popular impression, increasing the enforcement of certain core standards has the potential to generate significant increases in direct foreign investment. Disaggregating at the sectoral level (manufacturing/non-manufacturing) did not substantially alter the overall conclusions but deepened the understanding of some trends. For example, stronger civil liberties/freedom of association were more positively associated with manufacturing than non-manufacturing investment, and strikes more negatively affected manufacturing DFI.

The tentative results reached here are intended to contribute to an evolving body of literature and study and to focus greater attention to the Latin American and Caribbean region. Clearly variables with a "closer fit" with actual enforcement of labor standards should continue to be developed and explored. At the same time, we would like to caution that better enforcement variables may never resolve the controversy of whether there is a "race to the bottom" or not; proxy variables can always be criticized for not adequately capturing the enforcement of standards.

Much of the perception of the "race to the bottom" in Latin America and the Caribbean relates to impressions about investor decisions in key sectors. In some export sectors such as textiles and apparel, light manufacturing, agriculture and *maquiladoras* some foreign investors are believed to be trying to reduce labor costs through poor and even repressive working conditions (e.g. squeezing out unions, increasing hours without compensation), practices inconsistent with enforcement of core labor standards.

We would suggest that further research in this field might explore trends at the firm level, using firm level data and surveys of investors. This would allow concentration on the key industries or sectors of contention, which are difficult to analyze at the macro level at which FDI data are typically collected.

Annex I. Latin American and Caribbean Ratification of ILO Core Labor Standards Conventions

	Forced Labor		Freedom of Association		Discrimination		Child Labor	
	C. 29	C. 105	C. 87	C. 98	C. 100	C. 111	C. 138	C. 182
Argentina	14/03/1950	18/01/1960	18/01/1960	24/09/1956	24/09/1956	18/06/1968	11/11/1996	05/02/2001
Bahamas	25/05/1976	25/05/1976	14/06/2001	25/05/1976	14/06/2001	14/06/2001	31/10/2001	14/06/2001
Barbados	08/05/1967	08/05/1967	08/05/1967	08/05/1967	19/09/1974	14/10/1974	04/01/2000	23/10/2000
Belize	15/12/1983	15/12/1983	15/12/1983	15/12/1983	22/06/1999	22/06/1999	06/03/2000	06/03/2000
Bolivia	-	11/06/1990	04/01/1965	15/11/1973	15/11/1973	31/01/1977	11/06/1997	-
Brazil	25/04/1957	18/06/1965	-	18/11/1952	25/04/1957	26/11/1965	28/06/2001	02/02/2000
Chile	31/05/1933	01/02/1999	01/02/1999	01/02/1999	20/09/1971	20/09/1971	01/02/1999	17/07/2000
Colombia	04/03/1969	07/06/1963	16/11/1976	16/11/1976	07/06/1963	04/03/1969	02/02/2001	-
Costa Rica	02/06/1960	04/05/1959	02/06/1960	02/06/1960	02/06/1960	01/03/1962	11/06/1976	10/09/2001
Dominican Republic	05/12/1956	23/06/1958	05/12/1956	22/09/1953	22/09/1953	13/07/1964	15/06/1999	15/11/2000
Ecuador	06/07/1954	05/02/1962	29/05/1967	28/05/1959	11/03/1957	10/07/1962	19/09/2000	19/09/2000
El Salvador	15/06/1995	18/11/1958	-	-	12/10/2000	15/06/1995	23/01/1996	12/10/2000
Grenada	09/07/1979	09/07/1979	25/10/1994	09/07/1979	25/10/1994	-	-	-
Guatemala	13/06/1989	09/12/1959	13/02/1952	13/02/1952	02/08/1961	11/10/1960	27/04/1990	11/10/2001
Guyana	08/06/1966	08/06/1966	25/09/1967	08/06/1966	13/06/1975	13/06/1975	15/04/1998	15/01/2001
Haiti	04/03/1958	04/03/1958	05/06/1979	12/04/1957	04/03/1958	09/11/1976	-	-
Honduras	21/02/1957	04/08/1958	27/06/1956	27/06/1956	09/08/1956	20/06/1960	09/06/1980	25/10/2001
Jamaica	26/12/1962	26/12/1962	26/12/1962	26/12/1962	14/01/1975	10/01/1975	-	-
Mexico	12/05/1934	01/06/1959	01/04/1950	-	23/08/1952	11/09/1961	-	30/06/2000
Nicaragua	12/04/1934	31/10/1967	31/10/1967	31/10/1967	31/10/1967	31/10/1967	02/11/1981	06/11/2000
Panama	16/05/1966	16/05/1966	03/06/1958	16/05/1966	03/06/1958	16/05/1966	31/10/2000	31/10/2000
Paraguay	28/08/1967	16/05/1968	28/06/1962	21/03/1966	24/06/1964	10/07/1967	-	07/03/2001
Peru	01/02/1960	06/12/1960	02/03/1960	13/03/1964	01/02/1960	10/08/1970	13/11/2002	10/01/2002
Suriname	15/06/1976	15/06/1976	15/06/1976	05/06/1996	-	-	-	-
Trinidad and Tobago	24/05/1963	24/05/1963	24/05/1963	24/05/1963	29/05/1997	26/11/1970	-	23/04/2003
Uruguay	06/09/1995	22/11/1968	18/03/1954	18/03/1954	16/11/1989	16/11/1989	02/06/1977	03/08/2001
Venezuela	20/11/1944	16/11/1964	20/09/1982	19/12/1968	10/08/1982	03/06/1971	15/07/1987	-

Source: International Labor Organization, www.ilo.org

Annex II. Description of ILO Core Labor Standards Conventions

Forced Labor

No. 29 Forced Labor Convention (1930). Requires the suppression of forced on compulsory labor in all its forms. Certain exceptions are permitted, such as military service, convict labor, which is properly supervised, emergencies such as wars, fires, and earthquakes.

No. 105 Abolition of Forced Labor Convention (1957). Prohibits the use of any form of forced or compulsory labor as a means of political coercion or education, punishment for the expression of political or ideological views, workforce mobilization, labor discipline, punishment for participation in strikes, or discrimination.

Freedom of Association

No. 87 Freedom of Association and Protection of the Right to Organize Convention (1948). Establishes the right of all workers and employers to form and join organizations of their own choosing without prior authorization, and lays down a series of guarantees for the free functioning of organizations without interference by the public authorities.

No. 98 Right to Organize and Collective Bargaining Convention (1949). Provides for protection against anti-union discrimination, for protection of workers' and employers' organizations against acts of interference by each other, and for measures to promote collective bargaining.

Discrimination

No. 100 Equal Remuneration Convention (1951). Calls for equal pay and benefits for men and women for work of equal value.

No. 111 Discrimination (Employment and Occupation) Convention (1958). Calls for a national policy to eliminate discrimination in access to employment, training and working conditions, on grounds of race, color, sex, religion, political opinion, national extraction or social origin and to promote equality of opportunity and treatment.

Child Labor

No. 138 Minimum Age Convention (1973). Aims at the abolition of child labor, stipulating that the minimum age for admission to employment shall not be less than the age of completion of compulsory schooling.

No. 182 Convention concerning the Prohibition and Immediate Action for the Elimination of the Worst Forms of Child Labor (1999). The Convention and Recommendation seek the prohibition and immediate elimination of child labor involving slavery, prostitution and pornography, illicit activities such as drug trafficking and work which will endanger the health, safety or morals of the child. This prohibition will apply to all children under the age of 18.

References

Bales, Kevin (2000). Expendable People: Slavery in the Age of Globalization. *Journal of International Affairs*, **53**:2, 461 – 470.

Billington, Nicholas (1999). The Location of Foreign Direct Investment: an Empirical Analysis. *Applied Economics*, **31**, 65 – 76.

Blornström, Magnus and Ari Kokko (1995). Policies to Encourage Inflows of Technology through Foreign Multinationals. *World Development*, **23**:3 (March), 459 – 468.

Bureau of Economic Analysis (1995). A Guide to BEA Statistics on U.S. Multinational Companies. *Survey of Current Business*, (March).

Chau, Nancy and Ravi Kanbur (2002). The Adoption of International Labor Standards Conventions: Who, When and Why? *Brookings Trade Forum*, 2001, 113 – 156.

Cooke, William (1997). The Influence of Industrial Relations Factors on U.S. Foreign Direct Investment Abroad. *Industrial and Labor Relations Review*, **51**(1), 3 – 17.

Cooke, William and Deborah Noble (1998), Industrial Relations Systems and U.S. Foreign Direct Investment Abroad. *British Journal of Industrial Relations*, **36** (4), 581 – 609.

Daude, Christian and Marcel Fratzscher (2008). The Pecking Order of Cross-border Investment. *Journal of International Economics*, 74:1, 94 – 119.

Daude, Christian and Ernesto Stein (2007). The Quality of Institutions and Foreign Direct Investment. *Economics and Politics*, **19**:3, 317 – 344.

Daude, Christian, Eduardo Levy Yeyati and Ernesto Stein, (2004). The FTAA and the Location of FDI. In Antoni Estevadeordal, Dani Rodrik, Alan M. Taylor, and Andres Velasco, editors. *Integrating the Americas: FTAA and Beyond*, Cambridge, MA: Harvard University Press.

Dunning, John (1977). Trade, location of economic activity and the MNE: A Search for an Eclectic Approach. In *The International Allocation of Economic Activity*, London: MacMillan Press.

Dunning, John (1993). *Multinational Enterprises and the Global Economy.* New York: Addison-Wesley.

Dunning, John (1981). Explaining the International Direct Investment Position of Countries: Towards a Dynamic and development Approach. *Weltwirtschaftliches Archiv*, **117**, 30 – 64.

Eichengreen, Barry and Douglas A. Irvine (1995). Trade Blocs, Currency Blocks and the Reorientation of Trade in the 1930s. *Journal of International Economics*, **38**:1-2, 1 – 24.

Eichengreen, Barry and Douglas A. Irvine (1997). The Role of History in Bilateral Trade Flows. In Jeffrey A. Frankel, editor. *The Regionalization of the World Economy.* Chicago: University of Chicago Press.

Frankel, Jeffrey A. (1997). *Regional Trading Blocs.* Washington, DC: Institute for International Economics.

Freedom House. *Freedom in the World.* New York: Freedom House, annual reports, also available on www.freedomhouse.org

Harrison, Ann (1996). Determinants and Effects of direct foreign investment in Cote d'Ivoire, Morocco and Venezuela. In M. Roberts and J. Tybout, editors. *Industrial Evolution in Developing Countries: Micro Patterns of Turnover, Productivity and Market Structure.* Oxford, England: Oxford University Press.

Inter-American Development Bank (2002). *Economic and Social Progress in Latin America.* Washington, DC: Inter-American Development Bank.

Kucera, David (2001). The effects of core workers rights on labour costs and foreign direct investment: Evaluating the 'conventional wisdom.' *Discussion paper* #**130**. Geneva: International Labour Office.

Kucera, David (2002). Core Labour Standards and Direct Foreign Investment. *International Labour Review* **141**: 1-2, 31 – 69.

Maskus, Keith (1997). Should core labor standards be imposed through international trade policy? *Policy Research Working Paper* #**1817**. Washington, D.C.: World Bank.

Meyer, Klaus (1998). *Direct Investment in Economies in Transition.* Aldershot, UK and Northampton, MA: Edward Elgar.

OECD (1996). *Trade, Employment, and Labour Standards: A Study of Core Workers' Rights and International Trade.* Paris, France.

____ (2000). *International Trade and Core Labour Standards.* Paris, France.

Piore, Michael (1990). Labor Standards and Business Strategies. In Stephen Herzenberg and Jorge F. Perez-Lopez, editors. *Labor Standards and Development in the Global Economy.* Washington, D.C.: Department of Labor, 35 – 45.

Ozawa, Terutomo (1979). International Investment and Industrial Structure: New Theoretical Implications from the Japanese Experience. *Oxford Economic Papers* **31**:1 (March), 72 – 92.

Palley, Thomas I. (2002). A New Development Paradigm Domestic Demand-Led Growth: Why it is Needed and How to Make it Happen. *Foreign Policy in Focus Discussion Paper* (September).

________ (2000). Labor Standards, Economic Governance, and Income Distribution: Some Cross Country Evidence. Washington, DC: AFL-CIO Public Policy Department Economic Policy Paper.

Rama, Martin and Raquel Artecona (2002). A Database of Labor Market Indicators Across Countries. Paper prepared for World Bank research project "The Impact of Labor Market Policy and Institutions and Economic Performance", June.

Rama, Martin and Martin Ravallion, (2001). Labor Market Regulation and Inequality: a Cross-Country Analysis, *mimeo*, Washington, DC: The World Bank.

Raynaud, Andre and Jean-Pierre Vidal (1998). *Labour Standards and International Competitiveness: A Comparative Analysis of Developing and Industrialized Countries.* Cheltenham, UK: Edward Elgar.

Rodrik, Dani (1996). Labor standards in international trade: Do they matter and what do we know about them. In R. Lawrence, D. Rodrik and J. Whalley, editors. *Emerging Agenda for Global Trade: High Stakes for Developing Countries.* Washington, D.C.: Overseas Development Council.

Safarian, Albert E. (1993). Multinational Enterprise and Public Policy: A Study of the Industrial Countries. *New Horizons in International Business Series.* Brookfield, VT: Ashgate.

Stein, Ernesto and Christian Daude (2007). Longitude Matters: Time Zones and the Location of Foreign Direct Investment. *Journal of International Economics,* **71**: 1, 96 – 112.

In: Foreign Direct Investment
Editor: Harrison G. Blaine, pp. 85-121

ISBN: 978-1-60456-921-6
© 2009 Nova Science Publishers, Inc.

Chapter 5

CHINA'S FDI INFLOWS AND MANUFACTURING STRUCTURAL ADJUSTMENTS: INTER-CITY COMPETITION IN THE GLOBALIZED DELTA ECONOMIES

Chyau Tuan and Linda Fung-Yee Ng*

Department of Decision Sciences and Managerial Economics,
Faculty of Business Administration,
The Chinese University of Hong Kong, Hong Kong

Abstract

After receiving more than two decades of heavy foreign direct investment (FDI) inflows since China's economic opening in 1979, two globalized delta economies (GDEs) in China, namely, the Yangtze River Delta region in east China and the Pearl River Delta region in south China, have not only become the two fastest growing regions in China but also served as the engines of rapid growth. This chapter examines first, the mobilization of FDI inflows and its agglomerative patterns in the two GDEs at the city level along with the regional output growth and trade performance; second, the similarity structure in manufacturing production by industry groups at the city level and its structural adjustments overtime; and third, the patterns of inter-city and intra-regional competition being derived. Specifically, production agglomerations and the subsequent industry output complementarity or specialization patterns at the city level would be investigated via the industry specialization (complementarity) index and clustering patterns among cities. The formation of industry and city clusters, the inter-city competitive patterns, and any implications on intra-regional competition in the two delta regions are explored and discussed.

Keywords: FDI, city and industry cluster, production agglomeration, city and regional competition, economic growth, globalization, China

* E-mail address: lindang@cuhk.edu.hk, tel/fax: (852)-2609-7812/(852)-2603-5104, Department of Decision Sciences and Managerial Economics, Faculty of Business Administration, The Chinese University of Hong Kong (Corresponding author)

I. Introduction

Despite of the fact that much literature have attempted to understand the quest of China's remarkable growth at the macro level since China's economic opening and reform in 1979, the more divergent pattern and accelerated unbalanced regional growth particularly during the second stage of the economic opening since 1992 remains a critical question to be answered. The authors have attempted to argue in a series of research that foreign direct investment (FDI) and the regional capabilities or favorable investment environment to mobilize FDI inflows do play critical roles in determining the growth performance by regions. The FDI influx into China has not only demonstrated its power in terms of volume but also in its nature, structure, and effects especially during the evolutions of the two major economic opened delta regions, namely, Yangtze River Delta (YRD) and Pearl River Delta (PRD), in accommodating the investments of joint ventures.

In response to the China's economic opening policy, PRD in Guangdong was first designed as a showroom for FDI promotion so as to materialize the geographical advantages as well as agglomeration economies generated by its core city Hong Kong, the famous largest metropolis in China. Replication of such FDI promotion experience was conducted in YRD with Shanghai serving as its city core to facilitate FDI flows in the region. Functional division of labor between the core city and its peripheral cities in YRD/PRD has been made possible. As the core city of its respective region, both Hong Kong and Shanghai have acted as major service providers equipped with superior capabilities of easier accession to finance, marketing services, global networking and facilities, and international market provided to the SMEs producing commodities in the peripheral cities in the region.

The FDI inflowing into YRD/PRD were mainly export-led SMEs manufacturing firms and productive service providers not only bringing in with them technological and management know-how to the local Chinese firms in the host cities but also stimulating local entrepreneurship, changing local production and industry structure, and enhancing value-added and productivities. Before China's economic opening, most cities of the industrialized regions had similar structure in the manufacturing sector, that is, a balanced and regional self-supporting manufacturing with a complete range of commodities and capital goods fully reflecting the philosophy of conservative economic planning implemented in these industrialized regions at that time. Manufacturing in YRD is a typical example. The Guangzhou city and its proximate area in PRD served as another less representative case. It is reasonable to assume that the influx of FDI effectively acted as a momentum to alter the profile and structure of the manufacturing sector in both delta economies.

According to the findings of our previous researches, manufacturing FDI in the two delta economies are mostly SMEs which inclined to form various forms of industry clusters by staying closer together and closer to the regional city core in order to exploit not only the cost advantages derived from labor, land rental, transportation, and timely delivery, but also the agglomeration economies generated by the core. In PRD, electronics joint ventures inclined to cluster near the core Hong Kong to minimize the penalty and the risk of late delivery while textiles/garments joint venture preferred to locate at more distant vicinity from the core so as to enjoy lower rental. These joint ventures together with the local-owned manufacturing firms belonging to the same type of industry formed clusters within the city in the region and hence, industry specialization among cities would become a matter of fact in the long run.

In order to investigate the critical role of FDI in this regard, the authors believe that one effective way is to study such significant effects through the changes in the industry profile and structure among cities from a regional perspective using more disaggregate data of industry outputs at the city level. The less similar or more specialized industry structure not only demonstrated the power of a free market economy, but also lower competition intensity derived from better diversification of manufacturing production among the cities in the region in response to FDI inflows overtime. This chapter examines (1) the mobilization of FDI inflows and its agglomerative patterns at the city level along with the output growth and trade performance in the two delta economies, YRD/PRD; (2) the similarity structure of manufacturing output production by industry groups at the YRD/PRD cities and its structural adjustments overtime; and (3) the patterns of inter-city and intra-regional competition being derived. In specific, production agglomerations and the subsequent industry output complementarity or specialization patterns at the city level would be investigated via the industry specialization (complementarity) index and its clustering pattern among cities. The formation of industry and city clusters, the inter-city competitive patterns, and any implications on intra-regional competition in the two delta regions are further explored and discussed.

II. The Role of Post-Reform FDI Inflows in China: Globalization of the Delta Economies in South and East China

1. A Simple Profile of GYRD/GPRD: Basic Economic Indicators

The two greater delta economies in China, namely, Greater Yangtze River Delta (GYRD) in east China (GYRD is consisted of one city and two provinces in which YRD has 16 selected cities) and Greater Pearl River Delta (GPRD) in south China (GPRD is consisted of one province in which PRD has nine cities) are depicted in Figure 1. These two greater regions, GYRD and GPRD, together constituted 16.6% (or 7.7% by 25 YRD/PRD cities) of China's total population and 4% (or 1.4% by 25 YRD/PRD cities) of the land area, have served as the two dominating regions to share 22.3% and 12.2%, respectively, or a total of 34.5% of the national GDP in 2005 (Table 1).

Starting from the late 1990s and particularly after China's WTO accession in 2001, rapid growth in the 16 YRD cities has been observed. YRD has taken over the predominant role of PRD (in Guangdong province) as the top national regional FDI recipient. It was recorded that in year 2000, YRD received 27.5% of the national inward FDI and PRD another 27.7%. In 2004, YRD exceeded PRD by receiving 34.6% of FDI while PRD only 16.5%. However, both YRD/PRD are still the two dominating regions to account for more than half of the total national FDI receipts in China.

Among all the other regions in China, these two greater delta regions, GYRD/GPRD also showed remarkable records to outperform China's real GDP growth of 10.2% by attaining 11.1%, 14.5%, and 12.8% in Shanghai (municipality), Jiangsu (province), and Zhejiang (province), respectively, in GYRD; and 19.4% in Guangdong (province) or GPRD in 2005. The same is true in terms of per capita income where the three sub-regions in GYRD achieved, respectively 3.7, 1.8, and 2.1 folds of China's per capita income, while GPRD, 2 folds in 2005 (Table 1).

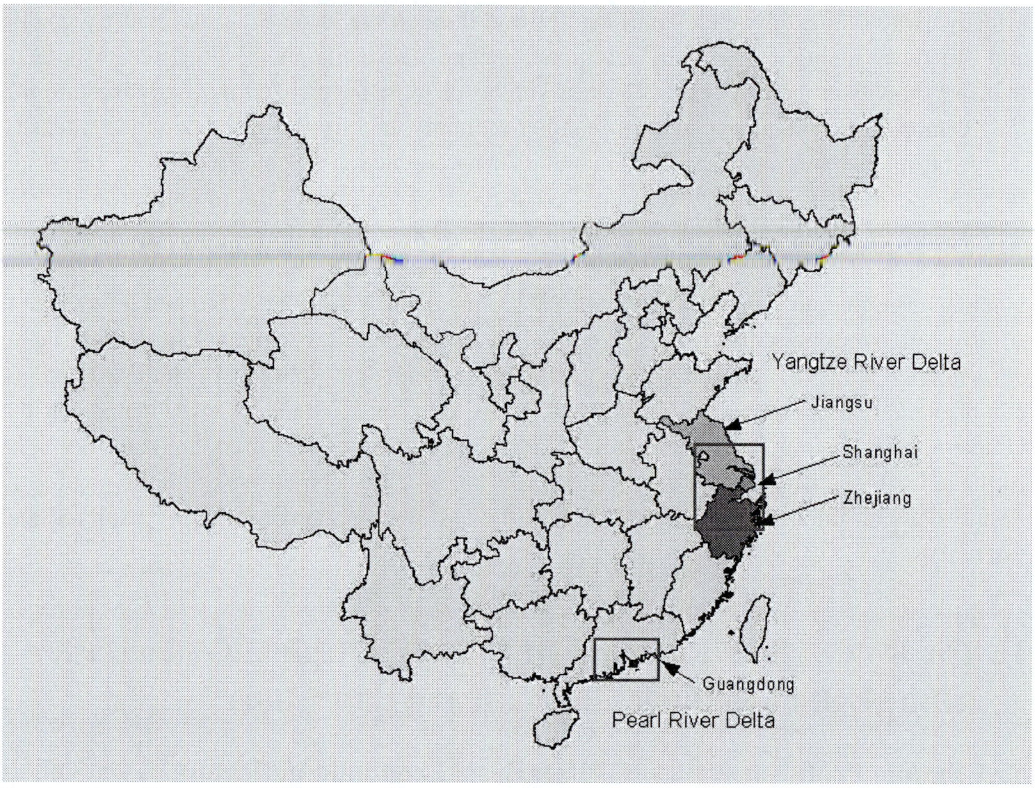

Source: Tuan, Ng, and Lin (2006).

Figure 1. A Map of China: Yangtze River Delta (YRD) and Pearl River Delta (PRD).

Together with the impressive growth and trade records, the two greater delta regions have been able to continuously attract heavy FDI flows since China's economic opening in 1979. Of the total US$ 60.3 billion of FDI flowing into China in 2005, GYRD shared 46.1% while GPRD another 20.5%, representing a total of 66.6% of the national FDI and an average FDI/GDP ratio of 5.3% as compared with China's 2.7% as in Table 1. In terms of external trade performance, the two greater delta regions also showed notable records both in imports and exports to GDP ratios as well as in openness or trade dependency. Among the four sub-regions in GYRD/GPRD, Guangdong and Shanghai, in particular, showed notable records in exports/GDP (87.5% and 81.4%, respectively), imports/GDP (69.8% and 85.8%, respectively), and openness (1.57 and 1.67, respectively), and followed by Jiangsu and Zhejiang. Some other major economic indicators showing the relative importance of GYRD/GPRD are also presented in Table 1.

Table 1. The Globalized Delta Economies in China: Basic Economic Indicators in Greater-YRD/PRD (2005)

Indicators	China	Greater Yangtze River Delta (GYRD[#])			Greater Pearl River Delta (GPRD[#])
	Total	Shanghai	Jiangsu	Zhejiang	Guangdong
Population (mil)	1307.6 (100)	17.8 (1.4)	74.7 (5.7)	46.0 (3.5)	79.0 (6.0)
Land Area (10 thou Km^2)	960.0 (100)	0.63 (0.07)	10.3 (1.1)	10.2 (1.1)	18.0 (1.9)
Output Performance					
Real GDP Growth (%)	10.2	11.1	14.5	12.8	13.8
Per Capita GDP (RMB)	14040.0	51541.6	24490.9	29199.5	28313.1
Current GDP (RMB 100 mil)	183084.8 (100)	9164.1 (5.0)	18305.7 (10.0)	13437.9 (7.3)	22366.5 (12.2)
Trade Performance					
Total Imports (US$100 mil)	7617.9 (100)	956.2 (14.5)	1049.6 (15.9)	305.9 (4.6)	1898.3 (28.8)
Total Exports (US$100 mil)	6599.5 (100)	907.4 (11.9)	1229.8 (16.1)	768.0 (10.1)	2381.7 (31.3)
Total Imports/GDP[(a)](%)	34.2	85.8	47.1	18.7	69.8
Total Exports/GDP[(a)](%)	29.6	81.4	55.2	47.0	87.5
Openness[(b)]	0.64	1.67	1.02	0.66	1.57
Investment					
Fixed Assets (RMB 100 mil)	88773.6 (100)	3542.6 (4.0)	8739.7 (9.8)	6696.3 (7.5)	7164.1 (8.1)
FDI (US$100 mil)	603.3 (100)	68.5 (11.4)	131.8 (21.9)	77.2 (12.8)	123.6 (20.5)
Fixed Assets/GDP (%)	48.5	38.7	47.7	49.8	32.0
FDI/GDP[(a)] (%)	2.71	6.14	5.92	4.72	4.54
Industry Base					
Manufacturing Output (RMB 100 mil)	87046.7 (100)	4452.9 (5.1)	10355.0 (11.9)	7166.2 (8.2)	11339.9 (13.0)
Services Output (RMB 100 mil)	72967.7 (100)	4620.9 (6.3)	6489.1 (8.9)	5378.9 (7.4)	9598.3 (13.2)
Manufacturing/GDP (%)	47.5	48.6	56.6	53.3	50.7
Service/GDP (%)	39.9	50.4	35.4	40.0	42.9

Notes: [#]GYRD denotes the greater region (at provincial level) of Yangtze River Delta province to include Shanghai (municipality), Jiangsu province, and Zhejiang province; and GPRD denotes the greater region of Pearl River Delta to include Guangdong province; [(a)]US$ is converted to RMB at 1:8.22; [(b)]openness (or trade dependency) is defined as (exports+imports)/GDP; percentage of China's total in parentheses.

Source: China Statistical Yearbook, 2006, National Bureau of Statistics of China; Guangdong, Shanghai, Jiangsu, and Zhejiang Provincial Statistics, various issues.

2. Globalization via FDI Absorption and Diffusion: FDI Agglomeration by Greater Regions

China's economic opening and continuous improvements of her investment environment in attracting global investors have played significant roles in mobilizing FDI inflows. The FDI absorption have promoted internationalization and globalization of local activities at YRD/PRD in terms of production techniques, management know-how, and distribution network via the FDI production activities and in particular, the demonstration effects brought about by the joint ventures through the interactions between foreign and local firms. The continuous improvements in the investment environment, deepening institutional reform, and refined law-making at the later stage of economic opening have further enhanced continuous heavy FDI inflows and facilitated not only rapid economic growth, but also technology up-grade and the building of a favorable investment environment for local Chinese entrepreneurship.

The critical role of FDI and its relations to China's regional economic growth especially in the globalization of the two delta economies can be well observed and illustrated by some recent FDI, growth, and trade statistics. During the past two decades since China's economic opening in 1979, the economic activities in the two delta economies were highly globalized through continuous absorption and diffusion of FDI and much enhanced particularly in terms of manufacturing production and trade. Table 2 presents the shares of realized FDI and trade in the two greater delta regions for the period of 1985-2005. During the earlier years of economic opening, Guangdong (GPRD) which was first designed as the showroom and well implemented by preferential FDI policies to receive FDI, recorded the highest share to account for at least 1/3 of the national FDI, while GYRD accounted for around 10%. For the period of 1985-2005, GPRD constituted 29.1%, on the average, of the national total, while GYRD shared another 23.4%, which together making a total of more than half (52.5%) of the total realized FDI receipts in China.

While GPRD remained receiving about 30%, on the average, of the national total FDI for the period of 1985-2005, the dominant position of Guangdong was surpassed by GYRD in the later stage of economic opening since 1992. The leading position of GPRD in FDI receipts has been overtaken by GYRD where FDI increased by 4.6 folds in 2005 relative to that of in 1985. In 2005, the three sub-regions in GYD accounted for 11.4% in Shanghai, 21.9% in Jiangsu, and 12.8% in Zhejiang, or a total of 46% as compared to GPRD's 20.5% (Table 2).

By the two sub-periods of economic opening of 1985-1991 versus 1992-2005, FDI in GPRD and GYRD shared an annual average of 33.9% and 11.7%, respectively, during the earlier stage of 1985-1991, and 27.7% and 29.3%, respectively, during the later stage of 1992-2005. Such a notable record of GYRD in FDI absorption was mainly achieved by Jiangsu (increased from 2.9% to 15.3% or by 5.3 folds) and followed by Shanghai (increased from 7.4% to 8.7% or by 1.9 folds) and Zhejiang (increased from 1.4% to 5.3% or by 3.7 folds) (Table 2).

Table 2. Realized FDI Absorption and Trade Performance in the Greater Delta Regions: FDI and Trade Shares (1979-2005)

Year[a]	Greater YRD (GYRD)				Greater PRD (GPRD)
Nation=100	**Total**	**Shanghai**	**Jiangsu**	**Zhejiang**	**Guangdong**
FDI Share (%)					
1985	10.09	6.47	2.01	1.60	31.02
1987	12.27	9.25	2.01	1.01	25.71
1992	19.95	4.48	13.29	2.18	32.26
2004	41.83	10.79	20.02	11.02	16.52
2005	46.00	11.35	21.85	12.80	20.49
1985 : 2005	1:4.56	1:1.75	1:10.97	1:8.0	1:0.66
Period Average					
(1) 1985-1991	11.67	7.35	2.91	1.41	33.94
(2) 1992-2005	29.25	8.72	15.30	5.25	26.69
(1) : (2)	1:2.51	1:1.86	1:5.26	1:3.72	1:0.79
1985-2005	23.39	8.27	11.17	3.96	29.10
Trade Share (%)					
1979	15.90	13.22	2.31	0.37	6.66
1987	12.54	7.25	3.48	1.81	25.45
1992	13.12	5.89	4.21	3.02	39.72
2004	36.04	13.86	14.80	7.38	30.93
2005	36.70	13.11	16.03	7.56	30.10
1979 : 2005	1:2.31	1:0.99	1:6.94	1:20.43	1:4.51
Period Average					
(1) 1979-1991	13.30	8.44	3.23	1.63	17.03
(2) 1992-2005	24.07	9.79	9.01	5.29	34.33
(1) : (2)	1:1.81	1:1.16	1:2.79	1:3.25	1:2.02
1979-2005	18.89	9.13	6.23	3.53	27.28

Notes: [a]1979, 1987, and 1992 represent the economic opening up of China's Special Economic Zones (SEZs), PRD, and YRD, respectively. For details of the stages of China economic openings and institutional effects, please see Ng & Tuan (2001).

Source: compiled from China official provincial statistical yearbooks, various issues (1980-2006)

3. FDI Spatial Pattern: FDI Agglomeration at the City-Level

The FDI spatial distribution in the two GDEs is characterized by concentration or agglomeration of FDI activities as described by the spatial agglomeration pattern at major cities. As distinguished from GYRD and GPRD, YRD is defined officially to consist of three sub-regions including Shanghai (Municipality), eight selected cities in Jiangsu province (namely, Suzhou, Wuxi, Nanjing, Changzhou, Nantong, Zhenjiang, Yangzhou, and Taizhou), and seven selected cities in Zhejiang province (namely, Ningbo, Hangzhou, Jiaxing, Shaoxing, Huzhou, Taizhou, and Zhoushan) (Figure 2, Panel a); while PRD is consisted of nine selected cities in Guangdong province (namely, Guangzhou, Shenzhen, Dongguan, Huizhou, Jiangmen, Zhuhai, Zhongshan, Zhaoqing, and Foshan) (Figure 2, Panel b).

Panel a: Yangtze River Delta (YRD) - Sixteen YRD Cities

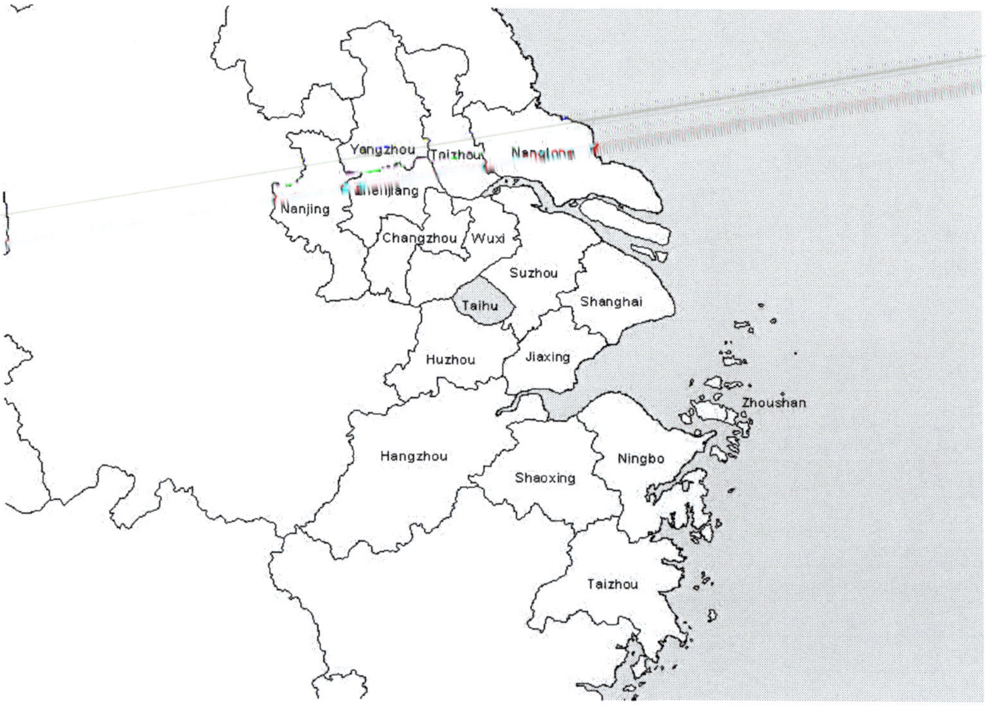

Panel b: Pearl River Delta (PRD) – Nine Cities

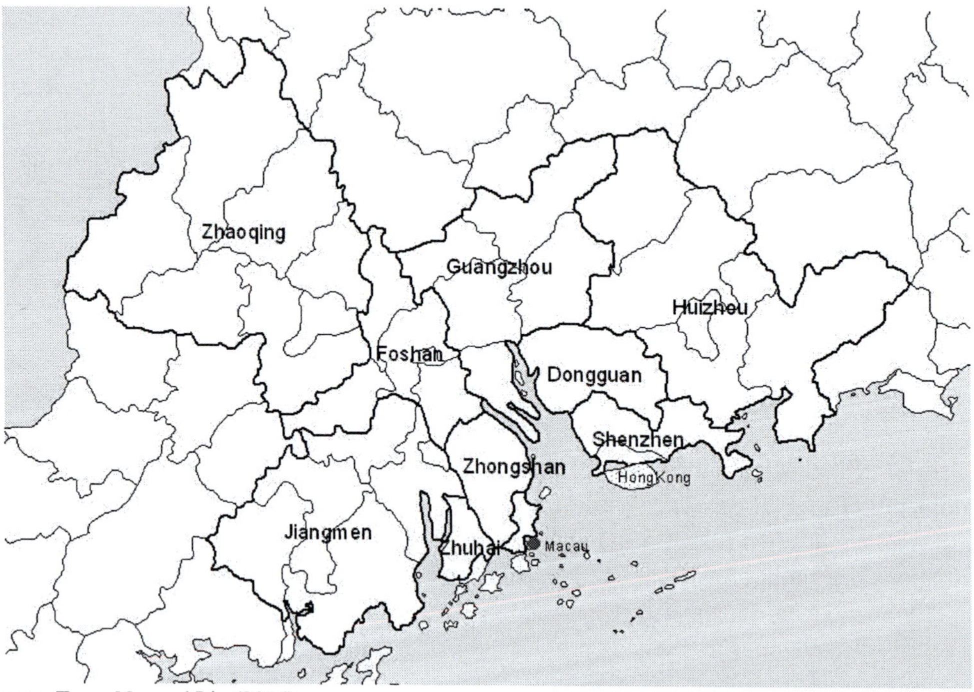

Source: Tuan, Ng, and Lin (2006).

Figure 2. A Map of Yangtze River Delta (YRD) and Pearl River Delta (PRD).

The statistics presented in Table 3 illustrate the spatial patterns of FDI and its agglomerative behavior at the city level in terms of FDI share in both globalized delta economies (GDEs) for the period of 1995-2004. Among the three sub-regions in YRD, Shanghai and Jiangsu (seven cities excluding Taizhou) had accounted for a majority of the FDI receipts by sharing an annual average of 32% and 52.9%, respectively, or a total of 85% of YRD's regional FDI, while Zhejiang (seven cities) accounted for only 15.1% (Table 3).

Table 3. Distributions of Realized FDI in the Globalized Delta Economies: FDI Shares by Major City (1995-2004)

Unit=%	1995	2001	2004	1995-2004 Average	1995 : 2004
Yangtze River Delta (=100)					
Shanghai	35.93	33.84	24.37	32.04	1:0.68
Jiangsu (7 Cities)	51.23	50.11	51.84	52.89	1:1.01
Suzhou	25.73 (25.73)	23.28 (23.28)	18.75 (18.75)	24.27 (24.27)	1:0.73
Wuxi	9.48 (35.21)	10.46 (33.74)	12.14 (30.89)	9.52 (33.79)	1:1.28
Nanjing	4.45 (39.66)	6.95 (40.69)	9.56 (40.45)	6.83 (40.62)	1:2.15
Changzhou	3.63 (43.29)	4.79 (45.48)	2.16 (42.61)	4.42 (45.04)	1:0.60
Nantong	4.57 (47.86)	1.35 (46.83)	4.11 (46.72)	3.38 (48.42)	1:0.90
Zhenjiang	2.42 (50.28)	2.51 (49.34)	2.09 (48.81)	3.35 (51.77)	1:0.86
Yangzhou	0.95 (51.23)	0.77 (50.11)	3.03 (51.84)	1.12 (52.89)	1:3.19
Zhejiang (7 Cities)	12.83	16.06	23.79	15.08	1:1.85
Ningpo	4.41 (4.41)	6.74 (6.74)	7.84 (7.84)	5.74 (5.74)	1:1.78
Hangzhou	4.72 (9.13)	3.88 (10.62)	5.25 (13.09)	4.06 (9.80)	1:1.11
Jiaxing	0.89 (10.02)	2.09 (12.71)	3.81 (16.9)	1.87 (11.67)	1:4.28
Shaoxing	1.43 (11.45)	1.22 (13.93)	3.07 (19.97)	1.57 (13.24)	1:2.15
Huzhou	0.71 (12.16)	1.62 (15.55)	2.61 (22.58)	1.19 (14.43)	1:3.68
Taizhou	0.41 (12.57)	0.43 (15.98)	1.13 (23.71)	0.54 (14.97)	1:2.76
Zhoushan	0.26 (12.83)	0.08 (16.06)	0.08 (23.79)	0.11 (15.08)	1:0.31
Pearl River Delta (=100)					
Guangzhou	30.67 (30.67)	28.67 (28.67)	24.36 (24.36)	28.53 (28.53)	1:0.79
Shenzhen	18.74 (49.41)	24.75 (53.42)	23.85 (48.21)	23.49 (52.02)	1:1.27
Dongguan	9.62 (59.03)	10.96 (64.38)	21.70 (69.91)	12.41 (64.43)	1:2.26
Huizhou	11.41 (70.44)	9.17 (73.55)	6.42 (76.33)	9.79 (74.22)	1:0.56
Jiangmen	9.03 (79.47)	7.90 (81.45)	8.84 (85.17)	7.61 (81.83)	1:0.98
Zhuhai	7.71 (87.18)	8.26 (89.71)	4.77 (89.94)	7.52 (89.35)	1:0.62
Zhongshan	6.44 (93.62)	6.14 (95.85)	5.17 (95.11)	5.67 (95.02)	1:0.80
Zhaoqing	6.37 (100.00)	4.15 (100.00)	4.89 (100.00)	4.99 (100.00)	1:0.77

Notes: Cumulative percentages in parentheses; YRD included Shanghai, eight cities in Jiangsu province (seven cities as reported above and Taizhou was excluded due to the lack of data) and seven cities in Zhejiang province; PRD included nine cities in Guangdong province (eight cities as reported above and Foshan was excluded due to the lack of data).

Source: Compiled from China's official provincial statistical yearbooks, various issues, 1996-2006.

Agglomeration of FDI activities was further conducted in a few major cities in GDEs where only four cities in their respective GDEs had accounted for over 70% of the FDI flowing into the area. At the city level as illustrated in Table 3, the top three FDI recipient cities in Jiangsu, namely, Suzhou, Wuxi, and Nanjing, were found to share, on the average, 24.3%, 9.5%, and 6.8%, respectively, or a total of 40.6% of YRD's total FDI receipts during the period. When Shanghai was included, the four cities together constituted almost ¾ or 72.6% of the total. Similar FDI agglomeration behavior was also observed in the case of PRD. Among the nine PRD cities (except Foshan) receiving FDI, the top three cities, namely, Guangzhou, Shenzhen, and Dongguan, had accounted for a total of 64.4%, on the average, and together with the fourth, Huizhou, constituted almost ¾ or 74.2% of PRD's total FDI receipts during the same period of 1995-2004.

Continual diffusion of FDI inflows into the selected YRD/PRD cities was also observed. Statistics in Table 3 illustrate that among the top three major Jiangsu cities receiving the majority of FDI inflows, FDI receipts in Wuxi and Nanjing increased by 1.28 folds and 2.15 folds, respectively, between the two years of 1995 and 2004. Although Suzhou showed a decline in FDI share, it still accounted for the highest average share (24.3% for 1995-2004) among the three top cities during the period. Moreover, even though Yangzhou had the smallest FDI share among the seven Jiangsu cities, its rapid increase in FDI share by 3.2 folds from 0.95% to 3.03% between 1995 and 2004 is also significant. Besides, all the cities in Zhejiang except Zhoushan recorded continuous gain in FDI share by 1.1 to 4.3 folds between the two years with Ningbo, Hangzhou, and Jiaxing ranked as the top three FDI recipients. In PRD, other than Guangzhou which accounted for an annual average of 28.5% of the regional FDI, Shenzhen and Dongguan were the other two top FDI recipients to record continuous increases in FDI inflows by 1.27 folds and 2.26, respectively, between 1995 and 2004 (Table 3).

III. Industrial Production and Trade Performance in the GDEs

1. Agglomerations of Industrial Production in the Delta Regions

Output Performance by Greater Regions (1979-2005)

While China was found to achieve an annual average growth rate of about 10% per annum for more than a decade, the two GDEs continued to outperform all other regions in terms of output growth. Table 4 presents the regional real GDP growth and trade performance in terms of trade dependency (openness) of GYRD/GPRD since 1979 and by the two sub-periods of economic opening. Both GYRD/GPRD outperformed the whole nation in GDP growth during the post-economic opening period. In 2005, China's national real GDP index increased by about 10 folds, while Shanghai, Jiangsu, and Zhejiang in GYRD by 13.4, 22.5, and 25.8 folds, respectively; and Guangdong (GPRD) by 29.1 folds when compared with the base year of 1979.

Table 4. GDP and Trade Performance in the Greater Delta Regions: Real GDP Index and Trade Dependency Ratio (1979-2005)

Year[(a)]	Nation	Greater YRD (GYRD)			Greater PRD (GPRD)
Real GDP Index (%)*		**Shanghai**	**Jiangsu**	**Zhejiang**	**Guangdong**
1979=100	100.00	100.00	100.00	100.00	100.00
1987	217.57	187.90	243.62	289.69	280.65
1992	327.32	271.14	426.42	466.87	558.34
2004	959.29	1079.70	1872.88	2182.73	2435.94
2005	960.16	1343.85	2253.43	2582.62	2907.89
1979:2005	1:9.6	1:13.4	1:22.5	1:25.8	1:29.1
Period Average					
(1) 1979-1991	182.96	164.01	204.13	229.51	235.18
(2) 1992-2005	629.27	657.52	1107.84	1278.37	1453.86
(1) : (2)	1:3.4	1:4.0	1:5.4	1:5.6	1:6.2
Trade Dependency Ratio					
1979	0.11	0.21	0.04	-	0.14
1987	0.26	0.41	0.12	0.09	0.93
1992	0.34	0.48	0.18	0.20	1.48
2004	0.70	1.78	0.91	0.63	1.84
2005	0.78	1.67	1.02	0.66	1.57
1979:2005	1:7.1	1:8.0	1:25.5	1:7.3*	1:11.2
Period Average					
(1) 1979-1991	0.21	0.33	0.09	0.12**	0.56
(2) 1992-2005	0.46	0.94	0.44	0.36	1.52
(1) : (2)	1:2.19	1:2.67	1:4.44	1:2.83	1:2.71

Note: *represents 1987:2005; **data available only from 1986; trade dependency ratio =(exports+imports)/GDP; [(a)]1979, 1987, and 1992 represent the economic opening up of China's Special Economic Zones (SEZs) in Guangdong, PRD, and YRD, respectively.

Source: compiled from China official provincial statistical yearbooks, various issues, 1980-2006.

When real GDP index was compared between the two sub-periods of economic opening, much faster GDP growth was recorded in the later stage of economic opening (1992-2004) than the earlier stage (1979-1991). Shanghai, Jiangsu, and Zhejiang in GYRD demonstrated an above national record increase of 4, 5.4, and 5.6 folds, respectively; and GPRD, 6.2 folds (Table 4).

Distributions of Industrial Production in GDEs: Regional Agglomerations of Outputs and Formation of Industry Clusters

(1) Agglomeration of Industrial Outputs in the Delta Regions (1978-2004)

Agglomeration of output production was observed to concentrate within the YRD/PRD economic opened delta regions in GPRD/GYRD. Table 5 presents the volume of industrial

production measured by real GDP in the GDEs in selected years from 1978-2004. The output production in the 16 YRD cities, which accounted for a majority of 78.4% of the total regional output in 1980, had become more concentrated within YRD overtime to reach 84.4% of the regional total in 2004. Similar concentration behavior of output production was also well observed in PRD in that about half or 50.4% of the total industrial output in Guangdong (GPRD) was produced by the nine major PRD cities in 1980 and the share increased drastically to 83.5% in 2004.

Table 5. Distributions of Industrial Outputs in the Globalized Delta Economies (1978-2004): YRD/PRD versus GYRD/GPRD

Region	1978	1980	1990	2000	2003	2004
Yangtze River Delta (YRD)						
YRD to GYRD (%)	83.1	78.4	83.5	84.2	84.7	84.4
YRD Total	547.8 (100)	635.8 (100)	2416.3 (100)	15944.8 (100)	23798.3 (100)	28775.4 (100)
Shanghai	272.8 (49.8)	311.9 (44.8)	756.5 (31.3)	4551.2 (28.5)	6250.8 (26.3)	7450.3 (25.9)
Nanjing	34.4 (6.3)	42.5 (6.7)	176.5 (7.3)	1021.3 (6.4)	1576.3 (6.6)	1910.0 (6.6)
Suzhou	32.0 (5.8)	40.7 (6.4)	202.1 (8.4)	1540.7 (9.7)	2801.6 (11.8)	3450.0 (12.0)
All Others	208.6 (38.1)	240.7 (42.1)	1281.2 (53.0)	8831.6 (55.4)	13169.6 (55.3)	15965.1 (55.5)
Pearl River Delta (PRD)						
PRD to Guangdong (GPRD) (%)	49.7	50.4	65.5	76.2	83.2	83.5
PRD Total	91.8 (100)	123.9 (100)	964.3 (100)	7360.9 (100)	11333.8 (100)	13394.0 (100)
Guangzhou	43.1 (46.9)	57.6 (46.4)	319.6 (33.1)	2375.9 (32.3)	3496.9 (30.9)	4115.8 (30.7)
Shenzhen	-	2.7 (2.1)	171.67 (33.1)	1665.5 (22.6)	2895.4 (25.5)	3422.8 (25.6)
Zuhai	-	2.6 (2.1)	41.4 (4.3)	330.3 (4.5)	473.3 (4.2)	546.3 (4.1)
All Others	-	61.0 (49.2)	431.6 (44.8)	2989.2 (40.6)	4468.2 (39.4)	5309.1 (39.6)

Notes: Unit: RMB100 mil; percentage in parentheses.

Source: Compiled from *Yangtze River Delta and Pearl River Delta and Hong Kong Special Administrative Region Statistical Yearbook, 2005*; *China Statistical Yearbook, 2006.*

Agglomeration of industrial outputs was also well observed in some major cities within YRD/PRD. Statistics from Table 5 further show that three of the 16 YRD cities including Shanghai, Nanjing, and Suzhou consistently shared about half of the total output in YRD since economic opening. Shanghai being the major city sharing 49.8% of the total YRD output in 1978, was still contributing a total of 25.9% in 2004. Shanghai together with two other major cities, Nanjing and Suzhou, produced 44.5% of the total YRD output in the same

year. More profound agglomeration behavior of output production activities was discovered in PRD. The top three major PRD cities, namely, Guangzhou, Shenzhen, and Zuhai, contributed a total of about half or 50.8% of PRD's output in 1980 and the share increased to 60.4% in 2004. In 2004, Guangzhou alone had accounted for 30.7% while Shenzhen another 25.6% and the two together making a total of more than half or 56.3% of PRD's total output.

(2) Agglomeration of Manufacturing Production by Industry Groups (2003)

Agglomeration of manufacturing outputs by major industry groups was observed in GDEs. Table 6 presents the distributions of the Top-10 SIC manufacturing industry groups constructed from a total of 30 industry groups in YRD/PRD in 2003. A checklist of the 30 industry groups by SIC is shown in Appendix I. The statistics from Table 6 show that the Top-3 industry groups (namely, ISC420, 403-411, and 375) had accounted for at least 1/3 of the total manufacturing outputs in both YRD/PRD, the Top-5 about half of the total, and the Top-10 about 70%. The Top-3 industry groups in the three sub-regions in YRD, Shanghai, Zhejiang, and Jiangsu had accounted for 41.1%, 29%, and 32.2%, respectively, of the total city/regional output; and in PRD, 43.9%. The respective figures for the Top-5 were 53.9%, 40.5%, and 46.5% in YRD and 52.5% in PRD; and the Top-10 were 73.8%, 63%, and 70.1% in YRD; and 71.1% in PRD.

Table 6. Distributions of Manufacturing Production of the Top-Ten Manufacturing Industry Groups in GDEs (2003)

Unit=%	Yangtze River Delta (YRD)			Pearl River Delta (PRD)
Industry Group (SIC Code)	Shanghai	Zhejiang (7 Cities)	Jiangsu (7 Cities)	Guangdong (9 Cities)
420 Communication Equipment, Computers and other Electronic Equipment	18.44 (1)	5.09 (7)	12.33 (1)	28.21 (1)
403-411 Transportation Equipment	15.12 (2)	5.77 (4)	4.96 (7)	4.37 (4)
375 Smelting & Pressing of Ferrous Metals	7.54 (3)	*	6.72 (6)	*
390 General Purpose Machinery	6.90 (4)	6.65 (3)	6.92 (5)	*
412 Electrical Machinery & Equipment	5.93 (5)	8.62 (2)	7.37 (4)	10.27 (2)
348 Chemical Raw Materials & Products	5.58 (6)	5.28 (6)	9.63 (3)	5.43 (3)
347 Petroleum, Coking, Processing of Nuclear Fuel	4.91 (7)	*	4.16 (9)	*
377 Metal Products	3.70 (8)	3.97 (9)	4.30 (8)	4.22 (5)
329 Textile Wearing Apparel, Footwear & Caps	2.85 (9)	5.75 (5)	10.21 (2)	3.64 (9)
321 Textiles	2.83 (10)	13.72 (1)	*	3.73 (8)
334 Leather, Furs, Feather and Related Products	*	4.33 (8)	*	*
364 Plastic Products	*	3.81 (10)	3.46 (10)	3.81 (7)
365 Non-metallic Mineral Products	*	*	*	3.26 (10)

Table 6. Continued

Unit=%	Yangtze River Delta (YRD)			Pearl River Delta (PRD)
Industry Group (SIC Code)	Shanghai	Zhejiang (7 Cities)	Jiangsu (7 Cities)	Guangdong (9 Cities)
501 Electric Power & Heating Supplies	*	*	*	4.19 (6)
Top-3 (Cumulative %)	41.10	28.99	32.16	43.91
Top-5 (Cumulative %)	53.93	40.51	46.46	52.50
Top-10 (Cumulative %)	73.81	63.00	70.05	71.12
Total Manufacturing Output (RMB 100 mil)	10631.26	12754.91	17745.69	21028.90

Notes: Ranking in descending order of importance in parentheses; *represents values smaller than that of T-10 industry group.

From the statistics showing the industry agglomeration behavior in both YRD/PRD from Table 6, seven groups (YRD has six groups) of the total 30 SIC industry groups were found among the Top-3 industry groups, nine groups among the Top-5 (PRD has seven groups), and 14 groups (YRD has 11 groups) among the Top-10. In particular, the Top-5 SIC industry groups located in both YRD/PRD, which accounted for at least 40% of the total industry output, were shared by seven common SIC industry groups. These seven groups included Communication equipment, computers and other electronic equipment (SIC420), Transportation equipment (SIC403-411), Smelting & pressing of ferrous metals (SIC375), General purpose machinery (SIC390), Electrical machinery & equipment (SIC412), Textile (SIC321), Wearing apparel, footwear, & caps (SIC329), Chemical raw materials & products (SIC348), and Metal products (SIC377). Again from Table 6, the distributions of the Top-5 of the seven SIC groups by sub-regions are summarized as follows.

- Shanghai (YRD): SIC420 (18.4%), SIC403-411 (15.1%), SIC375 (7.5%), SIC390 (6.9%), and SIC412 (5.9%) or a total of 53.4%
- Zhejiang (YRD): SIC321 (13.7%), SIC412 (8.6%), SIC390 (6.7%), SIC403-411 (5.8%), and SIC329 (5.8%) or a total of 40.1%
- Jiangsu (YRD): SIC420 (12.3%), SIC329 (10.2%), SIC348 (9.6%), SIC412 (7.4%), SIC390 (6.9%) or a total of 46.5%
- Guangdong (PRD): SIC420 (28.2%), SIC412 (10.3%), SIC348 (5.4%), SIC403-411 (4.4%), and SIC377 (4.2%) or a total of 52.5%

(3) Agglomeration of Manufacturing Output by Cities: Formation of Industry Clusters in the YRD/PRD Cities (2003)

The agglomeration behavior of manufacturing outputs by industry groups and by cities in GDEs is further investigated. Table 7 presents the distributions of the manufacturing output production of the Top-5 SIC industry groups in 25 YRD/PRD cities in 2003. Three main characteristics of output agglomeration were observed:

Table 7. Distributions of Manufacturing Output Production in GDEs: Top-Five Industry Groups by Major Cities (2003)

Industry Group (SIC)	Output Value*	Output (%)	Industry Group (SIC)	Output Value*	Output (%)
Yangtze River Delta (YRD)					
Shanghai					
420	1960.87	18.44	390	733095	6.90
403-411	1607.28	15.12	412	630.20	5.93
375	801.72	7.54	Top-5 Total	5734.02	53.94
Jiangsu Province					
Nanjing			Nantong		
348	433.94	17.57	321	218.56	19.5
420	413.79	16.76	329	125.22	11.17
403-411	229.95	9.31	348	87.22	7.78
375	195.41	7.91	390	82.18	7.33
347	187.92	7.61	301	79.49	7.09
Top-5 Total	1461.02	59.16	Top-5 Total	592.68	52.89
Wuxi			Yangzhou		
429-435	1136.11	25.80	362	96.03	11.96
321	437.80	9.94	412	91.83	11.44
375	414.51	9.41	403-411	71.57	8.92
420	347.04	7.88	321	58.40	7.27
348	248.27	5.64	390	57.45	7.16
Top-5 Total	2583.73	58.67	Top-5 Total	375.28	46.75
Changzhou			Zhenjiang		
321	211.62	13.90	377	114.38	13.60
348	163.59	10.74	348	106.14	12.62
390	155.22	10.19	344	80.56	9.58
375	128.65	8.45	412	58.54	6.96
420	127.51	8.37	403-411	49.90	5.93
Top-5 Total	786.58	51.66	Top-5 Total	409.51	48.70
Suzhou					
420	1566.13	31.57			
321	485256	9.79			
375	338.65	6.83			
348	313.68	6.32			
412	294.69	5.94			
Top-5 Total	2998.70	60.44			
Zhejiang Province					
Hangzhou			Shaoxing		
321	371.18	13.84	321	689.11	37.20
420	321.12	11.97	362	123.51	6.67
403-411	237.15	8.84	390	122.66	6.62
390	178.31	6.65	348	114.33	6.17
348	144.82	5.40	329	106.57	5.75
Top-5 Total	1252.58	46.70	Top-5 Total	1156.18	62.41

Table 7. Continued

Industry Group (SIC)	Output Value*	Output (%)	Industry Group (SIC)	Output Value*	Output (%)
Ningbo			Zhoushan		
412	333.70	12.74	301	70.56	46.57
347	287.87	10.99	396-401	19.26	12.71
390	202.01	7.71	403-411	15.93	10.51
329	194.14	7.41	501	7.66	5.06
420	185.86	7.10	362	6.70	4.42
Top-5 Total	1203.59	45.95	Top-5 Total	120.11	79.28
Jiaxing			Taizhou		
321	185.00	16.72	403-411	144.05	15.26
329	133.32	12.05	390	90.30	9.57
334	125.84	11.37	412	88.84	9.41
362	115.66	10.45	364	78.37	8.30
365	54.91	4.96	356	72.20	7.65
Top-5 Total	614.73	55.56	Top-5 Total	473.76	50.19
Huzhou					
321	134.65	24.30			
365	57.15	10.31			
412	46.75	8.44			
501	39.16	7.07			
342	35.70	6.44			
Top-5 Total	313.41	56.57			
Pearl River Delta (PRD)					
Guangzhou			Zhongshan		
403-411	630.21	15.86	420	206.87	15.89
348	525.59	13.23	412	194.08	14.90
420	438.06	11.03	329	110.29	8.47
412	266.45	6.71	364	81.66	6.27
347	170.92	4.30	429-435	79.91	6.14
Top-5 Total	2031.23	51.13	Top-5 Total	672.81	51.67
Shenzhen			Jiangmen		
420	3080.88	60.77	377	148.60	13.58
412	293.42	5.79	412	146.95	13.43
429-435	249.17	4.91	348	108.51	9.92
501	249.11	4.91	321	86.63	7.92
102	151.70	2.99	403-411	71.26	6.51
Top-5 Total	4024.28	79.37	Top-5 Total	561.95	51.35
Zhuhai			Foshan		
420	355.96	36.28	412	682.13	26.56
412	173.07	17.64	365	243.83	9.49
429-435	73.05	7.44	420	205.78	8.01
348	57.34	5.84	377	150.74	5.87
501	45.55	4.64	376	143.14	5.57
Top-5 Total	704.97	71.85	Top-5 Total	1425.62	55.51

Table 7. Continued

Industry Group (SIC)	**Output Value***	**Output (%)**	**Industry Group (SIC)**	**Output Value***	**Output (%)**
Huizhou			Zhaoqing		
420	659.86	64.94	420	62.04	14.44
412	94.29	9.28	377	41.47	9.65
364	32.98	3.25	321	36.27	8.44
377	29.17	2.87	334	35.96	8.37
321	21.23	2.09	365	24.87	5.79
Top-5 Total	837.53	82.42	Top-5 Total	200.61	46.68
Dongguan					
420	784.71	37.18			
412	210.64	9.98			
429-435	115.08	5.45			
321	113.57	5.38			
501	113.41	5.37			
Top-5 Total	1337.41	63.37			

Notes: * in RMB mil; for descriptions of industry groups by SIC, please see Appendix I.

(a) Regional agglomeration of industry outputs as industry clusters

As a common phenomenon in both GDEs, some major SIC industry groups were found to highly concentrate in the YRD/PRD cities to account for about half of the total manufacturing production in each city. Statistics from Table 7 shows that the Top-5 SIC industry groups had accounted for at least 45% of the city output by clustering within the city. In YRD, the Top-5 accounted for 53.9% of the total output in Shanghai, 46.8% (in Yangzhou) to 60.4% (in Suzhou) in Jiangsu, and 46.0% (in Ningbo) to 62.4% (in Shaoxing) in Zhejiang; and in PRD, 46.7% (in Zhaoqing) to 82.4% (in Huizhou).

(b) Agglomeration of industry output in major cities

High concentration or agglomeration of industry outputs was particularly observed in some major cities to account for over 70% of the city's total industrial outputs within the region. This is true in three cities in Zhejiang in YRD including Zhoushan (SIC301 sharing 45.6% and Top-5 total=79.3%), Shaoxing (SIC321 sharing 37.2% and Top-5 total=62.4%), and Huzhou (SIC321 sharing 24.3% and Top-5 total=56.6%) and two cities in Jiangsu including Suzhou (SIC420 sharing 31.6% and Top-5 total=60.4%) and Wuxi (SIC 429-435 sharing 25.8% and Top-5 total=58.7%); and in five PRD cities including Shenzhen (SIC420 sharing 60.8% and Top-5 total=79.4%), Zhuhai (ISC420 sharing 36.3% and Top-5 total=71.9%), Huizhou (SIC420 sharing 64.9% and Top-5 total=82.4%), Dongguan (SIC420 sharing 37.2% and Top-5 total=63.4%) and Foshan (ISC412 sharing 26.6% and Top-5 total=55.5%). Output agglomeration or cluster of SIC 420 in PRD in four of the five industry clusters is typical and of particular significance in PRD.

(c) Agglomeration of major types of industry outputs within and across cities

In both GDEs, a few common industry groups had accounted for a majority of the production share in the city in which the production locates and such behavior is also true across major cities in the region. Nine out of the total 30 major manufacturing industry groups, namely, SIC 420, 321, 412, 377, 348, 403-411, 429-435, 362, and 301, showed high concentration and significant shares in the city's total industry outputs both within and across cities in both region; while another five industry groups, namely, SIC 375, 390, 329, 501, and 365, were commonly located across various cities in both regions.

The distributions of the nine manufacturing industry groups classified the Top and among the Top-5 and concentrated within and commonly located across cities in GDEs were summarized as follows (Table 7):

- SIC 420: The Top industry group found in two YRD cities including Suzhou and Shanghai sharing respectively 31.6% and 18.5% of the total city output; and in six PRD cities including Huizhou 64.9%, Shenzhen 60.8%, Dongguan 37.2%, Zhuhai 36.3%, Zhongshan 15.9%, and Zhaoqing 14.4%. When included in the Top-5, SIC 420 was also found in five cities in YRD including Nanjing sharing 16.8% (Top-2), Wuxi 7.9% (Top-4), Changzhou 8.4% (Top-5), Hangzhou 12.0% (Top-2), and Ningpo 7.1% (Top-5); and the two other cities in PRD including Guangzhou 11.0% (Top-3) and Foshan 8.0% (Top-3).
- SIC 321: The Top industry group in six cities in YRD including Shaoxing, Huzhou, Nantong, Jiaxing, Changzhou, and Hangzhou sharing, respectively, 37.2%, 24.3%, 19.5%, 16.7%, 13.9%, and 13.8% of the total city output. When included in the Top-5, SIC 321 was found in three other cities in YRD including Wuxi, Suzhou, and Yangzhou sharing, respectively, 9.9% (Top-2), 6.8% (Top-2), and 7.3% (Top-4) of the total city output; and four cities in PRD including Zhaoqing 8.4% (Top-3), Jiangmen 7.9% (Top-4), Dongguan 5.4% (Top-4), and Huizhou 2.1% (Top-5).
- SIC 412: The Top industry group in Ningbo in YRD sharing 12.7% and Foshan in PRD 26.6%; and among the Top-five in YRD in Yangzhou 11.4% (Top-2), Taizhou 9.4% (Top-3), Huzhou 8.4% (Top-3), Zhenjiang 7.0% (Top-5), and Shanghai 5.9% (Top-5); and in PRD in Zhuhai 17.6% (Top-2), Zhongshan 14.9% (Top-2), Jiangmen 13.4% (Top-2), Dongguan 10.0% (Top-2), Huizhou 9.3% (Top-2), Guangzhou 6.7% (Top-4), and Shenzhen 5.8% (Top-2).
- SIC 377: The Top industry group in Zhenjiang in YRD sharing 13.6% and Jiangmen in PRD sharing 13.6%; and among the Top-5 in PRD in Zhaoqing 9.7% (Top-2), Foshan 5.9% (Top-4), and Huizhou 2.8% (Top-4).
- SIC 348: The Top industry group in Nanjing sharing 17.6% and among the Top-5 in seven cities in YRD including Zhenjiang 12.6% (Top-2), Changzhou 10.7% (Top-2), Nantong 7.8% (Top-3), Suzhou 6.3% (Top-4), Shaoxing 6.2% (Top-4), Wuxi 5.6% (Top-4), and Hangzhou 5.4% (Top-5); and in three cities in PRD including Guangzhou 13.2% (Top-2), Jiangmen 9.9% (Top-3), and Zhuhai 5.8% (Top-4).
- SIC 403-411: The Top industry group in Taizhou in YRD and Guangzhou in PRD sharing, respectively, 15.3% and 15.9% of the total city output. It is also found among the Top-5 industry groups in six YRD cities including Shanghai sharing 15.1% (Top-2), Zhoushan 12.7% (Top-2), Yangzhou 11.4% (Top-3), Nanjing 9.3% (Top-3), Hangzhou 8.8% (Top-3), Zhenjiang 5.9% (Top-5); and in PRD, in Jiangmen 6.5% (Top-5).

- SIC 429-435: The Top industry group in Wuxi in YRD sharing 25.8% of the total city output and among the Top-5 industry groups in two PRD cities including Zhongshan and Dongguan sharing 6.1% (Top-5), and 5.5% (Top-3), respectively.
- SIC 362: The Top industry group in Yangzhou in YRD sharing 12.0% of the total city output and among the Top-5 industry groups in Jiaxing 10.5% (Top-4), Shaoxing 6.7% (Top-2), and Zhoushan 4.4% (Top-5) in YRD.
- SIC 301: The Top industry group in YRD, in Zhoushan sharing 46.6% of the total city output and among the Top-5 industry groups in Nantong in YRD sharing 7.1% (Top 5); and in PRD, in Shenzhen sharing 4.9% (Top-4).

The distributions of the remaining five industry groups classified among the Top-5 industry groups and commonly located across cities within the region were summarized as follows (Table 7):

- SIC 375: Among the Top-5 industry groups in five YRD cities including Shanghai 7.5% (Top-3) and four other YRD cities in Jiangsu including Wuxi 9.4% (Top-3), Changzhou 8.5% (Top-4), Nanjing 7.9% (Top-4), and Suzhou 6.8% (Top-3).
- SIC 390: Among the Top-5 industry groups in eight YRD cities including Changzhou 10.2% (Top-3), Taizhou 9.6% (Top-2), Ningbo 7.7% (Top-3), Nantong 7.3% (Top-4), Yangzhou 7.2% (Top-5), Shanghai sharing 6.9% (Top-5), Hangzhou 6.7% (Top-4), and Shaoxing 6.6% (Top-3).
- SIC 329: Among the Top-5 industry groups in four YRD cities including Jiaxing sharing 12.1% (Top-2), Nantong 11.2% (Top-2), Ningbo 7.4% (Top-4), and Shaoxing 5.8% (Top-5); and in PRD, Zhongshan 14.9% (Top-2).
- SIC 501: Among the Top-5 industry groups in Huzhou sharing 7.1% (Top-4) and Zhoushan 5.1% (Top-4) in YRD; and in PRD, Dongguan 5.4% (Top-5), Shenzhen 4.9% (Top-4), and Zhuhai 4.6% (Top-5).
- SIC 365: Among the Top-5 industry groups in two YRD cities in Huzhou sharing 10.3% (Top-2) and Jiaxing 5.0% (Top-5); and in two PRD cities in Foshan 9.5% (Top-2) and Zhaoqing 5.6% (Top-5).

2. Globalization of Industrial Outputs: Trade Performance in the Globalized Delta Economies

Trade Shares by Greater Regions (1979-2005)

Similar remarkable growth was observed in the trade performance in GDEs since China's economic opening and reform. Table 2 also presents the distributions of trade in terms of trade shares of GYRD/GPRD. Rapidly increasing trade shares in both greater delta regions were observed since economic opening and by its sub-periods. Both GYRD/GPRD as a total accounted for 66.8% of the national trade in 2005 as compared to only 22.6% in 1979. GPRD achieved the highest share, on the average, to account for 27.3% of national total trade representing a gain of 4.5 folds during the post-reform period, while GYRD accounted for an average of 18.9% representing a gain of 2.3 folds with Shanghai, Jiangsu, and Zhejiang sharing an average of 9.1% (1 fold), 6.2% (6.9 folds), and 3.5% (20.4 folds), respectively (Table 2). Nevertheless, the more rapid increase in the trade share in GYRD has surpassed that of GPRD since 2003. Among the four sub-regions in GDEs, Zhejiang had the most rapid growth and gain in trade during the same period.

By sub-periods of economic opening, it is further observed that the trade shares of GYRD/GPRD increased more rapidly at the later stage than that of the first stage. Again from Table 2, the respective figures of trade share by the two sub-periods for GYRD increased from 13.3% to 23.1% representing an increase by 1.8 folds, and that of GPRD from 17% to 37.3% or by 2 folds. All three sub-regions in GYRD gained in trade shares in descending order of Zhejiang, Jiangsu, and Shanghai, by 3.3, 2.8, and 1.2 folds, respectively.

Trade Dependency by Greater Regions (1979-2005)

In considering trade performance in terms of trade dependency or openness in GDEs, the statistics in Table 4 further illustrate that both delta regions have become more dependent on external trade. It is observed that both Shanghai in YRD and Guangdong (GPRD) relied more heavily on external trade than the other two sub-regions, namely, Jiangsu and Zhejiang in YRD. Among the four sub-regions, Guangdong was the most open and fastest growing region in terms of trade dependency to record a ratio of 1.1, on the average, and following by Shanghai's 0.64, Zhejiang's 0.33, and Jiangsu's 0.28 for the period of 1979-2005.

Relative to the nation's trade dependency ratio to increase from 0.11 to 0.78 or by 7.1 folds for 1979-2005, the dependency ratio in GYRD/GPRD had increased at a much faster pace. Between 1979 and 2005, the openness in GPRD had increased from 0.14 to 1.57 or 11.2 folds, while in GYRD, Shanghai from 0.21 to 1.8 or 8 folds, Jiangsu from 0.04 to 1.0 or 25.5 folds, and Zhejiang from 0.09 (in 1987) to 0.66 or 7.3 folds. By sub-periods of economic opening, both greater delta regions also recorded more rapid growth in trade dependency at the later stage with GPRD from 0.56 to 1.52 or an increase of 2.7 folds, and in GYRD, Shanghai from 0.33 to 0.94 or 2.7 folds, Jiangsu from 0.09 to 0.44 or 4.4 folds, and Zhejiang from 0.12 to 0.36 or 2.8 folds. Therefore, Jiangsu had the fastest growth in openness among the four sub-regions and followed by Guangdong, Shanghai and Zhejiang.

From the simple statistics of FDI and together with both the GDP and trade growth records as presented above, important implications between the relationships among FDI inflows, output growth, and trade flows can be explored. The observations presented in the previous sections further provided supporting evidence to the understanding of the arguments in some recent literature regarding the close relationship between GDP growth and FDI from which external trade flows were further derived. Earlier FDI investing in GDEs and especially in PRD in labor-intensive and low technology industries, such as textiles, clothing, toys, clocks, electrical appliances, and plastics, were upgraded to the production of more technology-advanced electronics, communication and computers equipments, chemical products, and other high value-added production targeted for higher productivity and exporting purposes. Besides, FDI, through the joint ventures manufacturing activities in GDEs, further interacted with local manufacturing production and supplemented the manufacturing industry structure and output in GDEs where local production had been less capable to cater to international market needs.

IV. Inter-City and Intra-Regional Competition: Manufacturing Structural Adjustments in Globalized Delta Economies

The absorption of FDI and its role in enhancing the globalization of the delta economies has directed the flows and agglomerations of industrial output production to concentrate in major cities in GDEs as illustrated in the previous section. Such impacts of FDI flows on manufacturing structural and output adjustments and the subsequent competition patterns generated among cities (and city pairs) in the form of industry and city clusters would be examined through the industry complementarity or specialization behavior of the cities in GDEs. Reflections from the inter-city and intra-regional competitive patterns being derived would be further discussed in this section.

1. Industry Complementarities and Manufacturing Structural Adjustments: Measurements

Industry Complementarities (I): Modified Industry Specialization Index

Manufacturing industry agglomeration (or production clusters) and industry complementarity (or specialization) behavior and its adjustments overtime would be estimated and examined by the modified Krugman's industry specialization index (ISI) using output share (S) as follows:

$$ISI_{jkr} = \Sigma_i \mid S_{ijr} - S_{ikr} \mid \quad (1)$$

where ISI_{jkr} is the industry specialization index between the jth and k^{th} city in region r. S_{ijr} and S_{ikr} represent the output shares of ith industry in j^{th} and k^{th} city in region r; respectively, where i=1 to i; j=1 to j; k=1 to k, and r=1 to r. Then, $S_{ijr} = Q_{ijr}/Q_{jr}$ and $S_{ikr} = Q_{ikr}/Q_{kr}$ where Q_{ijr} and Q_{ikr} are the values of ith industry output in city j and k in region r, respectively; and Q_{jr} and Q_{kr} are the total industry output values in city j and k in region r, respectively.

ISI_{jkr} is defined as the sum of the absolute values of the differences in output shares between S_{ijr} and S_{ikr} over i industries in city j and k in region r. It follows that the range of ISI_{jkr} is '0' to '2' where '0' stands for perfect substitution among i industries, that is, no complementarity which implied perfect identical industry structure between city j and k in r; while '2' stands for no substitution, that is, perfect complementarity which implied perfect differential industry structure between city j and k in region r. ISI_{jk} would be computed for a total of 30 manufacturing industry groups (that is, i=1 to 30) classified at the SIC 3-digit level by city pairs between j and k cities in both delta regions r (that is, r=2; for PRD, j=1 to 9 and for YRD, k=1 to 16).

Table 8. Industry Specialization Structure among YRD Cities (2003)

ISI_{jk}, γ_{jk}	Yangtze River Delta (YRD)														
	SH	Zhejiang							Jiangsu						
YRD Cities	YRD1	YRD2	YRD3	YRD4	YRD5	YRD6	YRD7	YRD8	YRD9	YRD10	YRD11	YRD12	YRD13	YRD14	YRD15
Shanghai	-	0.526	0.683	0.898	1.099	1.147	1.075	1.289	0.795	0.379	0.785	0.654	0.544	0.848	0.799
Hangzhou	0.585	-	0.742	0.896	0.760	0.924	0.800	1.294	0.914	0.662	0.686	0.558	0.588	0.620	0.697
Ningbo	0.780	0.358	-	0.626	0.930	0.986	0.956	1.265	0.885	0.785	0.841	0.663	0.839	0.689	0.549
Jiaxing	0.216	0.437	0.307	-	0.834	1.068	1.029	1.379	0.756	1.043	1.032	0.878	1.001	0.800	0.644
Huzhou	0.272	0.227	0.162	0.433	-	0.832	0.754	1.373	1.185	1.100	1.043	0.891	0.829	0.550	0.750
Shaoxing	0.295	0.489	0.386	0.579	0.515	-	0.728	1.482	1.010	1.190	1.123	0.850	1.024	0.722	0.966
Zhoushan	0.368	0.373	0.479	0.431	0.238	0.543	-	1.377	1.084	1.156	0.974	0.757	0.979	0.610	0.787
Taizhou	0.310	0.258	0.254	0.234	0.441	0.498	0.379	-	1.203	1.355	1.364	1.304	1.400	1.207	1.115
Nanjing	0.889	0.531	0.732	0.267	0.245	0.277	0.313	0.303	-	1.047	1.133	0.841	1.116	0.993	0.696
Wuxi	0.729	0.637	0.581	0.414	0.231	0.564	0.462	0.312	0.530	-	1.898	0.695	03643	0.909	0.918
Changzhou	0.768	0.650	0.595	0.528	0.526	0.733	0.533	0.500	0.659	0.845	-	0.604	0.689	0.819	0.875
Suzhou	0.740	0.667	0.614	0.555	0.383	0.592	0.462	0.377	0.611	0.917	0.891	-	0.626	0.566	0.687
Nantong	0.603	0.551	0.663	0.654	0.443	0.751	0.673	0.440	0.638	0.664	0.831	0.744	-	0.757	0.871
Yangzhou	0.500	0.520	0.596	0.633	0.328	0.726	0.738	0.519	0.495	0.571	0.687	0.658	0.815	-	0.647
Zhenjiang	0.698	0.448	0.664	0.516	0.438	0.361	0.529	0.469	0.670	0.580	0.653	0.752	0.658	0.606	-

Notes: SH (Shanghai)=YRD1=Shanghai, YRD2=Hangzhou, YRD3=Ningbo, YRD4=Jiaxing, YRD5=Huzhou, YRD6=Shaoxing, YRD7=Zhoushan, YRD8=Taizhou YRD9=Nanjing, YRD10=Wuxi, YRD11=Changzhou, YRD12=Suzhou, YRD13=Nantong, YRD14=Yangzhou, YRD15=Zhenjiang; figures on the upper hand diagonal represent industry specialization index (ISI_{jk}) obtained from the modified Krugman's formulae with a range of '0' (no complementarity or identical industrial structure) to '2' (complete specialization or differential industry structure); figures on the lower hand diagonal represent rank (Spearman) correlation coefficients (γ_{jk}) obtained from the ranked output with a range of '0' (complete specialization or differential industry structure) to '1' (no complementarity or identical industrial structure); the estimates of ISI_{jk} and γ_{jk} for other selected years would be available from the authors upon request.

Since ISI measures and reflects industry output structure, it should be rather stable and no drastic fluctuations within a short period of time is expected. Therefore, computing annual ISI is not warranted in view of cost effectiveness. In this regard, ISI in YRD would be computed and compared for four selected years subject to data availability since the economic opening of YRD in 1992 until 2003; and in PRD, five selected years since the economic opening of the "larger" PRD in 1987 until 2003. While the number of city pairs is depending upon the availability of data (city) in a particular year, a maximum number of 105 city pairs for YRD and 36 pairs for PRD would be expected for 2003. The estimated industry specialization (complementarity) structure by cities measured by ISI_{jk} in 2003 for YRD and PRD were presented in Table 8 and 9 (upper-hand corner), respectively, and that of other selected years would be available from the authors.

Table 9. Industry Specialization Structure among PRD Cities (2003)

ISI_{jk}, γ_{jk}	Pearl River Delta (PRD)								
PRD Cities	**PRD1**	**PRD2**	**PRD3**	**PRD4**	**PRD5**	**PRD6**	**PRD7**	**PRD8**	**PRD9**
Guangzhou	-	0.657	1.262	1.072	1.288	1.003	0.865	0.470	0.786
Shenzhen	0.355	-	1.117	0.944	1.141	0.935	0.758	0.678	0.827
Zuhai	0.498	0.797	-	0.591	0.279	0.543	0.998	1.314	1.167
Huizhou	0.611	0.637	0.640	-	0.688	0.388	0.672	1.000	0.803
Dongguan	0.386	0.687	0.688	0.774	-	0.606	1.014	1.228	1.385
Zhongshan	0.482	0.652	0.699	0.816	0.870	-	0.582	0.962	0.855
Jiangmen	0.613	0.494	0.570	0.796	0.576	0.653	-	0.593	0.607
Foshan	0.531	0.571	0.658	0.815	0.709	0.735	0.668	-	0.714
Zhaoqing	0.413	0.421	0.518	0.710	0.512	0.630	0.713	0.619	-

Notes: PRD1=Guangzhou, PRD2=Shenzhen, PRD3=Zuahi, PRD4=Huizhou, PRD5=Dongguan, PRD6=Zhongshan, PRD7=Jiangmen, PRD8=Foshan, and PRD9=Zhaoqing; figures on the upper hand diagonal represent industry specialization index (ISI_{jk}) obtained from modified Krugman's formulae with a range of '0' (no complementarity or identical industrial structure) to '2' (complete specialization or differential industry structure); figures on the lower hand diagonal represent rank (Spearman) correlation coefficients (γ_{jk}) obtained from the ranked output with a range of '0' (complete specialization or differential industry structure) to '1' (no complementarity or identical industrial structure); the estimates of ISI_{jk} and γ_{jk} for other selected years would be available from the authors upon request.

Industry Complementarity (II): Ranked (Spearman) Correlation Analyses

To address the limitations of Krugman's index which involved highly aggregated data as recognized by Krugman and the lower efficiency in interpreting a range from '0' to '2', the problem was reinvestigated using the method of rank (Spearman) correlation of output shares (S_{ij} and S_{ik}) with disaggregated city-level data. Following the rationale from the above, the output shares in each region in city i (S_{ijr} and S_{ikr}) computed would be first ranked in the order of size, $\forall i,j$ and $\forall i,k$ in r. Rank (Spearman) correlation analyses between S_{ijr} and S_{ikr}, $\forall i,j$ and $\forall i,k$, and $\forall r$ would be performed.

The rank (Spearman) correlation (γ_{jk}) between S_{ijr} and S_{ikr} has a range of '0' to '1' where '0' (that is, $\gamma_{jk}=0$) represents absence of substitution (that is, complete complementarity) or perfect differential industry structure between two cities j and k; while '1' (that is, $\gamma_{jk}=1$) implies the reverse is true, that is, perfect substitution (or no complementarity) or identical industry structure between cities j and k. The estimated industry specialization (complementarity) structure measured by the rank (Spearman) correlation coefficient (γ_{jk}) in 2003 for YRD and PRD were presented in Table 8 and 9 (lower-hand corner), respectively, and that of other years would be available from the authors.

2. Inter-City and Intra-regional Competition and its Evolutions in GDEs: Results from Cluster Analyses (1987-2003)

Inter-city and intra-regional competition can be derived from the similarities of industry output structure (industry complementarities or specialization) among the YRD/PRD cities by comparing the industry complementarities (specialization) between two cities and among city-pairs using the estimated industry specialization indexes (ISI_{jkr}) and rank correlation coefficients (γ_{jkr}). However, γ_{jk} would be chosen for all latter computations and analyses due to its efficiency in interpretations. Cluster analyses were further performed on the γ_{jkr} measurements for all city pairs in both GDEs for the selected periods in an attempt to classifying the city pairs into groups or clusters of cities characterized by "low" versus "high" industry complementarities and correspondingly, "high" versus "low" intensity of competition.

Industry Complementaries and Inter-City and Intra-regional Competition: Formation of City Clusters

Low Industry Complementarities: City Clusters with High Inter-City Competition

The statistical results of the city pairs with high estimated rank correlation coefficients (γ_{jk}) (where $\gamma_{jk}>0.8$) and hence, low industry complementarities or high inter-city competition were identified in YRD/PRD and presented in Tables 10-11, respectively. In YRD, six pairs of cities sharing common borders/expressway (within three-hour travelling zone) and showing high industry similarities were found (Table 10):

(i) Wuxi-Suzhou (all five selected years);
(ii) Wuxi-Changzhou (all five selected years);
(iii) Changzhou-Suzhou (all five selected years);
(iv) Shanghai-Nanjing (in 1997 and 2003);
(v) Shanghai-Changzhou (in 1992 and 1997); and
(vi) Shanghai-Suzhou (in 1997).

In PRD, however, only two pairs of cities were found (Table 11).

(i) Dongguan-Zhongshan (in 2000 and 2003) and
(ii) Huizhou-Dongguan (in 1987 and 1992).

Table 10. Evolution of Industry (High) Similarity Structure in YRD by Selected City (1992-2003): Results of Rank Correlation Analyses

	Spearman's R (γ_{jk}) [(a)]			
City Pairs	**1992**	**1997**	**2000**	**2003**
10 Wuxi				
10-12 Suzhou*	0.827 (5)*	0.870 (3)*	0.860 (2)*	0.917 (1)*
10-11 Changzhou*	0.899 (1)*	0.873 (2)*	0.909 (1)*	0.845 (4)*
11 Changzhou				
11-12 Suzhou*	0.874 (2)*	0.916 (1)*	0.851 (3)*	0.891 (2)*
11-13 Nantong	#	#	0.819 (5)	0.831 (5)
1 Shanghai				
1-9 Nanjing	#	0.800 (10)	#	0.889 (3)**
1-3 Ningbo^	#	#	#	0.780^
1-11 Changzhou*	0.828 (4)*	0.851 (4)*	#	#
1-12 Suzhou*	#	0.835 (6)*	#	#
1-10 Wuxi*	0.830 (3)*	0.843 (5)*	0.836 (4)*	#
13 Nantong				
13-14 Yangzhou	#	#	#	0.815 (6)
13-15 Zhengjiang	#	0.827 (7)	#	#
4 Jiaxing				
4-13 Nantong	#	0.823 (8)	#	#
12 Suzhou				
12-13 Nantong	#	0.816 (9)	#	#
γ_{jk} Average (N)	0.672	0.605	0.555	0.529
Top-3 City-pair Average	0.825	0.886	0.873	0.899
Range (min-max) (Difference Δ)	0.383-0.899 (0.516)	0.219-0.916 (0.697)	0.173-0.909 (0.736)	0.162-0.919 (0.755)
C.V.	0.189	0.253	0.290	0.331
City-Pairs (N)	36	91	91	105

Notes: [(a)]ranking of γ_{jk} in descending order in parentheses where $\gamma_{jk}>0.8$ are reported for simplicity; # represents $\gamma_{jk}<0.8$; *indicates cities sharing common border and/or connected by expressways (within 3-hours travelling zone); ^cross harbor highway under construction; range of γ_{jk} = 0 (zero degree of similarity) to 1 (perfect degree of similarity);

YRD city codes: 1=Shanghai; 2=Hangzhou; 3=Ningbo; 4=Jiaxing; 5=Wuzhou; 6=Shaoxing; 7=Zhoushan; 8=Taizhou; 9=Nanjin; 10=Wuxi; 11=Changzhou; 12=Suzhou; 13=Nantong; 14=Yangzhou; 15=Zhengjiang

The statistical results obtained from cluster analyses showing the formation of city clusters consisting of city-pairs characterized by low industry complementarities (that is, similar or identical industry structure and hence, high level of competition) in YRD/PRD were presented in Tables 12-13, respectively. Three major clusters of city pairs with high level of inter-city competition ($\gamma_{jk}>0.74$) were found in all the selected year in YRD (except in 1997) (Table 12) as well as in PRD (Table 13).

Table 11. Evolution of Industry (High) Similarity Structure in PRD by Selected Cities (1987-2003): Results of Rank Correlation Analyses

	Spearman's R (γ_{jk})[(a)]				
City Pairs	**1987**	**1992**	**1997**	**2000**	**2003**
5 Dongguan					
5-6 Zhongshan*	#	#	#	0.846 (2)*	0.870 (1)*
5-7 Jiangmen	#	#	#	0.821 (4)	#
4 Huizhou					
4-8 Foshan	#	#	#	0.863 (1)	0.815 (2)
4-6 Zhongshan	#	#	#	#	0.806 (3)
4-5 Dongguan*	0.801 (2)*	0.805 (2)*	#	#	#
2 Shenzhen					
2-3 Zhuhai	0.732	0.817 (1)	0.807 (1)	0.843 (3)	#
2-8 Foshan	0.851 (1)	#	#	#	#
3 Zuhai					
3-5 Dongguan	#	#	#	0.810 (5)	#
γ_{jk} Average (N)	0.629	0.655	0.619	0.616	0.625
Top-3 City-pair Average	0.805	0.823	0.805	0.851	0.830
Range (Min-Max) (Difference Δ)	0.411-0.851 (0.440)	0.394-0.838 (0.444)	0.335-0.807 (0.472)	0.279-0.863 (0.584)	0.355-0.870 (0.515)
C.V.	0.223	0.200	0.191	0.252	0.205
City-Pairs (N)	21	36	36	36	36

Notes: [(a)]ranking of γ_{jk} in descending order where $\gamma_{jk}>0.8$ are reported for simplicity; # represents $\gamma_{jk}<0.8$; *indicates cities sharing common border and/or connected by expressways (within 3-hours travelling zone); range of $\gamma_{jk}= 0$ (zero degree of similarity) to 1 (perfect degree of similarity);

PRD city codes: 1=Guangzhou; 2=Shenzhen; 3=Zhuhai; 4=Huizhou; 5=Dongguan; 6=Zhongshan; 7=Jiangmen; 8=Foshan; 9=Zhaoxing.

High Industry Complementarities: City Clusters with Low Inter-City Competition

The statistical result obtained from cluster analyses showing the formation of city clusters consisting of city-pairs characterized by high industry complementarities (that is, differential or distinct industry structure and hence, low level of competition) in YRD/PRD were further presented in Tables 14-15, respectively. In YRD, three clusters of city pairs with low inter-city competition ($\gamma_{jk}<0.45$) were found in all the selected years (Table 14); and in PRD, two clusters (except in 2000) (Table 15).

Table 12. Evolutions of YRD City Clusters and Intra-Regional Competition: Results from Cluster Analysis of Low Industry Complementarities (1992-2003)

1992		1997		2000		2003	
City Pair	**γ_{jk} (Rank)**	**City Pair**	**γ_{jk} (Rank)**	**City Pair**	**γ_{jk} (Rank)**	**City Pair**	**γ_{jk} (Rank)**
Cluster #1		Cluster #1		Cluster #1		Cluster #1	
10-11 Wuxi-Changzhou	0.899 (1)*	11-12 Changzhou-Suzhou	0.916 (1)^	10-11 Wuxi-Changzhou	0.909 (1)*	10-12 Wuxi-Suzhou	0.917 (1)*
11-12 Changzhou-Suzhou	0.874 (2)^					11-12 Changzhou-Suzhou	0.891 (2)^
						1-9 Shanghai-Nanjing	0.889 (3)**
Cluster #2		Cluster #2		Cluster #2		Cluster #2	
1-10 Shanghai-Wuxi	0.830 (3)^	10-11 Wuxi-Changzhou	0.873 (2)*	10-12 Wuxi-Suzhou	0.860 (2)*	10-11 Wuxi-Changzhou	0.845 (4)*
1-11 Shanghai-Changzhou	0.828 (4)^	10-12 Wuxi-Suzhou	0.870 (3)^	11-12 Changzhou-Suzhou	0.851 (3)^	11-13 Changzhou-Nantong	0.831 (5)
10-12 Wuxi-Suzhou	0.827 (5)*			1-10 Shanghai-Wuxi	0.836 (4)^	13-14 Nantong-Yangzhou	0.815 (6)
				11-13 Changzhou-Nantong	0.819 (5)		
Cluster #3		Cluster #3		Cluster #3		Cluster #3	
10-14 Wuxi-Yangzhou	0.804 (6)	1-11 Shanghai-Changzhou	0.851 (4)^	1-12 Shanghai-Suzhou	0.787 (6)*	1-3 Shanghai-Ningbo	0.780 (7)^^
10-13 Wuxi-Nantung	0.789 (7)	1-10 Shanghai-Wuxi	0.843 (5)^	13-14 Nantong-Yangzhou	0.774 (7)	1-11 Shanghai-Changzhou	0.768 (8)^
13-14 Nantong-Yangzhou	0.789 (8)	1-12 Shanghai-Suzhou	0.835 (6)*	6-11 Shaoxing-Changzhou	0.772 (8)		
11-13 Changzhou-Nantong	0.787 (9)	13-15 Nantong-Zhenjiang	0.827 (7)	1-11 Shanghai-Changzhou	0.770 (9)^		
		4-13 Jiaxing-Nantong	0.823 (8)	1-9 Shanghai-Nanjing	0.768(10)#		
		12-13 Suzhou-Nantong	0.816 (9)	12-13 Suzhou-Nantong	0.767 (11)		
		Cluster #4		6-13 Shaoxing-Nantong	0.760 (12)		
		1-9 Shanghai-Nanjing	0.800 (10)#	12-15 Suzhou-Zhenjiang	0.742 (13)		

Notes: Assumptions: (1) Wald criterion used for estimations of cluster analyses and (2) for low degree of industry complementarity (hat is, high degree of competition) or high correlation $\gamma_{jk} > 0.8$; Ranking in descending order in parentheses; *cities sharing common borders; ^cities connected by expressway (within one-hour travelling zone); ^^cross-harbor expressway under construction and completion in 2009; #Nanjing is the capital city of Jiangsu province and Shanghai as the core city of YRD;

YRD city codes: 1=Shanghai; 2=Hangzhou; 3=Ningbo; 4=Jiaxing; 5=Huzhou; 6=Shaoxing; 7=Zhoushan; 8=Taizhou; 9=Nanjing; 10=Wuxi; 11=Changzhou; 12=Suzhou; 13=Nantong; 14=Yangzhou; 15=Zhenjiang

Table 13. Evolutions of PRD City Clusters and Intra-Regional Competition: Results from Cluster Analysis of Low Industry Complementarities (1987-2003)

1987		1992		1997		2000		2003	
City Pair	**γ_{jk} (Rank)**	**City Pair**	**γ_{jk} (Rank)**	**City Pair**	**γ_{jk} (Rank)**	**City Pair**	**γ_{jk} (Rank)**	**City Pair**	**γ_{jk} (Rank)**
Cluster #1		Cluster #1		Cluster #1		Cluster #1		Cluster #1	
2-8 Shenzhen-Foshan	0.851(1)	6-7 Zhongshan-Jiangmen	0.838(1)*	2-3 Shenzhen-Zhuhai	0.807(1)	4-8 Huizhou-Foshan	0.863(1)	5-6 Dongguan-Zhongshan	0.870(1)^
				3-4 Zhuhai-Huizhou	0.806(2)	5-6 Dongguan-Zhongshan	0.846(2)^		
				6-8 Zhongshan-Foshan	0.801(3)*	2-3 Shenzhen-Zhuhai	0.843(3)		
Cluster #2		Cluster #2		Cluster #2		Cluster #2		Cluster #2	
3-7 Zhuhai-Jiangmen	0.787(2)*	2-3 Shenzhen-Zhuhai	0.817(2)	6-7 Zhongshan-Jiangmen	0.793(4)*	5-7 Dongguan-Jiangmen	0.821(4)	4-8 Huizhou-Foshan	0.815(2)
8-9 Foshan-Zhaoqing	0.777(3)*	3-8 Zhuhai-Foshan	0.815(3)	7-8 Jiangmen-Foshan	0.783(5)*	3-5 Zhuhai-Dongguan	0.810(5)	4-6 Huizhou-Zhongshan	0.806(3)
		4-5 Huizhou-Dongguan	0.805(4)*			2-4 Shenzhen-Huizhou	0.790(6)*	2-3 Shenzhen-Zhuhai	0.797(4)
								4-7 Huizhou-Jiangmen	0.796(5)
Cluster #3		Cluster #3		Cluster #3		Cluster #3		Cluster #3	
7-9 Jiangmen-Zhaoqing	0.750(4)	3-6 Zhuhai-Zhongshan	0.788(5)*	4-5 Huizhou-Dongguan	0.746(6)*	4-5 Huizhou-Dongguan	0.770(7)	4-5 Huizhou-Dongguan	0.774(6)*
3-9 Zhuhai-Zhaoqing	0.735(5)	6-8 Zhongshan-Foshan	0.783(6)*			5-8 Dongguan-Foshan	0.766(8)^		
2-3 Shenzhen-Zuhai	0.732(6)	2-5 Shenzhen-Dongguan	0.783(7)*			2-5 Shenzhen-Dongguan	0.759(9)*		
		3-7 Zhuhai-Jiangmen	0.776(8)*						

Notes: Assumptions: (1) Wald criterion used for estimations of cluster analyses and (2) for high degree of industry complementarity (that is, high degree of competition): high correlation γ_{jk} >0.80; Ranking in descending order in parentheses; *cities sharing common borders; ^cities connected by expressway (within one-hour travelling zone);

PRD city codes: 1=Guangzhou; 2=Shenzhen; 3=Zhuhai; 4=Huizhou; 5=Dongguan; 6=Zhongshan; 7=Jiangmen; 8=Foshan; and 9=Zhaoqing

Table 14. Evolutions of YRD City Clusters and Intra-Regional Competition: Results from Cluster Analysis of Low Industry Complementarities (1992-2003)

1992		1997		2000		2003	
City Pair	**γ_{jk} (Rank)**	**City Pair**	**γ_{jk} (Rank)**	**City Pair**	**γ_{jk} (Rank)**	**City Pair**	**γ_{jk} (Rank)**
Cluster #1		**Cluster #1**		**Cluster #1**		**Cluster #1**	
2-3 Hangzhou-Ningbo	0.383(1)	3-8 Ningbo-Taizhou	0.219(1)*	4-8 Jiaxing-Taizhou	0.173(1)	3-5 Ningbo-Huzhou	0.162(1)
		4-9 Jiaxing-Nanjing	0.270(2)				
		4-8 Jiaxing-Taizhou	0.278(3)				
		Cluster #2		**Cluster #2**		**Cluster #2**	
		7-9 Zhoushan-Nanjing	0.339(4)	1-8 Shanghai-Taizhou	0.229(2)	1-4 Shanghai-Jiaxing	0.216(2)*
		8-10 Taizhou-Wuxi	0.342(5)	3-8 Ningbo-Taizhou	0.245(3)*	2-5 Hangzhou-Huzhou	0.227(3)*
				4-9 Jiaxing-Nanjing	0.253(4)		
		Cluster #3		**Cluster #3**		**Cluster #3**	
		8-12 Taizhou-Suzhou	0.389(5)	2-8 Hangzhou-Taizhou	0.298(5)	5-10 Huzhou-Wuxi	0.231(4)*
		7-10 Zhoushan-Wuxi	0.393(6)	1-4 Shanghai-Jiaxing	0.309(6)*	4-8 Jiaxing-Taizhou	0.234(5)
		2-3 Hangzhou-Ningbo	0.396(7)	7-9 Zhoushan-Nanjing	0.321(7)	5-7 Huzhou-Zhoushan	0.238(6)
		2-8 Hangzhou-Taizhou	0.399(8)	8-12 Taizhou-Suzhou	0.322(8)	5-9 Huzhou-Nanjing	0.245(7)
				8-10 Taizhou-Wuxi	0.323(9)	3-8 Ningbo-Taizhou	0.254(8)*
				6-9 Shaoxing-Nanjing	0.327(10)	2-8 Hangzhou-Taizhou	0.258(9)
				2-4 Hangzhou-Jiaxing	0.349(11)*	4-9 Jiaxing-Nanjing	0.267(10)
						1-5 Shanghai-Huzhou	0.272(11)
						6-9 Shaoxing-Nanjing	0.277(12)

Notes: Assumptions: (1) Wald criterion used for estimations of cluster analyses and (2) low degree of industry complementarity (that is, low degree of competition) or low correlation, that is, $\gamma_{jk} < 0.4$ (1992 and 1997), $\gamma_{jk} < 0.35$ (2000), and $\gamma_{jk} < 0.28$ (2003); Ranking in descending order in parentheses; *cities sharing common borders;

YRD city codes: 1=Shanghai; 2=Hangzhou; 3=Ningbo; 4=Jiaxing; 5=Huzhou; 6=Shaoxing; 7=Zhoushan; 8=Taizhou; 9=Nanjing; 10=Wuxi; 11=Changzhou; 12=Suzhou; 13=Nantong; 14=Yangzhou; 15=Zhengjiang

Table 15. Evolutions of PRD City Clusters and Intra-Regional Competition: Results from Cluster Analysis of High Industry Complementarities (1987-2003)

1987		1992		1997		2000		2003	
City Pair	**γ_{jk} (Rank)**	**City Pair**	**γ_{jk} (Rank)**	**City Pair**	**γ_{jk} (Rank)**	**City Pair**	**γ_{jk} (Rank)**	**City Pair**	**γ_{jk} (Rank)**
Cluster #1		**Cluster #1**		**Cluster #1**		**Cluster #1**		**Cluster #1**	
1-7 Guangzhou-Jiangmen	0.411(1)	1-5 Guangzhou-Dongguan	0.383 (1)*	2-9 Shenzhen-Zhaoqing	0.334 (1)	2-9 Shenzhen-Zhaoqing	0.279(1)	1-2 Guangzhou-Shenzhen	0.355(1)^
1-4 Guangzhou-Hiuzhou	0.412(2)*			3-9 Zhuhai-Zhaoqing	0.377 (2)			1-5 Guangzhou-Dongguan	0.386(2)*
Cluster #2		**Cluster #2**		**Cluster #2**		**Cluster #2**		**Cluster #2**	
1-9 Guangzhou-Zhaoqing	0.436(3)	1-7 Guangzhou-Jiangmen	0.410 (2)	1-5 Guangzhou-Dongguan	0.430 (3)*	3-9 Zhuhai-Zhaoqing	0.359(2)	1-9 Guangzhou-Zhaoqing	0.413(3)^
		1-8 Guangzhou-Foshan	0.415 (3)*	5-9 Dongguan-Zhaoqing	0.448 (4)	2-7 Shenzhen-Jiangmen	0.372(3)	2-9 Shenzhen-Zhaoqing	0.421(4)^
		1-6 Guangzhou-Zhongshan	0.415 (4)	1-9 Guangzhou-Zhaoqing	0.452 (5)	1-9 Guangzhou-Zhaoqing	0.388(4)		
						Cluster #3			
						1-2 Guangzhou-Shenzhen	0.423(5)		

Notes: Assumptions: (1) Wald criterion used for estimations of cluster analyses and (2) low degree of industry complementarity (that is, low intensity of competition) or low correlation, that is , γ_{jk} <0.45; Ranking in descending order in parentheses; *cities sharing common borders; ^cities connected by expressway (within one-hour travelling zone in 2003);

PRD city codes: 1=Guangzhou; 2=Shenzhen; 3=Zhuhai; 4=Huizhou; 5=Dongguan; 6=Zhongshan; 7=Jiangmen; 8=Foshan; and 9=Zhaoqing

Evolution of Industry Complementarities and Intra-regional Competition

Intra-regional competition in GDEs can be inferred and compared via the statistical results obtained from the industry similarity structure and its structural adjustment overtime (Tables 10-15). Both GDEs had diversified and become more specialized in industry output structure during the study period. Moreover, increasing competition was also observed in some city clusters characterized by low industry complementarities and high-γ_{jk} city clusters had becoming more alike in terms of industry structure overtime. Three major features were observed.

(i) Higher diversification of industry production and structure

- YRD showed a wider change in the range of γ_{jk} (0.38-0.90 or a difference of 0.52 in 1992 versus 0.16-0.91 or a difference of 0.76 in 2003) during 1992-2003. The higher diversification or larger variation in regional industrial production can also be verified by the increasing coefficient of variation (C.V.) from 0.19 to 0.33 during the same period (Table 10).
- Similar but modest effect is observed in PRD as shown by its narrower γ_{jk} range (0.41-0.85 or a difference of 0.44 in 1987 versus 0.36-0.87 or a difference of 0.52 in 2003) during 1987-2003 (Table 11). Smaller adjustments in the industry structure among PRD cities overtime was experienced when compared with YRD.

(ii) Decreasing intra-regional competition via increasing specialization of industry production and structure

- Both GDEs diversified and became more specialized in industry production and structure overtime and with YRD adjusted at a much faster pace. The overall average γ_{jk} had decreased in both GDEs with YRD from 0.67 in 1992 to 0.53 in 2003 (Table 10) and PRD a smaller drop from 0.66 to 0.63 in the respective years (Table 11).
- YRD had experienced lower intra-regional competition, on the average, as illustrated by the smaller average γ_{jk}=0.53 for 1992-2003 (Table 10) when compared with PRD's γ_{jk}=0.63 for 1987-2003 (Table 11);

(iii) Increasing inter-city competition by city clusters

- Although both GDEs had become more specialized in industry production and structure, some YRD/PRD cities were still competing more vigorously with each other in terms of industry production overtime.
- The Top-3 (with high γ_{jk}) YRD city clusters had also experienced higher inter-city competition when compared with that of PRD. YRD had steadily increasing average γ_{jk} in the Top-3 city clusters from 0.83 to 0.90 (a change of 0.7 and average γ_{jk}=0.87) for 1992-2003 (Table 10); and in PRD, from 0.81 to 0.83 (a change of 0.2 and average γ_{jk}=0.82) for 1987-2003 (Table 11).

Evolution of Industry Complementarities and Inter-City Competition

By examining the changing behavior of the industry specialization index among city pairs, the statistical results from Tables 10-11 and Tables 12-13 also provide the inter-city competitive patterns by city-pairs and by city clusters, respectively. The evolutions of the inter-city competitive behavior can be summarized as below (Tables 10-11):

(i) In YRD, three city-pairs sharing common borders and/or expressway were found competing more vigorously overtime. The three city-pairs included Wuxi-Suzhou (γ_{jk} increased from 0.87 in 1997 to 0.92 in 2003), Changzhou-Suzhou (γ_{jk} increased from 0.87 in 1992 to 0.89 in 2003), and Shanghai-Nanjing (γ_{jk} increased from 0.8 in 1997 to 0.92 in 2003). Furthermore, strong competition remained between Wuxi-Changzhou although increasing industry specialization (γ_{jk} decreased from 0.9 in 1992 to 0.85 in 2003) or decreasing inter-city competition was observed in these two cities overtime.

(ii) Among the PRD cities, only Dongguan-Zhongshan had been competing against each other more vigorously overtime (γ_{jk} increased from 0.85 to 0.87 for 2000-2003). PRD had demonstrated a more effective diversification in industry structure overtime in this regard.

Formation of Effective City Clusters via Industry Specialization

Groupings with Low Industry Complementarities: City-pairs with High Competition

The statistical analyses from the above sections provide information for deriving the competitive patterns among the city pairs with high inter-city competition from which the pattern of intra-regional competition can also be deduced. The linkages among competitive city-pairs and city clusters depicted by groupings of city pairs with high industry competitive patterns in YRD/PRD were presented in Tables 12-13, respectively, and illustrated below. In this connection, better diversification of industry structure in these city groups in the future may be warranted.

(i) Two groups of city clusters were formed in YRD (where $\gamma_{jk}>0.76$) in 2003.
- Grouping #1: Wuxi-Suzhou-Changzhou-Wuxi (R=1, C=1; R=2, C=1; R=4, C=2)
- Grouping #2: Ningpo-Shanghai-Changzhou (R=7, C=3; R=8, C=1)

(ii) One group of city clusters was formed in PRD (where $\gamma_{jk}>0.76$) in 2003.
- Grouping #1: Zhongshan-Dongguan-Huizhou (R=1, C=1; R=6, C=3)

Groupings with High Industry Complementarities: City-pairs with Low Competition

City-pairs sharing common borders with high industry complementarities (low γ_{jk}) could well form effective city clusters to leverage on the comparative advantages generated by their industry complementarities or differential industry structures. The groupings of effective city clusters with low competition in YRD/PRD were presented in Tables 14-15, respectively, and illustrated as below.

(i) Three effective groups of city clusters were formed in YRD (where $\gamma_{jk}<0.3$) in 2003.
- Grouping #1: Shanghai-Jiaxing (R=2, C=2)
- Grouping #2: Hangzhou-Huzhou-Wuxi (R=3, C=2; R=4, C=3)

- Grouping #3: Ningbo-Taizhou (R=8, C=3).

(ii) One group of effective city cluster was formed in PRD (where $\gamma_{jk}<0.4$) in 2003.

- Grouping #1: Dongguan-Guangzhou-Zhaoqing (R=2, C=1; R=3, C=2)

V. Concluding Remarks

By examining FDI absorption and the industry similarity structure of manufacturing production at the city level in the two delta economies since China's economic opening, the main findings can be summarized as follows:

(1) Globalization of the two delta economies in terms of manufacturing output production and enhancement of external trade and regional economic growth via FDI absorption.
(2) Regional specialization of manufacturing activities in terms of output production structure such that both GDEs diversified and became more specialized in industry structure overtime.
(3) Formation of city clusters in GDEs revealed both high versus low inter-city competition patterns, that is, similar versus distinct industry output structure existed among GDEs cities.
(4) Evolutions of industry complementarities or inter-city competitive patterns in both GDEs illustrated the patterns of inter-city and intra-regional competition. Some cities are competing more vigorously against each other overtime while effective city clusters were also formed to leverage on the comparative advantages generated by industry complementarities.
(5) Specifically in YRD/PRD, (i) higher industry complementarities or diversification and lower (intra-regional) competition in YRD than that in PRD; (ii) higher rate of adjustments in industry structure in YRD overtime than that in PRD; (iii) the higher inter-city competition in some YRD city-pairs relative to PRD revealed the fact that PRD, in general, had been more effective in diversifying manufacturing output production and shaping industry complementarities within the region.

The results of this study reasonably suggest that the decades of manufacturing FDI influx into the two delta regions had been coupled with an evolving manufacturing production structure mainly characterized by outward orientation production of export-led manufactures catering to external trade and the global market. The spatial pattern of manufacturing production agglomerations would continue and remain as incentives for further FDI absorption and inflows into the area. Besides, such spatial agglomerations of FDI and manufacturing production activities would further enhance the outward orientation nature and city/regional growth of the two delta regions. Moreover, the formation of effective city clusters exemplified by successful output diversification and industry complementarities among the cities within the region would definitely facilitate industry productivities and city/regional competitiveness. In this connection, continual regional disparities and diversities in terms of income and city/regional growth would remain a critical problem to be investigated and resolved in China in the years to come.

Appendix I. A List of Manufacturing Industry in GDEs by SIC Group

SIC	Industry Sector
301	Processing of Food from Agricultural Products
309	Manufacture of Foods
316-319	Manufacture of Beverages
320	Manufacture of Tobacco
321	Manufacture of Textile
329	Manufacture of Textile Wearing Apparel, Footwear, and Caps
334	Manufacture of Leather, Fur, Feather and Related Products
342	Processing of Timber, Manufacture of Wood, Bamboo, Rattan, Palm, and Straw Products
343	Manufacture of Furniture
344	Manufacture of Paper and Paper Products
345	Printing, Reproduction of Recording Media
346	Manufacture of Articles For Culture, Education and Sport Activity
347	Processing of Petroleum, Coking, Processing of Nuclear Fuel
348	Manufacture of Raw Chemical Materials and Chemical Products
356	Manufacture of Medicines
362	Manufacture of Chemical Fibers
363	Manufacture of Rubber
364	Manufacture of Plastics Products
365	Manufacture of Non-metallic Mineral Products
375	Smelting and Pressing of Ferrous Metals
376	Smelting and Pressing of Non-ferrous Metals
377	Manufacture of Metal Products
390	Manufacture of General Purpose Machinery
396-401	Manufacture of Special Purpose Machinery
403-411	Manufacture of Transport Equipment
412	Manufacture of Electrical Machinery and Equipment
420	Manufacture of Communication Equipment, Computers and Other Electronic Equipment
429-435	Manufacture of Measuring Instruments and Machinery for Cultural Activity and Office Work
437-439	Manufacturing of Artwork and Other Manufacturing
501	Production and Distribution of Electric Power and Heat Power

References

Alonso, W. (1964). Location and land use. New York: Harvard University Press.

Aitken, B. and Harrison, A., 1999. Do Domestic Firms Benefit from Foreign Direct Investment?, *American Economic Review*, **89**, 605-618.

Baldwin, R.E. (1997). Agglomeration and endogenous capital, *European Economic Review*, **43**(2), 253-280.

Berthelemy, J.C. and Sylvie, D. (2000). Foreign direct investment and economic growth: theory and applications to China, *Review of Development Economics*, **4**(2), 140-155.

Black, D. and Henderson, V. (1999). A theory of urban growth, *Journal of Political Economy*, **107**(2), 252-284.

Blonigen, B.A., Ellis, C.J., and Fausten, D. (2005). Industrial groupings and foreign direct investment, *Journal of International Economics*, **65**(1), 75-91.

Borensztein E, De Gregorio, J. and Lee, J.W. (1998). How does foreign investment affect economic growth, *Journal of International Economics*, **45**, 115-135.

Ciccone, A. (2002). Agglomeration effects in Europe, *European Economic Review*, **46**(2), 213-228.

Curzio, A.Q. and Fortis, M. (eds.) (2002). *Complexity and industrial clusters*. New York: Physica-Verlag.

de Mello, L.R. Jr. (1997). *Foreign direct investment in developing countries and growth: a selective survey. The Journal of Development Studies*, **34**(1), 1-34.

de Mello, L.R. Jr. (1999). Foreign direct investment-led growth: evidence from time series and Panel Data, *Oxford Economic Papers*, **51**, 133-151.

de la Potterie, B.P. and Lichtenberg, F., 2001. Does Foreign Direct Investment Transfer Technology across Borders?, *The Review of Economics and Statistics*, **83**(3), 490-497.

Dunning, J.H. (1979). Explaining patterns of international production: in defense of the eclectic theory, *Oxford Bulletin of Economics and Statistics*, **41**, 269-295.

Dunning, J.H. (1988). The eclectic paradigm of international production: a restatement of some possible extensions, *Journal of International Business Studies*, **19**, 1-19.

Dunning, J.H. (1993). *Multinational enterprises and the global economy*. MA: Addison-Wesley.

Fujita, M. and Hu, D. (2001). Regional diversity in China 1985-1994: The effects of globalization and economic liberalization, *Annals of Regional Science*, **35**(3), 3-37.

Fujita, M., Krugman, P. and Venables, A.J. (1999). *The spatial economy: cities, regions, and international trade*. Massachusetts: MIT Press.

Fujita, M. and Thisse, J.F. (1996). Economics of agglomeration, *Journal of the Japanese and International Economics*, **10**, 339-378.

Fujita, M. and Thissa, J.F. (2002). *Economics of Agglomeration: Cities, Industrial Location, and Regional Growth*. Cambridge: Cambridge University Press.

Gao, T. (2002). The impact of foreign trade and investment reform on industry location: the case of China, *The Journal of International Trade and Economic Development*, **11**(4), 367-386.

Giersch, H. (1995). (ed.), *Urban Agglomeration and Economic Growth*. Berlin: Springer-Veriag.

Henderson, J.V. (1974). The sizes and types of cities, *American Economic Review*, **64**, 640-656.

Henderson, J.V. (1988). *Urban development: Theory, facts, and illusion*. New York: Oxford University Press.

Kohno, H., Nijkamp, P., and Poot, J. (2000). *Regional cohesion and competition in the age of globalization*. MA: Edward Elgar.

Krugman, P. (1991a). Increasing returns and economic geography, *Journal of Political Economy*, **99**, pp. 483-499.

Krugman, P. (1991b). *Geography and Trade*. Cambridge, Mass: MIT Press.

Krugman, P. (1998). Space: the final frontier, *Journal of Economic Perspectives*, **12**(2), pp.161-174.

Lim, E.G. (2001). Determinants of, and the relation between, foreign direct investment and growth: A summary of the recent literature, *IMF Working Paper*, WP/01/175.

Mccann, P. and Mudambe, R. (2004). The location behavior of the multinational enterprise: some analytical issues, *Growth and Change*, **35** (4), 491-524.

Mei, W. (2004). Relocation and agglomeration of Chinese industry, *Journal of Development Economics*, **73**(1), 329-347.

Mullen, J.K. and Williams, M. (2005). Foreign direct investment and regional economic performance, *Kyklos*, **58**(2), 265-282.

Ng, L.F.Y. and Tuan, C. (2001). FDI promotion policy in China: Governance and Effectiveness, *The World Economy*, **24**(8), 1051-1074.

Ng, L.F.Y. and Tuan, C. (2002). Building a favorable investment environment: evidence for the facilitation of FDI in China, *The World Economy*, **25**(8), 1095-1114.

Ng, L.F.Y. and Tuan, C. (2003). Location decisions of manufacturing FDI in China: Implications of China's WTO accession, *Journal of Asian Economics*, **14**, 51-72.

Ng, L.F.Y. and Tuan, C. (2005). Industry technology performance of manufacturing FDI: Micro-level evidence from joint ventures in China, *International Journal of Technology Management*, **32**(3/4), 246-263.

Ng, L.F.Y. and Tuan, C. (2006). Spatial Agglomeration, FDI, and Regional Growth in China: Locality of Local and Foreign Manufacturing Investments. *Journal of Asian Economics*, **17**, 691-713.

Palivos, T. and Wang, P. (1996). Spatial agglomeration and endogenous growth, *Regional Science and Urban Economics*, **26**(6), 645-669.

Paul, C.J.M. and Siegel, D.S. (1999). Scale economies and industry agglomeration externalities: A dynamic cost function, *American Economic Review*, **89**(March), 272-290.

Porter, M. (1998). *Clusters and the new economics of competition. Harvard Business Review* **76**(6): 77-90.

Porter, M. (1998). *On Competition*. MA: Harvard Business School Press.

Propris, L.D. and Driffield, N. (2006). The importance of clusters for spillovers from foreign direct investment and technology sourcing, *Cambridge Journal of Economics,* **30**, 277-291.

Puga, D. and Venables, A.J. (1996). The spread of industry: spatial agglomeration in economic development", *CEPR Discussion Paper Series*, **1354**, CEPR, London.

Quah, D. (2002). Spatial agglomeration dynamics, *American Economic Review*, **92**(2), 247-252.

Quigley, J.M. (1998). "Urban Diversity and Economic Growth", *Journal of Economic Perspectives*, **12**(2), pp. 127-138.

Richardson, H.W. (1995). "Economies and Diseconomies of Agglomeration", in Giersch, H. (ed.), *Urban Agglomeration and Economic Growth*. Berlin: Springer-Veriag.

Rosenthal, S.S. and Strange, W.C. (2003). Geography, industrial organization and agglomeration, *Review of Economics and Statistics*, **85**, 377-393.

Rosenthal, S.S. and Strange, W.C. (2004). Evidence on the nature and sources of agglomeration economies, in V. Henderson and J. Thisse (eds.), *Handbook of Urban and Regional Economics*, Vol. 4.

Sun, H. and Parikh, A. (2001). Exports, inward foreign direct investment (FDI) and regional economic growth in China, *Regional Studies*, **35**(3), 187-196.

Taube, M. and Ogutcu, M. (2002). Main issues on foreign investment in China's regional development: prospects and policy challenges, *Foreign Direct Investment in China: Challenges and Prospects for Regional Development*, OECD.

Teece, D.J., 1977. Technology transfer by multinationals firms: The resource cost of transferring technological know-how, *The Economic Journal*, **87**(6), 242-262.

Tuan, C. and Ng, L.F.Y. (1995). Hong Kong's outward investment and regional economic integration with Guangdong: Process and implications, *Journal of Asian Economics*, **6**(3), 385-405.

Tuan, C. and Ng, L.F.Y. (2001). Regional division of labor from agglomeration economies' perspective: Some evidence, *Journal of Asian Economics*, **12**, 65-85.

Tuan, C. and Ng, L.F.Y. (2002). FDI facilitated by agglomeration economies: Evidence from manufacturing and services joint ventures in China, *Journal of Asian Economics*, **13**(6), 749-765.

Tuan, C. and Ng, L.F.Y. (2003). *A Miracle via Agglomerations: The HK-PRD Connections*, monograph (UNDP#CPR/91/161). The Chinese University of Hong Kong (in Chinese).

Tuan, C. and Ng, L.F.Y. (2004a). FDI and industrial restructuring in post-WTO Greater PRD: Implications on regional growth in China, *The World Economy*, **27**(10), pp. 1609-1630.

Tuan, C. and Ng, L.F.Y. (2004b). Manufacturing agglomeration as incentives to Asian FDI in China after WTO. *Journal of Asian Economics*, **15**, 673-693.

Tuan, C. and Ng, L.F.Y. (2006). FDI inflows and growth of private business in China, *Journal of Entrepreneurship Research*, **9**(1), 101-132.

Tuan, C. and Ng, L.F.Y. (2007). The place of FDI in China's regional economic development: Emergence of the globalized delta economies, *Journal of Asian Economics*, **18**, 348-364.

Tuan, C., Ng, L.F.Y., and Lin, H. (2006). *The Globalized Delta Economies in China (Yangtze-River Delta and Pearl-River Delta): Visualized Economic Indicators for Investment Environment.* Institute of Space and Earth Information Science, The Chinese University of Hong Kong. Website: www.jlgis.cuhk.edu.hk/business

Vogel, E.F. (1989). *One step ahead in China: Guangdong under reform.* Mass: Harvard University Press.

Whalley, J. and Xin, X. (2006). China's FDI and non-FDI economies and the sustainability of future high Chinese growth, *NBER Working Paper Series*, #**12249**, National Bureau of Economic Research.

Wolff, R. (1985). Efficient growth of an agglomeration regional economy, *Regional Science and Urban Economics*, **15**(4), 555-573

Yehouse, E.B. (2005). *Clusters as a Driving Engine for FDI. IMF Papers WP/05/193.*

Zhang, Q. and Felmingham, B. (2002). The role of FDI, exports and spillovers effects in the regional development of China, *The Journal of Development Studies*, **38**(4), 157-178.

Zhao, Z.P. (2001). *FDI utilization and economic growth in China.* Beijing: People's Press (in Chinese).

In: Foreign Direct Investment
Editor: Harrison G. Blaine, pp. 123-144
ISBN 978-1-60456-921-6
© 2009 Nova Science Publishers, Inc.

Chapter 6

FOREIGN DIRECT INVESTMENT AND CURRENCY HEDGING

Kit Pong Wong*
School of Economics and Finance, University of Hong Kong,
Pokfulam Road, Hong Kong

Abstract

This paper examines the behavior of a risk-averse multinational firm (MNF) under exchange rate uncertainty. The MNF has an investment opportunity in a foreign country. To hedge the exchange rate risk, the MNF can avail itself of customized derivative contracts that are fairly priced. Foreign direct investment (FDI) is irreversible and costly expandable in that the MNF can acquire additional capital at a higher unit price after the spot exchange rate has been publicly revealed. The MNF as such possesses a real (call) option that is rationally exercised whenever the foreign currency has been substantially appreciated relative to the domestic currency. The ex-post exercise of the real option convexifies the MNF's ex-ante domestic currency profit with respect to the random spot exchange rate, thereby calling for the use of currency options as a hedging instrument. We show that the MNF's optimal initial level of sequential FDI is always lower than that of lumpy FDI, while the expected optimal aggregate level of sequential FDI can be higher or lower than that of lumpy FDI. We further show that currency hedging, no matter perfect or imperfect, improves the MNF's ex-ante and ex-post incentives to make FDI, a result consistent with the complementary nature of operational and financial hedging strategies.

JEL classification: D81; F23; F31

Keywords: Foreign direct investment; Real options; Currency hedging

1. Introduction

Foreign direct investment (FDI) is a sequential process that determines the volume and direction of resources transferred across borders (Kogut, 1983). The ability of multinational

*E-mail address: kpwong@econ.hku.hk. Tel.: (852) 2859-1044, fax: (852) 2548-1152,

firms (MNFs) to arbitrage institutional restrictions (e.g., tax codes, relative exchange rates, and remittance forms) creates a string of options that are written on various contingent outcomes. In this regard, MNFs are best described as a collection of valuable options that permit discretionary choices among alternative real economic activities and financial flows from one country to the other.

One important strand of the literature on MNFs under exchange rate uncertainty focuses on the effect of currency hedging on the behavior of MNFs. (see, e.g., Broll, 1992; Broll and Zilcha, 1992; Broll, Wong, and Zilcha, 1999, Chang and Wong, 2003; Wong, 2003a). The typical scenario is that a risk-averse MNF makes its FDI and hedging decisions simultaneously prior to the resolution of the exchange rate uncertainty. Two notable results emanate. First, the separation theorem states that the MNF's optimal FDI decision is affected neither by its risk attitude nor by the underlying exchange rate uncertainty when there is a currency forward/futures market. Second, the full-hedging theorem states that the MNF optimally opts for a full-hedge to completely eliminate its exchange rate risk exposure should the currency forward/futures market be unbiased.

Taking FDI as a sequential process into account, we depart from the extant literature by allowing the MNF to make sequential, rather than lumpy, FDI decisions. To this end, the MNF has the right, but not the obligation, to alter its level of FDI after the exchange rate uncertainty has been completely resolved. We model FDI to be irreversible and costly expandable in that the MNF can purchase additional, but cannot sell redundant, capital in the domestic country at a higher unit price of capital when adjustments in FDI are called for.[1] The flexibility of making sequential FDI, vis-à-vis lumpy FDI, proffers the MNF a real (call) option that is rationally exercised whenever the foreign currency has been substantially appreciated relative to the domestic currency. The ex-post exercise of the real option as such convexifies the MNF's ex-ante domestic currency profit with respect to the random spot exchange rate.

To examine how the MNF's optimal FDI decisions are affected by the interaction between operational and financial hedging, we allow the MNF to avail itself of fairly priced derivatives that can be tailor-made for its hedging need. We show that the MNF optimally tailors its customized derivative contract in a way that its hedged domestic currency profit is stabilized at the expected level, thereby eliminating all the exchange rate risk. The MNF's optimal initial level of FDI is thus identical to the one when the MNF is risk neutral, which is always lower than the optimal level of lumpy FDI. The expected optimal aggregate level of sequential FDI, however, can be higher or lower than that of lumpy FDI. We further show that the MNF's optimal customized derivative contract can be perfectly replicated by trading the unbiased currency futures and a continuum of fairly priced currency put and call option contracts of all exercise prices, a result consistent with the prevalent use of currency options by non-financial firms (Bodnar, Hayt, and Marston, 1998).

If the MNF is banned from engaging in currency hedging, we show that the MNF's ex-ante and ex-post incentives to make FDI are reduced as compared to those with perfect currency hedging. Since a financial hedge is absent, the MNF has to rely on an operational hedge via lowing its FDI. We further show that an increase in the fixed or setup cost incurred by the MNF gives rise to similar perverse effects on FDI should the MNF's risk preferences

[1] Dixit and Pindyck (1994) argue that asset specificity, information asymmetry, and government regulations are plausible reasons why FDI is irreversible and costly expandable. See also Wong (2006).

exhibit the reasonable property of decreasing absolute risk aversion. Given that the change in the fixed or setup cost may be due to a change in the investment tax credits offered by the host government, or due to a change in the severity of entry barriers in the host country, FDI flows are expected to react in a predictable manner when these government policies and market conditions shift over time. These implications are largely consistent with the empirical findings of Anand and Kogut (1997) and Hines (2001).

If the MNF is restricted to use the unbiased currency futures contracts as the sole hedging instrument, we show that risk aversion has no effect on the expected marginal return to the initial level of FDI, but has a negative effect on the option value of waiting to make subsequent FDI. The former is due to the spanning property that arises from the tradability of the random spot exchange rate via trading the unbiased currency futures contracts. The latter is due to the non-tradability of the real option embedded in sequential FDI so that spanning is not possible, making the MNF's risk preferences impact negatively on the pricing of the option in this incomplete market context. The MNF's ex-ante and ex-post incentives to make FDI are therefore enhanced as compared to those with perfect currency hedging. This implies immediately that futures hedging promotes FDI, a result consistent with the complementary nature of operational and financial hedging strategies (Allayannis, Ihrig, and Weston, 2001; Kim, Mathur, and Nam, 2006).

The rest of this paper is organized as follows. Section 2 delineates a dynamic model of a risk-averse MNF that makes sequential FDI decisions in response to the intertemporal resolution of exchange rate uncertainty. Section 3 derives the MNF's optimal FDI and hedging decisions when there are fairly priced derivatives that can be tailor-made for the MNF's hedging need. Section 4 compares the MNF's optimal FDI decisions in the case of sequential FDI to those in the case of lumpy FDI. Section 5 examines the effects of banning the MNF from engaging in currency hedging on its optimal sequential FDI decisions. Section 6 restricts the MNF to use the unbiased currency futures contracts as the sole hedging instrument and shows that futures hedging improves the MNF's ex-ante and ex-post incentives to make FDI. The final section concludes.

2. The Model

Consider a multinational firm (MNF) that invests in a foreign country under exchange rate uncertainty. There is one period with three dates, indexed by $t = 0$, 1, and 2. The prevailing spot exchange rate at $t = 2$, which is denoted by $\tilde{e}$ and is expressed in units of the domestic currency per unit of the foreign currency, is uncertain at $t = 0$.[2] The MNF regards $\tilde{e}$ as a positive random variable distributed according to a known cumulative distribution function, $F(e)$, over support $[\underline{e}, \overline{e}]$, where $0 \leq \underline{e} < \overline{e} \leq \infty$.[3] The exchange rate uncertainty, however, is completely resolved at $t = 1$, at which time the true realization of $\tilde{e}$ is publicly observed.

[2]Throughout the paper, random variables have a tilde ($\tilde{\ }$) while their realizations do not.

[3]An alternative way to model the exchange rate uncertainty is to apply the concept of information systems that are conditional cumulative distribution functions over a set of signals imperfectly correlated with $\tilde{e}$ (Eckwert and Zilcha, 2001, 2003; Drees and Eckwert, 2003; Broll and Eckwert, 2006). The advantage of this more general and realistic approach is that one can study the value of information by comparing the information content of different information systems. Since the focus of this paper is not on the value of information, we adopt a simpler structure to save notation.

The riskless rate of interest is known and constant for the period. To simplify notation, we henceforth suppress the interest factors by compounding all cash flows to their future values at $t = 2$.

To begin, the MNF incurs a fixed cost, $c \geq 0$, for the access to a project in the foreign country. If the MNF makes foreign direct investment (FDI) of k units of capital that are acquired in the home country, the project yields a deterministic cash flow of $f(k)$ at $t = 2$, where $f(k)$ is denominated in the foreign currency with $f(0) = 0$, $f'(k) > 0$ and $f''(k) < 0$ for all $k \geq 0$, $\lim_{k \to 0} f'(k) = \infty$, and $\lim_{k \to \infty} f'(k) = 0$. FDI has the properties of being sequential, irreversible, and costly expandable. Succinctly, at $t = 0$, the MNF acquires k_0 units of capital at a known unit price, $p_0 > 0$, in the home country, where p_0 is denominated in the domestic currency. At $t = 1$, after the complete resolution of the exchange rate uncertainty, the MNF has the right, but not the obligation, to acquire additional k_1 units of capital at a known unit price, p_1, in the home country, where p_1 is denominated in the domestic currency and $p_1 > p_0$ to reflect costly expandability of FDI. The MNF's aggregate level of FDI is thus equal to $k_0 + k_1$.

To hedge the exchange rate risk at $t = 0$, the MNF avails itself of customized derivatives at $t = 0$. The payoff of a customized derivative contract at $t = 2$ is delineated by a function, $\phi(e)$, whose functional form is chosen by the MNF at $t = 0$. To focus on the MNF's hedging motive, vis-à-vis its speculative motive, we assume that the contract is fairly priced in that $\mathrm{E}[\phi(\tilde{e})] = 0$, where $\mathrm{E}(\cdot)$ is the expectation operator with respect to $F(e)$. That is, we interpret $\phi(\tilde{e})$ as net of the price of the contract.[4]

Given a realized spot exchange rate, $\tilde{e} = e$, an initial level of FDI, k_0, and a customized derivative contract, $\phi(e)$, the MNF chooses an additional level of FDI, k_1, so as to maximize its domestic currency profit at $t = 2$ under certainty:

$$\max_{k_1 \geq 0} \; ef(k_0 + k_1) - p_0 k_0 - p_1 k_1 - c + \phi(e). \tag{1}$$

The Kuhn-Tucker condition for program (1) is given by[5]

$$ef'[k_0 + k_1(e, k_0)] - p_1 \leq 0, \tag{2}$$

where $k_1(e, k_0)$ is the solution to program (1). If $e \leq p_1/f'(k_0)$, it follows from condition (2) that $k_1(e, k_0) = 0$. On the other hand, if $e > p_1/f'(k_0)$, condition (2) holds as an equality:

$$ef'[k_0 + k_1(e, k_0)] - p_1 = 0. \tag{3}$$

Since $f''(k) < 0$, it is easily verified that $k_1(e, k_0)$ is strictly increasing in e for all $e > p_1/f'(k_0)$. The flexibility of making sequential FDI decisions thus proffers the MNF a real (call) option to buy additional capital at $t = 1$, which is rationally exercised whenever the realized spot exchange rate is sufficiently favorable, i.e., $e > p_1/f'(k_0)$.

The MNF's random domestic currency profit at $t = 2$ is given by

$$\pi(\tilde{e}) = \tilde{e}f[k_0 + k_1(\tilde{e}, k_0)] - p_0 k_0 - p_1 k_1(\tilde{e}, k_0) - c + \phi(\tilde{e}), \tag{4}$$

[4]If $\mathrm{E}[\phi(\tilde{e})] > (<)\ 0$, the positive (negative) risk premium induces the MNF to speculate by selling (purchasing) the customized derivative contract.

[5]The second-order condition for program (1) is satisfied given the strict concavity of $f(k)$.

where $k_1(e, k_0) = 0$ for all $e \leq p_1/f'(k_0)$ and $k_1(e, k_0)$ is defined in Eq. (3) for all $e > p_1/f'(k_0)$. The MNF is risk averse and possesses a von Neumann-Morgenstern utility function, $u(\pi)$, defined over its domestic currency profit at $t = 2$, π, with $u'(\pi) > 0$ and $u''(\pi) < 0$.[6] The MNF's ex-ante decision problem is to choose an initial level of FDI, k_0, and a customized derivative contract, $\phi(\tilde{e})$, at $t = 0$ so as to maximize the expected utility of its domestic currency profit at $t = 2$:

$$\max_{k_0 \geq 0, \phi(e)} \; \mathrm{E}\{u[\pi(\tilde{e})]\} \quad \text{s.t.} \quad \mathrm{E}[\phi(\tilde{e})] = 0, \tag{5}$$

where $\pi(\tilde{e})$ is defined in Eq. (4).

Figure 1 depicts how the sequence of events unfolds in the model.

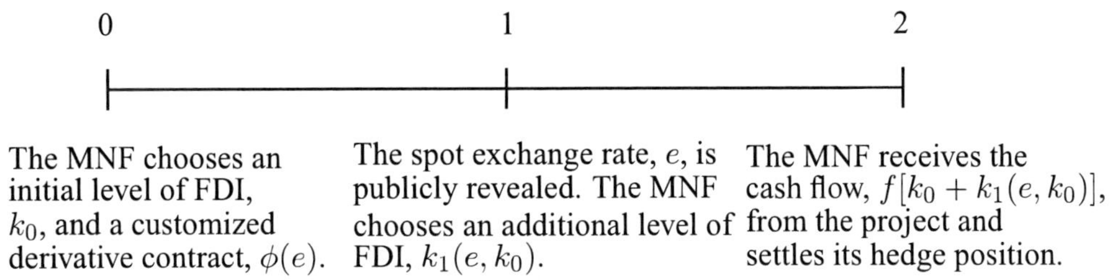

Figure 1. Time line. The underlying exchange rate uncertainty, $\tilde{e}$, is exogenously given and is resolved at $t = 1$. The MNF chooses an initial level of FDI, k_0, at the unit price of capital, p_0, and devises a customized derivative contract, $\phi(e)$, at $t = 0$. After observing the realized spot exchange rate at $t = 1$, the MNF chooses an additional level of FDI, $k_1(k_0, e)$, at the unit price of capital, $p_1 > p_0$. The MNF receives the project's cash flow, $f[k_0 + k_1(e, k_0)]$, at $t = 2$ and settles its hedge position at that time.

3. Optimal FDI and Hedging Decisions

Given the Inada conditions on $f(k)$ and the fact that $p_1 > p_0$, the solution to program (5) must be an interior one. The first-order conditions for program (5) are given by[7]

$$\int_{\underline{e}}^{p_1/f'(k_0^*)} u'[\pi^*(e)][ef'(k_0^*) - p_0] \,\mathrm{d}F(e) + \int_{p_1/f'(k_0^*)}^{\overline{e}} u'[\pi^*(e)](p_1 - p_0) \,\mathrm{d}F(e) = 0, \tag{6}$$

and

$$u'[\pi^*(e)] - \lambda^* = 0 \quad \text{for all } e \in [\underline{e}, \overline{e}], \tag{7}$$

[6] The risk-averse behavior of the MNF can be motivated by managerial risk aversion (Stulz, 1984), corporate taxes (Smith and Stulz, 1985), costs of financial distress (Smith and Stulz, 1985), and capital market imperfections (Stulz, 1990; Froot, Scharfstein, and Stein, 1993). See Tufano (1996) for evidence that managerial risk aversion is a rationale for corporate risk management in the gold mining industry.

[7] The second-order conditions for program (5) are satisfied given risk aversion and the strict concavity of $f(k)$.

where Eq. (6) follows from Leibniz's rule and Eq. (3), λ is the Lagrange multiplier, and an asterisk $(^*)$ signifies an optimal level. If $p_1 = p_0$, it is evident from Eq. (6) that we have a corner solution to program (5) in that $k_0^* = 0$.

Solving Eqs. (6) and (7) yields our first proposition.

Proposition 1. *If the MNF is allowed to make sequential FDI and to use customized derivatives that are fairly priced for hedging purposes, the MNF's optimal initial level of FDI, k_0^*, solves*

$$\mathrm{E}(\tilde{e})f'(k_0^*) = p_0 + \mathrm{E}\{\max[\tilde{e}f'(k_0^*) - p_1, 0]\}, \tag{8}$$

and the optimal customized derivative contract, $\phi^*(e)$, is given by

$$\phi^*(e) = \nu^* - ef[k_0^* + k_1(e, k_0^*)] + p_1 k_1(e, k_0^*), \tag{9}$$

where $\nu^* = \mathrm{E}\{\tilde{e}f[k_0^* + k_1(\tilde{e}, k_0^*)] - p_1 k_1(\tilde{e}, k_0^*)\}$.

Proof. Using Eq. (4), we can write Eq. (7) as

$$ef[k_0^* + k_1(e, k_0^*)] - p_0 k_0^* - p_1 k_1(e, k_0^*) - c + \phi^*(e) = u'^{-1}(\lambda^*) \quad \text{for all } e \in [\underline{e}, \overline{e}], \tag{10}$$

where $u'^{-1}(\lambda^*)$ is a constant. It then follows from $\mathrm{E}[\phi^*(\tilde{e})] = 0$ and Eq. (10) that $u'^{-1}(\lambda^*) = \nu^* - p_0 k_0^* - c$, thereby implying equation (9). Substituting equation (7) into equation (6) yields

$$\int_{\underline{e}}^{p_1/f'(k_0^*)} [ef'(k_0^*) - p_0]\, \mathrm{d}F(e) + \int_{p_1/f'(k_0^*)}^{\overline{e}} (p_1 - p_0)\, \mathrm{d}F(e) = 0. \tag{11}$$

Rearranging terms of Eq. (11) yields

$$\int_{\underline{e}}^{\overline{e}} ef'(k_0^*)\, \mathrm{d}F(e) - \int_{p_1/f'(k_0^*)}^{\overline{e}} [ef'(k_0^*) - p_1]\, \mathrm{d}F(e) - p_0 = 0. \tag{12}$$

Eq. (12) is identical to Eq. (8). □

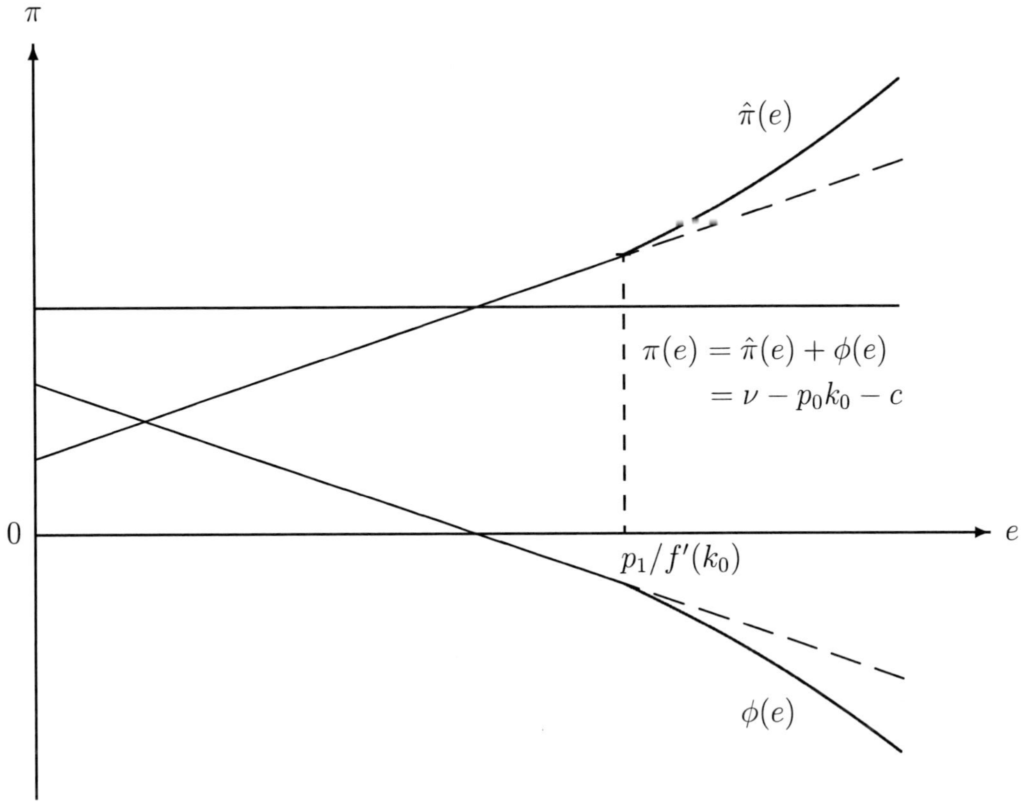

Figure 2. Hedged and unhedged domestic currency profits of the MNF. The MNF's unhedged domestic currency profit at $t = 2$ is denoted by $\hat{\pi}(e) = ef[k_0 + k_1(e, k_0)] - p_0 k_0 - p_1 k_1(e, k_0) - c$. The customized derivative contract is given by $\phi(e) = \nu - ef[k_0 + k_1(e, k_0)] + p_1 k_1(e, k_0)$, where $\nu = \mathrm{E}\{\tilde{e}f[k_0 + k_1(\tilde{e}, k_0)] - p_1 k_1(\tilde{e}, k_0)\}$. The MNF's hedged domestic currency profit at $t = 2$ is thus given by $\pi(e) = \hat{\pi}(e) + \phi(e) = \nu - p_0 k_0 - c$, which is invariant to e.

To see the intuition of Proposition 1, we refer to Figure 2. Using Eq. (4) and setting $\phi(e) \equiv 0$, the MNF's unhedged domestic currency profit at $t = 2$ is given by

$$\hat{\pi}(\tilde{e}) = \tilde{e}f[k_0 + k_1(\tilde{e}, k_0)] - p_0 k_0 - p_1 k_1(\tilde{e}, k_0) - c. \tag{13}$$

If the MNF devises its customized derivative contract to be

$$\phi(e) = \nu - ef[k_0 + k_1(e, k_0)] + p_1 k_1(e, k_0), \tag{14}$$

where $\nu = \mathrm{E}\{\tilde{e}f[k_0 + k_1(\tilde{e}, k_0)] - p_1 k_1(\tilde{e}, k_0)\}$, then its hedged domestic currency profit at $t = 2$ is the sum of Eqs. (13) and (14), i.e., $\pi(\tilde{e}) = \hat{\pi}(\tilde{e}) + \phi(\tilde{e}) = \nu - p_0 k_0 - c$, which is non-stochastic. In this case, the MNF's ex-ante decision problem becomes

$$\max_{k_0 \geq 0} \int_{\underline{e}}^{p_1/f'(k_0)} ef(k_0)\,\mathrm{d}F(e)$$

$$+\int_{p_1/f'(k_0)}^{\overline{e}} \{ef[k_0 + k_1(e, k_0)] - p_1 k_1(e, k_0)\}\,\mathrm{d}F(e) - p_0 k_0 - c. \qquad (15)$$

The solution to program (15) renders Eq. (8). Eq. (8) states that the optimal initial level of FDI, k_0^*, is the one that equates the expected marginal return to FDI made at $t = 0$, $\mathrm{E}(\tilde{e})f'(k_0^*)$, to the unit price of capital at $t = 0$, p_0, plus the forgone option value of waiting to invest that unit of capital at $t = 1$, $\mathrm{E}\{\max[\tilde{e}f'(k_0^*) - p_1, 0]\}$. Substituting k_0^* into Eq. (14) yields Eq. (9).

Two remarks are in order. First, the MNF tailors its optimal customized derivative contract, $\phi^*(e)$, in a way that its hedged domestic currency profit at $t = 2$ is stabilized at the expected level, $\nu^* - p_0 k_0^* - c$. The MNF as such faces no risk exposure to $\tilde{e}$. Second, the optimal initial level of FDI, k_0^*, is preference-free. These results resemble the celebrated separation and full-hedging theorems (see, e.g., Broll, 1992; Broll and Zilcha, 1992; Broll, Wong, and Zilcha, 1999; Chang and Wong, 2003; Wong, 2003a) with one caveat: While k_0^* is independent of the MNF's utility function, $u(\pi)$, it does depend on the distribution of the underlying exchange rate uncertainty, $F(e)$, as is evident from Eq. (8).

The optimal customized derivative contract, $\phi^*(e)$, as specified in Eq. (9), takes on a rather complicated form. It is unclear how we can structure this contract in a practical manner. The spanning of $\phi^*(e)$ by a portfolio of plain vanilla derivatives, i.e., currency futures and options that are more readily available, is thus worth examining. We characterize such a replicating portfolio in the following proposition.[8]

Proposition 2. *If the MNF has access to the unbiased currency futures and a continuum of fairly priced currency put and call option contracts of all exercise prices for hedging purposes, the MNF's optimal customized derivative contract, $\phi^*(e)$, can be replicated by trading these plain vanilla derivatives exclusively in the following way:*

$$\phi^*(e) = [e - \mathrm{E}(\tilde{e})]\phi^{*\prime}[\mathrm{E}(\tilde{e})] + \int_{\underline{e}}^{\mathrm{E}(\tilde{e})} [\max(x - e, 0) - v_p(x)]\phi^{*\prime\prime}(x)\,\mathrm{d}x$$

$$+\int_{\mathrm{E}(\tilde{e})}^{\overline{e}} [\max(e - x, 0) - v_c(x)]\phi^{*\prime\prime}(x)\,\mathrm{d}x, \qquad (16)$$

where $v_p(x) = \mathrm{E}[\max(x - \tilde{e}, 0)]$ *and* $v_c(x) = \mathrm{E}[\max(\tilde{e} - x, 0)]$.

Proof. Using the fundamental theorem of calculus, we have

$$\phi^*(e) = \phi^*[\mathrm{E}(\tilde{e})] - I_{\{e<\mathrm{E}(\tilde{e})\}} \int_{e}^{\mathrm{E}(\tilde{e})} \phi^{*\prime}(y)\,\mathrm{d}y + I_{\{e>\mathrm{E}(\tilde{e})\}} \int_{\mathrm{E}(\tilde{e})}^{e} \phi^{*\prime}(y)\,\mathrm{d}y$$

[8]Due to the put-call parity, the replicating portfolio is by no means unique.

$$= \phi^*[\mathrm{E}(\tilde{e})] - I_{\{e<\mathrm{E}(\tilde{e})\}} \int_e^{\mathrm{E}(\tilde{e})} \left\{ \phi^{*\prime}[\mathrm{E}(\tilde{e})] - \int_y^{\mathrm{E}(\tilde{e})} \phi^{*\prime\prime}(x)\,\mathrm{d}x \right\} \mathrm{d}y$$

$$+ I_{\{e>\mathrm{E}(\tilde{e})\}} \int_{\mathrm{E}(\tilde{e})}^{e} \left\{ \phi^{*\prime}[\mathrm{E}(\tilde{e})] + \int_{\mathrm{E}(\tilde{e})}^{y} \phi^{*\prime\prime}(x)\,\mathrm{d}x \right\} \mathrm{d}y, \qquad (17)$$

where $I_{\{\cdot\}}$ is an indicator function that takes on unity if the event described in the curly brackets occurs, and zero otherwise. Applying Fubini's theorem, we can write Eq. (17) as

$$\phi^*(e) = \phi^*[\mathrm{E}(\tilde{e})] + [e - \mathrm{E}(\tilde{e})]\phi^{*\prime}[\mathrm{E}(\tilde{e})] + I_{\{e<\mathrm{E}(\tilde{e})\}} \int_e^{\mathrm{E}(\tilde{e})} \int_e^{x} \phi^{*\prime\prime}(x)\,\mathrm{d}y\,\mathrm{d}x$$

$$+ I_{\{e>\mathrm{E}(\tilde{e})\}} \int_{\mathrm{E}(\tilde{e})}^{e} \int_x^{e} \phi^{*\prime\prime}(x)\,\mathrm{d}y\,\mathrm{d}x. \qquad (18)$$

Taking the integral over y in Eq. (18) yields

$$\phi^*(e) = \phi^*[\mathrm{E}(\tilde{e})] + [e - \mathrm{E}(\tilde{e})]\phi^{*\prime}[\mathrm{E}(\tilde{e})] + I_{\{e<\mathrm{E}(\tilde{e})\}} \int_e^{\mathrm{E}(\tilde{e})} (x-e)\phi^{*\prime\prime}(x)\,\mathrm{d}x$$

$$+ I_{\{e>\mathrm{E}(\tilde{e})\}} \int_{\mathrm{E}(\tilde{e})}^{e} (e-x)\phi^{*\prime\prime}(x)\,\mathrm{d}y\,\mathrm{d}x$$

$$= \phi^*[\mathrm{E}(\tilde{e})] + [e - \mathrm{E}(\tilde{e})]\phi^{*\prime}[\mathrm{E}(\tilde{e})] + \int_0^{\mathrm{E}(\tilde{e})} \max(x-e,0)\phi^{*\prime\prime}(x)\,\mathrm{d}x$$

$$+ \int_{\mathrm{E}(\tilde{e})}^{\infty} \max(e-x,0)\phi^{*\prime\prime}(x)\,\mathrm{d}x. \qquad (19)$$

Taking expectations on both side of Eq. (19) with respect to $F(e)$ yields

$$\mathrm{E}[\phi^*(\tilde{e})] = \phi^*[\mathrm{E}(\tilde{e})] + \int_{\underline{e}}^{\mathrm{E}(\tilde{e})} v_p(x)\phi^{*\prime\prime}(x)\,\mathrm{d}x + \int_{\mathrm{E}(\tilde{e})}^{\overline{e}} v_c(x)\phi^{*\prime\prime}(x)\,\mathrm{d}x, \qquad (20)$$

where $v_p(x) = \mathrm{E}[\max(x-\tilde{e},0)]$ and $v_c(x) = \mathrm{E}[\max(\tilde{e}-x,0)]$. Substituting Eq. (20) into Eq. (19) and using the fact that $\mathrm{E}[\phi^*(\tilde{e})] = 0$ yields Eq. (16). □

Proposition 2 describes how we can replicate the optimal customized derivative contract, $\phi^*(e)$, as characterized in Eq. (9) by trading the unbiased currency futures and a continuum of fairly priced currency put and call option contracts of all exercise prices. According to Eq. (16), the replicating portfolio consists of buying $\phi^{*\prime}[\mathrm{E}(\tilde{e})]$ units of the futures contracts, $\phi^{*\prime\prime}(x)$ units of the put option contracts with the exercise price, x, for all $x \in [\underline{e}, \mathrm{E}(\tilde{e})]$, and $\phi^{*\prime\prime}(x)$ units of the call option contracts with the exercise price, x, for all $x \in [\mathrm{E}(\tilde{e}), \overline{e}]$. The futures position creates a tangent to the MNF's unhedged domestic currency profit at $\mathrm{E}(\tilde{e})$. The put and call option positions are used to bend the tangent line so as to match the MNF's unhedged domestic currency profit perfectly for all $e \in [\underline{e}, \overline{e}]$. As such, the MNF's hedged domestic currency profit at $t = 2$ is ultimately stabilized at the expected level.[9]

[9]For any given twice continuously differentiable function of a terminal stock price, Carr and Madan (2001) show how this function can be replicated by positions in pure discount bonds, the underlying stock, and call and put options of all exercise prices. See also Wong (2003b). Proposition 2 is along the line of their results.

Differentiating Eq. (13) twice with respect to e yields

$$\hat{\pi}''(e) = \begin{cases} 0 & \text{if } e \in [\underline{e}, p_1/f'(k_0)], \\ -f'[k_0 + k_1(e, k_0)]^2/ef''[k_0 + k_1(e, k_0)] & \text{if } e \in (p_1/f'(k_0), \overline{e}], \end{cases} \tag{21}$$

where we have used Eq. (3). It is evident from Eq. (21) that the MNF's unhedged domestic currency profit at $t = 2$ is a convex function of the realized spot exchange rate (see also Figure 2). The MNF's implicit real hedge thus introduces a convex component into its exchange rate risk exposure, thereby calling for the use of currency options for hedging purposes. In the 1998 Wharton survey of financial risk management by US non-financial firms, Bodnar, Hayt, and Marston (1998) report that 68% of the 200 derivatives-using firms indicated that they had used some form of options within the past 12 months. Proposition 2 thus offers a rationale for the hedging demand for currency options by MNFs that make sequential FDI under exchange rate uncertainty.

4. Lumpy versus Sequential FDI.

In this section, we consider the case wherein the MNF is unable to adjust its irreversible FDI at $t = 1$ or, equivalently, we set $p_1 = \infty$.

At $t = 0$, the MNF chooses a level of lumpy FDI, k_0, and a customized derivative contract, $\phi(e)$, so as to maximize the expected utility of its domestic currency profit at $t = 2$:

$$\max_{k_0 \geq 0, \phi(e)} \mathrm{E}\{u[\tilde{e}f(k_0) - p_0 k_0 - c + \phi(\tilde{e})]\} \quad \text{s.t.} \quad \mathrm{E}[\phi(\tilde{e})] = 0. \tag{22}$$

The first-order conditions for program (22) are given by[10]

$$\mathrm{E}\{u'[\tilde{e}f(k_0^{\mathrm{o}}) - p_0 k_0^{\mathrm{o}} - c + \phi^{\mathrm{o}}(\tilde{e})][\tilde{e}f'(k_0^{\mathrm{o}}) - p_0]\} = 0, \tag{23}$$

and

$$u'[ef(k_0^{\mathrm{o}}) - p_0 k_0^{\mathrm{o}} - c + \phi^{\mathrm{o}}(e)] - \lambda^{\mathrm{o}} = 0 \quad \text{for all } e \in [\underline{e}, \overline{e}], \tag{24}$$

where λ is the Lagrange multiplier, and a nought (^{o}) indicates an optimal level.

Solving Eqs. (23) and (24) yields the following proposition.

Proposition 3. *If the MNF is unable to adjust its irreversible FDI at $t = 1$ and is allowed to use customized derivatives that are fairly priced for hedging purposes, the MNF's optimal level of lumpy FDI, k_0^{o}, solves*

$$\mathrm{E}(\tilde{e})f'(k_0^{\mathrm{o}}) = p_0, \tag{25}$$

and its optimal customized derivative contract, $\phi^{\mathrm{o}}(e)$, is given by

$$\phi^{\mathrm{o}}(e) = [\mathrm{E}(\tilde{e}) - e]f(k_0^{\mathrm{o}}). \tag{26}$$

[10]The second-order conditions for program (22) are satisfied given risk aversion and the strict concavity of $f(k)$.

Proof. It is evident from Eq. (24) that

$$ef(k_0^{\text{o}}) - p_0 k_0^{\text{o}} - c + \phi^{\text{o}}(e) = u'^{-1}(\lambda^{\text{o}}) \quad \text{for all } e \in [\underline{e}, \overline{e}], \tag{27}$$

where $u'^{-1}(\lambda^{\text{o}})$ is a constant. It then follows from $\text{E}[\phi^{\text{o}}(\tilde{e})] = 0$ and Eq. (27) that $u'^{-1}(\lambda^{\text{o}}) = \text{E}(\tilde{p})f(k_0^{\text{o}}) - p_0 k_0^{\text{o}} - c$, thereby implying Eq. (26). Substituting Eq. (24) into Eq. (23) yields Eq. (25). □

The intuition of Proposition 3 is as follows. The MNF could have completely eliminated its exchange rate risk exposure had it chosen $\phi(e) = [\text{E}(\tilde{e}) - e]f(k_0)$, which can be perfectly replicated by a full-hedge via shorting $f(k_0)$ units of the unbiased currency futures contracts at $t = 0$. Alternatively put, the degree of exchange rate risk exposure to be assumed by the MNF should be totally unrelated to its FDI decision at $t = 0$. The optimal level of lumpy FDI, k_0^{o}, is then chosen to maximize $\text{E}(\tilde{e})f(k_0) - p_0 k_0 - c$, thereby yielding Eq. (25). Since the currency futures contracts are unbiased, they offer actuarially fair "insurance" to the MNF. The risk-averse MNF as such optimally opts for full insurance by choosing a full-hedge. These results are simply the well-known separation and full-hedging theorems emanated from the literature on MNFs under exchange rate uncertainty (see, e.g., Broll, 1992; Broll and Zilcha, 1992; Broll, Wong, and Zilcha, 1999; Chang and Wong, 2003; Wong, 2003a).

Since $\max[\tilde{e}f'(k_0^*) - p_1, 0] \geq 0$, Eq. (8) implies that $\text{E}(\tilde{e})f'(k_0^*) > p_0$. It then follows from $f''(k) < 0$ and Eq. (25) that $k_0^* < k_0^{\text{o}}$, thereby invoking the following proposition.

Proposition 4. *If the MNF is allowed to use customized derivatives that are fairly priced for hedging purposes, the MNF's optimal initial level of FDI in the case of sequential FDI is less than that in the case of lumpy FDI, i.e., ,* $k_0^* < k_0^{\text{o}}$.

The intuition of Proposition 4 is as follows. The flexibility of making sequential FDI, vis-à-vis lumpy FDI, offers the MNF a real (call) option to buy additional capital at $t = 1$, which is exercised whenever $e > p_1/f'(k_0)$. It is well-known that the value of a call option increases with a decrease in its exercise price (Merton, 1973). Since $f''(k) < 0$, the MNF has incentives to cut down its initial level of FDI, k_0, so as to lower $p_1/f'(k_0)$, the exercise price of the real option created by the flexibility of making sequential FDI. Thus, we have $k_0^* < k_0^{\text{o}}$.

Proposition 4 states that the MNF is forced to undertake more FDI at $t = 0$ should FDI be lumpy rather than sequential. It is of interest to extend this result by comparing the MNF's expected optimal aggregate level of sequential FDI, $k_0^* + \text{E}[k_1(\tilde{e}, k_0^*)]$, with that of lumpy FDI, k_0^{o}. Since $k_0^* < k_0^{\text{o}}$ and $\text{E}[k_1(\tilde{e}, k_0^*)] > 0$, such a comparison is a non-trivial one. To see this, consider the extreme case wherein $p_1 = p_0$. In this case, we know from Eq. (6) that $k_0^* = 0$. It then follows from Eqs. (3) and (25) that $k_1[\text{E}(\tilde{e}), 0] = k_0^{\text{o}}$. Totally differentiating $ef'[k_1(e, 0)] = p_0$ with respect to e twice and rearranging terms yields

$$\frac{\partial^2 k_1(e,0)}{\partial e^2} = -\frac{f'[k_1(e,0)]}{e^2 f''[k_1(e,0)]}\left\{\frac{f'[k_1(e,0)]f'''[k_1(e,0)]}{f''[k_1(e,0)]^2} - 2\right\}. \tag{28}$$

It follows from Eq. (28) that $k_1(e, 0)$ is convex (concave) in e if $f'(k)f'''(k)/f''(k)^2$ is everywhere no less (no greater) than 2. By Jensen's inequality, the convexity (concavity) of $k_1(e,0)$ in e implies that $\mathrm{E}[k_1(\tilde{e},0)] > (<)\ k_1[\mathrm{E}(\tilde{e}),0] = k_0^{\mathrm{o}}$. We thus establish the following proposition.

Proposition 5. *Given that $p_1 = p_0$, the MNF's expected optimal aggregate level of sequential FDI, $\mathrm{E}[k_1(\tilde{e},0)]$, is greater or smaller than the optimal level of lumpy FDI, k_0^{o}, depending on whether $f'(k)f'''(k)/f''(k)^2$ is everywhere no less or no greater than 2, respectively.*

If $f'''(k) \leq 0$, then $f'(k)f'''(k)/f''(k)^2 \leq 0$ so that $k_1(e,0)$ is concave in e. In this case, we have $\mathrm{E}[k_1(\tilde{e},0)] < k_0^{\mathrm{o}}$. On the other hand, if $f(k) = k^{\alpha}$, where $0 < \alpha < 1$, then $f'(k)f'''(k)/f''(k)^2 = 2 + \alpha/(1-\alpha) > 2$ so that $k_1(e,0)$ is convex in e. In this case, we have $\mathrm{E}[k_1(\tilde{e},0)] > k_0^{\mathrm{o}}$. In general, without knowing the specific functional forms of $u(\pi)$, $f(k)$, and $F(e)$, we are a priori unable to make an unambiguous comparison between the MNF's expected optimal aggregate level of sequential FDI and the optimal level of lumpy FDI.

5. Sequential FDI without Currency Hedging

In this section, we consider the case wherein the MNF is banned from engaging in currency hedging. This is tantamount to setting $\phi(e) \equiv 0$.

At $t = 0$, the MNF chooses a level of FDI, k_0, so as to maximize the expected utility of its domestic currency profit at $t = 2$:

$$\max_{k_0}\ \mathrm{E}\{u[\hat{\pi}(\tilde{e})]\}, \tag{29}$$

where $\hat{\pi}(\tilde{e})$ is defined in Eq. (13). The first-order condition for program (29) is given by[11]

$$\int_{\underline{e}}^{p_1/f'(k_0^{\diamond})} u'[\hat{\pi}^{\diamond}(e)][ef'(k_0^{\diamond}) - p_0]\,\mathrm{d}F(e) + \int_{p_1/f'(k_0^{\diamond})}^{\overline{e}} u'[\hat{\pi}^{\diamond}(e)](p_1 - p_0)\,\mathrm{d}F(e) = 0, \tag{30}$$

where a diamond ($^{\diamond}$) indicates an optimal level.

Rearranging terms of Eq. (30) yields

$$\mathrm{E}\left\{\frac{u'[\hat{\pi}^{\diamond}(\tilde{e})]}{\mathrm{E}\{u'[\hat{\pi}^{\diamond}(\tilde{e})]\}}\tilde{e}\right\} f'(k_0^{\diamond}) = p_0 + \mathrm{E}\left\{\frac{u'[\hat{\pi}^{\diamond}(\tilde{e})]}{\mathrm{E}\{u'[\hat{\pi}^{\diamond}(\tilde{e})]\}}\max[\tilde{e}f'(k_0^{\diamond}) - p_1, 0]\right\}. \tag{31}$$

Define the following function:

$$G(e) = \int_{\underline{e}}^{e} \frac{u'[\hat{\pi}^{\diamond}(x)]}{\mathrm{E}\{u'[\hat{\pi}^{\diamond}(\tilde{e})]\}}\,\mathrm{d}F(x), \tag{32}$$

for all $e \in [\underline{e},\ \overline{e}]$. It is evident from Eq. (32) that $G'(e) > 0$, $G(\underline{e}) = 0$, and $G(\overline{e}) = 1$. We can as such interpret $G(e)$ as a cumulative distribution function of $\tilde{e}$. Substituting Eq. (32) into Eq. (31) yields

$$\mathrm{E}_G(\tilde{e})f'(k_0^{\diamond}) = p_0 + \mathrm{E}_G\{\max[\tilde{e}f'(k_0^{\diamond}) - p_1, 0]\}, \tag{33}$$

[11] The second-order condition for program (29) is satisfied given risk aversion and the strict concavity of $f(k)$.

where $\mathrm{E}_G(\cdot)$ is the expectation operator with respect to $G(e)$. Eq. (33) states that the optimal initial level of FDI, $k_0^\diamond$, is the one that equates the expected marginal return to FDI made at $t = 0$, $\mathrm{E}_G(\tilde{e})f'(k_0^\diamond)$, to the unit price of capital at $t = 0$, p_0, plus the foregone option value of waiting to invest that unit of capital at $t = 1$, $\mathrm{E}_G\{\max[\tilde{e}f'(k_0^\diamond) - p_1, 0]\}$, where the expectations are evaluated taking the MNF's risk attitude into account.

Using the covariance operator with respect to $F(e)$, $\mathrm{Cov}(\cdot,\cdot)$, we can write Eq. (31) as[12]

$$\left\{\mathrm{E}(\tilde{e}) + \frac{\mathrm{Cov}\{u'[\hat{\pi}^\diamond(\tilde{e})], \tilde{e}\}}{\mathrm{E}\{u'[\hat{\pi}^\diamond(\tilde{e})]\}}\right\} f'(k_0^\diamond)$$

$$= p_0 + \left\{\mathrm{E}\{\max[\tilde{e}f'(k_0^\diamond) - p_1, 0]\} + \frac{\mathrm{Cov}\{u'[\hat{\pi}^\diamond(\tilde{e})], \max[\tilde{e}f'(k_0^\diamond) - p_1, 0]\}}{\mathrm{E}\{u'[\hat{\pi}^\diamond(\tilde{e})]\}}\right\}. \quad (34)$$

From Eqs. (3) and (13), we know that $\hat{\pi}^{\diamond\prime}(e) = f[k_0^\diamond + k_1(e, k_0^\diamond)] > 0$. Since $u''(\pi) < 0$, we have $\mathrm{Cov}\{u'[\hat{\pi}^\diamond(\tilde{e})], \tilde{e}\} < 0$ and $\mathrm{Cov}\{u'[\hat{\pi}^\diamond(\tilde{e})], \max[\tilde{e}f'(k_0^\diamond) - p_1, 0]\} < 0$. Inspection of Eqs. (8), (33), and (34) reveals that the absence of currency hedging reduces both the expected marginal return to FDI made at $t = 0$ and the forgone option value of waiting to invest that unit of capital at $t = 1$, as compared to those in the presence of currency hedging. The former has a negative effect on the MNF's initial level of FDI while the latter has a positive effect. We show in the following proposition that the net effect is unambiguously negative.

Proposition 6. *Suppose that the MNF is banned from engaging in currency hedging. The MNF's ex-ante and ex-post incentives to make FDI are reduced as compared to those with perfect currency hedging, i.e.,* $k_0^\diamond < k_0^*$ *and* $k_0^\diamond + k_1(e, k_0^\diamond) \leq k_0^* + k_1(e, k_0^*)$, *where the inequality is strict for all* $e < p_1/f'(k_0^*)$.

Proof. Using the fact that $\tilde{e}f'(k_0^\diamond) - p_1 = \max[\tilde{e}f'(k_0^\diamond) - p_1, 0] - \max[p_1 - \tilde{e}f'(k_0^\diamond), 0]$, we can write Eq. (34) as

$$\mathrm{E}(\tilde{e})f'(k_0^\diamond) = p_0 + \mathrm{E}\{\max[\tilde{e}f'(k_0^\diamond) - p_1, 0]\} + \frac{\mathrm{Cov}\{u'[\hat{\pi}^\diamond(\tilde{e})], \max[p_1 - \tilde{e}f'(k_0^\diamond), 0]\}}{\mathrm{E}\{u'[\hat{\pi}^\diamond(\tilde{e})]\}}. \quad (35)$$

Since $\mathrm{Cov}\{u'[\hat{\pi}^\diamond(\tilde{e})], \max[p_1 - \tilde{e}f'(k_0^\diamond), 0]\} > 0$, Eq. (35) implies that $\mathrm{E}(\tilde{e})f'(k_0^\diamond) > p_0 + \mathrm{E}\{\max[\tilde{e}f'(k_0^\diamond) - p_1, 0]\}$. It then follows from Eq. (8) and the strict concavity of $f(k)$ that $k_0^\diamond < k_0^*$. From Eq. (3), we have $k_0^\diamond + k_1(e, k_0^\diamond) < k_0^*$ for all $e < p_1/f'(k_0^*)$ and $k_0^\diamond + k_1(e, k_0^\diamond) = k_0^* + k_1(e, k_0^*)$ for all $e \geq p_1/f'(k_0^*)$. □

To see the intuition underlying Proposition 6, we partially differentiate Eq. (13) with respect to k_0 to yield

$$\frac{\partial \hat{\pi}(e)}{\partial k_0} = ef'[k_0 + k_1(e, k_0)] - p_0, \quad (36)$$

which is negative for all $e < p_0/f'(k_0)$ and positive for all $e > p_0/f'(k_0)$. If the MNF is allowed to use customized derivatives for hedging purposes, the optimal initial level of FDI is k_0^*. When the MNF is banned from engaging in currency hedging, risk aversion implies

[12] For any two random variables, $\tilde{x}$ and $\tilde{y}$, we have $\mathrm{Cov}(\tilde{x}, \tilde{y}) = \mathrm{E}(\tilde{x}\tilde{y}) - \mathrm{E}(\tilde{x})\mathrm{E}(\tilde{y})$.

that the MNF has incentives to shift its domestic currency profits when the realizations of $\tilde{e}$ are high to those when the realizations of $\tilde{e}$ are low. This can be achieved by lowering k_0, as is evident from Eq. (36). Hence, we must have $k_0^\diamond < k_0^*$. It then follows from Eq. (3) that $k_0^\diamond + k_1(e, k_0^\diamond) < k_0^*$ for all $e < p_1/f'(k_0^*)$ and $k_0^\diamond + k_1(e, k_0^\diamond) = k_0^* + k_1(e, k_0^*)$ for all $e \geq p_1/f'(k_0^*)$. Thus, both the optimal initial level of FDI and the optimal aggregate level of FDI are lower in the absence than in the presence of currency hedging.

Unlike k_0^*, the optimal initial level of FDI in the absence of currency hedging, $k_0^\diamond$, is not preference free, as is evident from Eq. (33). It is of interest to examine how the MNF in this case alters its FDI decisions when it becomes more risk averse. To this end, we let $v(\pi)$ be a von Neumann-Morgenstern utility function that is more risk averse than $u(\pi)$. According to Pratt (1964), we can write $v(\pi) = \psi[u(\pi)]$, where $\psi(\cdot)$ is a strictly concave function.

The more risk-averse MNF's ex-ante decision problem is given by

$$\max_{k_0 \geq 0} \ \mathrm{E}\{v[\hat{\pi}(\tilde{e})]\}, \tag{37}$$

where $\hat{\pi}(\tilde{e})$ is defined in Eq. (13). Differentiating the objective function in program (37) with respect to k_0, and evaluating the resulting derivative at $k_0 = k_0^\diamond$ yields

$$\left.\frac{\mathrm{dE}\{v[\hat{\pi}(\tilde{e})]\}}{\mathrm{d}k_0}\right|_{k_0 = k_0^\diamond} = \int_{\underline{e}}^{p_1/f'(k_0^\diamond)} \psi'\{u[\hat{\pi}^\diamond(e)]\}u'[\hat{\pi}^\diamond(e)][ef'(k_0^\diamond) - p_0]\,\mathrm{d}F(e)$$
$$+ \int_{p_1/f'(k_0^\diamond)}^{\bar{e}} \psi'\{u[\hat{\pi}^\diamond(e)]\}u'[\hat{\pi}^\diamond(e)](p_1 - p_0)\,\mathrm{d}F(e). \tag{38}$$

Multiplying $\psi'\{u\{\hat{\pi}^\diamond[p_0/f'(k_0^\diamond)]\}\}$ to Eq. (30) and substituting the resulting equation to the right-hand side of Eq. (38) yields

$$\int_{\underline{e}}^{p_1/f'(k_0^\diamond)} \Big\{\psi'\{u[\hat{\pi}^\diamond(e)]\} - \psi'\{u\{\hat{\pi}^\diamond[p_0/f'(k_0^\diamond)]\}\}\Big\}u'[\hat{\pi}^\diamond(e)][ef'(k_0^\diamond) - p_0]\,\mathrm{d}F(e)$$
$$+ \int_{p_1/f'(k_0^\diamond)}^{\bar{e}} \Big\{\psi'\{u[\hat{\pi}^\diamond(e)]\} - \psi'\{u\{\hat{\pi}^\diamond[p_0/f'(k_0^\diamond)]\}\}\Big\}u'[\hat{\pi}^\diamond(e)](p_1 - p_0)\,\mathrm{d}F(e).$$

The above expression is unambiguously negative because the strict concavity of $\psi(\cdot)$ implies that $\psi'\{u[\hat{\pi}^\diamond(e)]\} > (<)\ \psi'\{u\{\hat{\pi}^\diamond[p_0/f'(k_0^\diamond)]\}\}$ for all $e < (>)\ p_0/f'(k_0^\diamond)$. Thus, the MNF must invest less than $k_0^\diamond$ at $t = 0$ when it becomes more risk averse, thereby invoking the following proposition.

Proposition 7. *Suppose that the MNF is banned from engaging in currency hedging. The perverse ex-ante and ex-post incentives to make FDI, as characterized in Proposition 6, are preserved in the case of increased risk aversion from $u(\pi)$ to $v(\pi)$.*

Finally, we want to examine how the fixed cost, c, for the access to the project would affect the MNF's ex-ante and ex-post incentives to make FDI. As is well known in the literature on decision making under certainty, risk aversion alone is usually too weak to yield intuitively appealing comparative statics. To reconcile these shortcomings, the literature suggests that it is reasonable and useful to impose the additional assumption of decreasing absolute risk aversion (Gollier, 2001). We say that the MNF's utility function, $u(\pi)$, exhibits decreasing absolute risk aversion if, and only if, its Arrow-Pratt measure of absolute risk aversion, $-u''(\pi)/u'(\pi)$, decreases with π.[13] We state and prove the following proposition.

Proposition 8. *Suppose that the MNF is banned from engaging in currency hedging. If the MNF's utility function exhibits decreasing absolute risk aversion, an increase in the fixed cost for the access to the project reduces the MNF's ex-ante and ex-post incentives to make FDI.*

Proof. Totally differentiating Eq. (30) with respect to c and rearranging terms yields

$$\frac{\mathrm{d}k_0^\diamond}{\mathrm{d}c} = \frac{1}{\Delta}\left\{ \int_{\underline{e}}^{p_1/f'(k_0^\diamond)} u''[\hat{\pi}^\diamond(e)][ef'(k_0^\diamond) - p_0]\,\mathrm{d}F(e) + \int_{p_1/f'(k_0^\diamond)}^{\overline{e}} u''[\hat{\pi}^\diamond(e)](p_1 - p_0)\,\mathrm{d}F(e) \right\}, \quad (39)$$

where $\Delta = \int_{\underline{e}}^{p_1/f'(k_0^\diamond)} u''[\hat{\pi}^\diamond(e)][ef'(k_0^\diamond) - p_0]^2\,\mathrm{d}F(e) + \int_{\underline{e}}^{p_1/f'(k_0^\diamond)} u'[\hat{\pi}^\diamond(e)]ef''(k_0^\diamond)\,\mathrm{d}F(e) + \int_{p_1/f'(k_0^\diamond)}^{\overline{e}} u''[\hat{\pi}^\diamond(e)](p_1 - p_0)^2\,\mathrm{d}F(e) < 0$. From Eqs. (3) and (13), we have $\hat{\pi}^{\diamond\prime}(e) = f[k_0^\diamond + k_1(e, k_0^\diamond)] > 0$. Since $u(\pi)$ satisfies decreasing absolute risk aversion, we have

$$-\frac{u''[\hat{\pi}^\diamond(e)]}{u'[\hat{\pi}^\diamond(e)]} > (<)\, R \quad \text{for all} \quad e < (>)\, p_0/f'(k_0^\diamond), \quad (40)$$

where R is the Arrow-Pratt measure of absolute risk aversion evaluated at $e = p_0/f'(k_0^\diamond)$. We multiply $-u'[\hat{\pi}^\diamond(e)][ef'(k_0^\diamond) - p_0]$ to both sides of inequality (40) for all $e < p_0/f'(k_0^\diamond)$, and $-u'[\hat{\pi}^\diamond(e)](p_1 - p_0)$ to both sides of inequality (40) for all $e > p_0/f'(k_0^\diamond)$. Taking the expectations on both sides of the resulting inequality with respect to $F(e)$ yields

$$\int_{\underline{e}}^{p_1/f'(k_0^\diamond)} u''[\hat{\pi}^\diamond(e)][ef'(k_0^\diamond) - p_0]\,\mathrm{d}F(e) + \int_{p_1/f'(k_0^\diamond)}^{\overline{e}} u''[\hat{\pi}^\diamond(e)](p_1 - p_0)\,\mathrm{d}F(e)$$

$$> -R\left\{ \int_{\underline{e}}^{p_1/f'(k_0^\diamond)} u'[\hat{\pi}^\diamond(e)][ef'(k_0^\diamond) - p_0]\,\mathrm{d}F(e) + \int_{p_1/f'(k_0^\diamond)}^{\overline{e}} u'[\hat{\pi}^\diamond(e)](p_1 - p_0)\,\mathrm{d}F(e) \right\}$$

$$= 0, \quad (41)$$

where the equality follows from Eq. (30). Hence, Eq. (39) and inequality (41) imply that $\mathrm{d}k_0^\diamond/\mathrm{d}c < 0$. □

The intuition of Proposition 8 is as follows. An increase in the fixed cost, c, reduces the MNF's domestic currency profit at $t = 2$ by the same amount for all $e \in [\underline{e}, \overline{e}]$. Given

[13]If the MNF's utility function satisfies increasing (constant) absolute risk aversion, it can be shown analogously that $\mathrm{d}k_0^\diamond/\mathrm{d}c > (=)\, 0$.

decreasing absolute risk aversion, the MNF becomes more risk averse. It then follows from Proposition 7 that the MNF's ex-ante and ex-post incentives to make FDI are reduced.

Changes in fixed or setup costs incurred by MNFs may be due to changes in investment tax credit offered by the host government, or due to changes in the severity of entry barriers in the host country. Proposition 8 thus implies that FDI flows are positively related to higher investment tax credits and negatively related to more barriers to entry. Hines (2001) finds that the volume of Japanese FDI in countries with whom Japan has "tax sparing" agreements is 1.4 to 2.4 times higher than it would have been otherwise. Furthermore, Anand and Kogut (1997) document that industrial concentration has a negative effect on the attraction of FDI. The implications of Proposition 8 are largely consistent with these empirical findings.

6. Sequential FDI with Futures Hedging Only

In this section, we consider the case wherein the MNF is restricted to use the unbiased currency futures contracts as the sole hedging instrument. This is tantamount to setting $\phi(e) \equiv [\mathrm{E}(\tilde{e}) - e]h$, where h is the number of the currency futures contracts sold (purchased if negative) by the MNF at $t = 0$.

The MNF's random domestic currency profit at $t = 2$ is given by

$$\pi(\tilde{e}) = \tilde{e}f[k_0 + k_1(\tilde{e}, k_0)] - p_0 k_0 - p_1 k_1(\tilde{e}, k_0) - c + [\mathrm{E}(\tilde{e}) - \tilde{e}]h, \tag{42}$$

where $[\mathrm{E}(\tilde{e}) - e]h$ is the gain or loss from its futures position, h. The MNF's ex-ante decision problem is to choose an initial level of FDI, k_0, and a futures position, h, at $t = 0$ so as to maximize the expected utility of its domestic currency profit at $t = 2$:

$$\max_{k_0 \geq 0, h} \ \mathrm{E}\{u[\pi(\tilde{e})]\}, \tag{43}$$

where $\pi(\tilde{e})$ is defined in Eq. (42). The first-order conditions for program (43) are given by[14]

$$\int_{\underline{e}}^{p_1/f'(k_0^{**})} u'[\pi^{**}(e)][ef'(k_0^{**}) - p_0]\,\mathrm{d}F(e) + \int_{p_1/f'(k_0^{**})}^{\overline{e}} u'[\pi^{**}(e)](p_1 - p_0)\,\mathrm{d}F(e) = 0, \tag{44}$$

and

$$\mathrm{E}\{u'[\pi^{**}(\tilde{e})][\mathrm{E}(\tilde{e}) - \tilde{e}]\} = 0, \tag{45}$$

where Eq. (44) follows from Leibniz's rule and Eq. (3), and a double asterisk (**) signifies an optimal level.

Solving Eqs. (44) and (45) yields our first proposition.

Proposition 9. *Suppose that the MNF is restricted to use the unbiased currency futures contracts as the sole hedging instrument. The MNF's optimal initial level of FDI in the case of sequential FDI is less than that in the case of lumpy FDI, i.e.,* $k_0^{**} < k_0^{\circ}$. *Furthermore,*

[14]The second-order conditions for program (43) are satisfied given risk aversion and the strict concavity of $f(k)$.

the MNF optimally opts for an over-hedge, i.e., $h^{**} > f(k_0^{**})$, in the case of sequential FDI and a full-hedge, i.e., $h^{\rm o} = f(k_0^{\rm o})$, in the case of lumpy FDI.

Proof. From Proposition 3, we know that the MNF optimally opts for a full-hedge via the unbiased currency futures contracts in the case of lumpy FDI, even when the MNF is allowed to use customized derivatives that are fairly priced for hedging purposes. Thus, the results in Proposition 3 hold when we restrict the MNF to use the unbiased currency futures contracts as the sole hedging instrument.

Rearranging terms of Eq. (44) yields

$$\mathrm{E}\{u'[\pi^{**}(\tilde{e})][\tilde{e}f'(k_0^{**}) - p_0]\} - \mathrm{E}\{u'[\pi^{**}(\tilde{e})]\max[\tilde{e}f'(k_0^{**}) - p_1, 0]\} = 0. \tag{46}$$

Multiplying $f'(k_0^{**})$ to Eq. (45) and adding the resulting equation to Eq. (46) yields

$$\mathrm{E}(\tilde{e})f'(k_0^{**}) = p_0 + \mathrm{E}\left\{\frac{u'[\pi^{**}(\tilde{e})]}{\mathrm{E}\{u'[\pi^{**}(\tilde{e})]\}}\max[\tilde{e}f'(k_0^{**}) - p_1, 0]\right\} > p_0, \tag{47}$$

where the inequality follows from $u'(\pi) > 0$ and $\max[\tilde{e}f'(k_0^{**}) - p_1, 0] \geq 0$. Since $f''(k) < 0$, Eqs. (25) and (47) imply that $k_0^{**} < k_0^{\rm o}$.

Using the covariance operator with respect to $F(e)$, we can write Eq. (45) as

$$\mathrm{Cov}\{u'[\pi^{**}(\tilde{e})], \tilde{e}\} = 0. \tag{48}$$

Partially differentiating $u'[\pi^{**}(e)]$ with respect to e yields

$$\frac{\partial}{\partial e}u'[\pi^{**}(e)] = u''[\pi^{**}(e)]\{f[k_0^{**} + k_1(e, k_0^{**})] - h^{**}\}, \tag{49}$$

where we have used Eq. (3). Suppose that $h^{**} \leq f(k_0^{**})$. Since $k_1(e, k_0^{**}) \geq 0$ and $f'(k) > 0$, Eq. (49) implies that $\mathrm{Cov}\{u'[\pi^{**}(\tilde{e})], \tilde{e}\} < 0$, which contradicts Eq. (48). Thus, it must be true that $h^{**} > f(k_0^{**})$. □

The intuition of Proposition 9 is as follows. In the case of sequential FDI, the MNF is endowed with a real (call) option to buy additional capital at $t = 1$, which is exercised whenever $e > p_1/f'(k_0)$. The value of such a call option increases with a decrease in its exercise price (Merton, 1973) so that the MNF has incentives to cut down its initial level of FDI, k_0, thereby implying that $k_0^{**} < k_0^{\rm o}$. Given the fact that its exchange rate risk exposure is at least $f(k_0^{**})$ and is strictly greater than $f(k_0^{**})$ when $e > p_1/f'(k_0^{**})$, the MNF opts for $h^{**} > f(k_0^{**})$ as its optimal futures position. Unlike in the case of lumpy FDI, the MNF has to bear some residual exchange rate risk that cannot be eliminated by trading the unbiased currency futures contracts only.

Using a sample of U.S. MNFs, Allayannis, Ihrig, and Weston (2001) find that operational hedging is not an effective substitute for financial hedging. In spite of this, operational hedging is capable of reducing exchange rate risk exposure and enhancing firm value when it is used in combination with financial hedging. This is confirmed by Pantzalis, Simkins, and Laux (2001) and Kim, Mathur, and Nam (2006) who also show that operational hedging serves as a real option for managing exchange rate risk. Furthermore, Allayannis, Ihrig, and Weston (2001) and Kim, Mathur, and Nam (2006) find that operational hedging is a complement to, not a substitute for, financial hedging. Since a full-hedge is the optimal futures position in the case of lumpy FDI, the over-hedging result of Proposition 9 when the MNF is allowed to make sequential FDI is consistent with the empirical finding that operational hedges and financial hedges are complements to each other.

Define the following function:

$$H(e) = \int_{\underline{e}}^{e} \frac{u'[\pi^{**}(x)]}{\mathrm{E}\{u'[\pi^{**}(e)]\}} \, \mathrm{d}F(x), \tag{50}$$

for all $e \in [\underline{e}, \overline{e}]$. It is evident from Eq. (50) that $H'(e) > 0$, $H(\underline{e}) = 0$, and $H(\overline{e}) = 1$. We can as such interpret $H(e)$ as a cumulative distribution function of $\tilde{e}$. Substituting Eq. (50) into Eq. (47) yields

$$\mathrm{E}(\tilde{e})f'(k_0^{**}) = p_0 + \mathrm{E}_H\{\max[\tilde{e}f'(k_0^{**}) - p_1, 0]\}, \tag{51}$$

where $\mathrm{E}_H(\cdot)$ is the expectation operator with respect to $H(e)$. The interpretation of Eq. (51) is similar to those of Eqs. (8) and (33) with two caveats. First, when the unbiased currency futures contracts are the sole hedging instrument, the MNF's risk preferences play no role in determining the expected return to FDI made at $t = 0$, which is governed solely by $F(e)$, as is evident from the left-hand side of Eq. (51). This is simply the spanning property that arises from the tradability of $\tilde{e}$ via the currency futures contracts. Second, the option value of waiting to make FDI at $t = 1$ is now priced based on $H(e)$, as is evident from the right-hand side of Eq. (51). Using the covariance operator with respect to $F(e)$, we can write this option value as

$$\mathrm{E}_H\{\max[\tilde{e}f'(k_0^{**}) - p_1, 0]\} = \mathrm{E}\{\max[\tilde{e}f'(k_0^{**}) - p_1, 0]\} + \frac{\mathrm{Cov}\{u'[\pi^{**}(\tilde{e})], \max[\tilde{e}f'(k_0^{**}) - p_1, 0]\}}{\mathrm{E}\{u'[\pi^{**}(\tilde{e})]\}}. \tag{52}$$

The wedge between this option value and the option value under perfect currency hedging is gauged by the covariance term on the right-hand side of Eq. (52). Due to the non-tradability of the real option embedded in sequential FDI, spanning is not possible and thus the MNF's risk preferences affect the pricing of the option in this incomplete market context.

Partially differentiating $\pi^{**}(e)$ with respect to e yields

$$\pi^{**'}(e) = f[k_0^{**} + k_1(e, k_0^{**})] - h^{**}, \tag{53}$$

where we have used Eq. (3). From Proposition 9, we know that $h^{**} > f(k_0^{**})$. Eq. (53) then implies that $\pi^{**}(e)$ is strictly decreasing for all $e < e_0$ and strictly increasing for all $e > e_0$, where e_0 solves $f[k_0^{**} + k_1(e_0, k_0^{**})] = h^{**}$. Since $\pi^{**}(e)$ is non-monotonic in e, the sign of the covariance term on the right-hand side of Eq. (52) is not immediately determinate. We prove in the following proposition that this term is unambiguously negative.

Proposition 10. *Suppose that the MNF is restricted to use the unbiased currency futures contracts as the sole hedging instrument. The MNF's ex-ante and ex-post incentives to* *make FDI are enhanced as compared to those with perfect currency hedging, i.e.,* $k_0^{**} > k_0^*$ *and* $k_0^{**} + k_1(e, k_0^{**}) \geq k_0^* + k_1(e, k_0^*)$*, where the inequality is strict for all* $e < p_1/f'(k_0^{**})$*.*

Proof. From Proposition 9, we know that $h^{**} > f(k_0^{**})$. Eq. (49) then implies that $u'[\pi^{**}(e)]$ is strictly increasing for all $e < e_0$ and strictly decreasing for all $e > e_0$, where e_0 solves $f[k_0^{**}, k_1(e_0, k_1^{**})] = h^{**}$. In other words, $u'[\pi^{**}(e)]$ is hump-shaped and attains a unique global maximum at $e = e_0$. Since $\mathrm{E}\{u'[\pi^{**}(\tilde{e})]\}$ is the expected value of $u'[\pi^{**}(\tilde{e})]$, there must exist at least one and at most two distinct points at which $u'[\pi^{**}(e)] = \mathrm{E}\{u'[\pi^{**}(\tilde{e})]\}$. Write Eq. (45) as

$$\int_{\underline{e}}^{\overline{e}} \Big\{ u'[\pi^{**}(e)] - \mathrm{E}\{u'[\pi^{**}(\tilde{e})]\} \Big\} (e - y) \, \mathrm{d}F(e) = 0, \tag{54}$$

for all $y \in [\underline{e}, \overline{e}]$. If there is only one point, $\hat{e}$, at which $u'[\pi^{**}(\hat{e})] = \mathrm{E}\{u'[\pi^{**}(\tilde{e})]\}$, then we have

$$\int_{\underline{e}}^{\overline{e}} \Big\{ u'[\pi^{**}(e)] - \mathrm{E}\{u'[\pi^{**}(\tilde{e})]\} \Big\} (e - \hat{e}) \, \mathrm{d}F(e) > (<)\, 0, \tag{55}$$

when $u'[\pi^{**}(\underline{e})] \leq (>)\ \mathrm{E}\{u'[\pi^{**}(\tilde{e})]\}$, a contradiction to Eq. (54). Thus, there must exist two distinct points, e_1 and e_2, with $\underline{e} < e_1 < e_0 < e_2 < \overline{e}$, such that $u'[\pi^{**}(e)] \geq \mathrm{E}\{u'[\pi^{**}(\tilde{e})]\}$ for all $e \in [e_1, e_2]$ and $u'[\pi^{**}(e)] < \mathrm{E}\{u'[\pi^{**}(\tilde{e})]\}$ for all $e \in [\underline{e}, e_1) \bigcup (e_2, \overline{e}]$, where the equality holds only at $e = e_1$ and $e = e_2$.

Consider the following function:

$$\begin{aligned} g(x) &= \mathrm{Cov}\{u'[\pi^{**}(\tilde{e})], \max[\tilde{e} - x, 0]\} \\ &= \int_{x}^{\overline{e}} \Big\{ u'[\pi^{**}(e)] - \mathrm{E}\{u'[\pi^{**}(\tilde{e})]\} \Big\} (e - x) \, \mathrm{d}F(e). \end{aligned} \tag{56}$$

Differentiating Eq. (56) with respect to x and using Leibniz's rule yields

$$g'(x) = -\int_{x}^{\overline{e}} \Big\{ u'[\pi^{**}(e)] - \mathrm{E}\{u'[\pi^{**}(\tilde{e})]\} \Big\} \, \mathrm{d}F(e). \tag{57}$$

Differentiating Eq. (57) with respect to x and using Leibniz's rule yields

$$g''(x) = \Big\{ u'[\pi^{**}(x)] - \mathrm{E}\{u'[\pi^{**}(\tilde{e})]\} \Big\} F'(x). \tag{58}$$

It follows from Eq. (58) that $g''(x) \geq 0$ for all $x \in [e_1, e_2]$ and $g''(x) < 0$ for all $x \in [\underline{e}, e_1) \bigcup (e_2, \overline{e}]$, where the equality holds only at $x = e_1$ and $x = e_2$. In words, $g(x)$ is strictly concave for all $x \in [\underline{e}, e_1) \bigcup (e_2, \overline{e}]$ and is strictly convex for all $x \in (e_1, e_2)$. It follows from Eq. (57) that $g'(\underline{e}) = g'(\overline{e}) = 0$. Hence, $g(x)$ attains two local maxima at $x = \underline{e}$ and $x = \overline{e}$. From Eq. (56), we have $g(\overline{e}) = 0$. Also, Eqs. (54) and (56) imply that

$$g(\underline{e}) = \int_{\underline{e}}^{\overline{e}} \Big\{ u'[\pi^{**}(e)] - \mathrm{E}\{u'[\pi^{**}(\tilde{e})]\} \Big\} (e - \underline{e}) \, \mathrm{d}F(e) = 0.$$

In words, $g(x)$ has an inverted bell-shape bounded from above by zero at $x = \underline{e}$ and $x = \overline{e}$. Hence, $g(x) < 0$ for all $x \in (\underline{e}, \overline{e})$.

In particular, we have $g[p_1/f'(k_0^{**})] < 0$ and thus $\mathrm{Cov}\{u'[\pi^{**}(\tilde{e})], \max[\tilde{e}f'(k_0^{**}) - p_1, 0]\} < 0$. Eq. (52) implies that $\mathrm{E}(\tilde{e})f'(k_0^{**}) < p_0 + \mathrm{E}\{\max[\tilde{e}f'(k_0^{**}) - p_1, 0]\}$. It then follows from Eq. (8) and the strict concavity of $f(k)$ that $k_0^{**} > k_0^*$. From Eq. (3), we have $k_0^{**} > k_0^* + k_1(e, k_0^*)$ for all $e < p_1/f'(k_0^{**})$ and $k_0^{**} + k_1(e, k_0^{**}) = k_0^* + k_1(e, k_0^*)$ for all $e \geq p_1/f'(k_0^{**})$. $\square$

The results of Proposition 10 should be contrasted with those of Proposition 6. If there are only the unbiased currency futures contracts available to the MNF for hedging purposes, risk aversion has no effect on the expected marginal return to FDI made at $t = 0$ but has a negative effect on the forgone option value of waiting to invest that unit of capital at $t = 1$, as is evident from Eq. (52). Thus, the MNF is induced to make more FDI at $t = 0$ as compared to the case of perfect currency hedging, thereby implying that $k_0^{**} > k_0^*$. It then follows from Eq. (3) that $k_0^{**} > k_0^* + k_1(e, k_0^*)$ for all $e < p_1/f'(k_0^{**})$ and $k_0^{**} + k_1(e, k_0^{**}) = k_0^* + k_1(e, k_0^*)$ for all $e \geq p_1/f'(k_0^{**})$. Thus, both the optimal initial level of FDI and the optimal aggregate level of FDI are higher when the MNF is restricted to use the unbiased currency futures contracts as the sole hedging instrument. The opposite results, however, hold when the MNF is banned from engaging in currency hedging (see Proposition 6). An immediate implication is that futures hedging promotes FDI, both ex ante and ex post, a result in line with the extant literature on lumpy FDI (see, e.g., Broll, 1992; Broll and Zilcha, 1992; Broll, Wong, and Zilcha, 1999; Wong, 2003b). This is consistent with the complementary nature of operational and financial hedging strategies as empirically documented by Allayannis, Ihrig, and Weston (2001) and Kim, Mathur, and Nam (2006).

7. Conclusion

Taking foreign direct investment (FDI) as a sequential process into account, we have examined the behavior of a risk-averse multinational firm (MNF) under exchange rate uncertainty. The MNF has an investment opportunity in a foreign country. FDI is irreversible and costly expandable in that the MNF can purchase additional, but cannot sell redundant, capital at a higher unit price after the spot exchange rate has been publicly revealed. The MNF as such possesses a real (call) option that is rationally exercised whenever the foreign currency has been substantially appreciated relative to the domestic currency. The ex-post exercise of the real option convexifies the MNF's ex-ante domestic currency profit with respect to the random spot exchange rate, thereby calling for the use of currency options as a hedging instrument. We have shown that the MNF's optimal initial level of sequential FDI is always lower than that of lumpy FDI, while the expected optimal aggregate level of sequential FDI can be higher or lower than that of lumpy FDI.

If the MNF is banned from engaging in currency hedging, we have show that the MNF's ex-ante and ex-post incentives to make FDI are reduced as compared to those with perfect currency hedging. An increase in the fixed or setup cost incurred by the MNF generates similar perverse effects on FDI if the MNF's utility function satisfies the reasonable property of decreasing absolute risk aversion. Given that the change in the fixed or setup cost may be due to a change in the investment tax credit offered by the host government, or due to a change in the severity of entry barriers in the host country, FDI flows are expected to react in a predictable manner when these government policies and market conditions shift over time (Anand and Kogut, 1997; Hines, 2001). If the MNF is restricted to use the unbiased currency futures contracts as the sole hedging instrument, we have shown that the MNF's ex-ante and ex-post incentives to make FDI are enhanced as compared to those with perfect currency hedging. This implies immediately that futures hedging promotes FDI, a result consistent with the complementary nature of operational and financial hedging strategies (Allayannis, Ihrig, and Weston, 2001; Kim, Mathur, and Nam, 2006).

References

Allayannis, G., Ihrig, J., Weston, J. P., 2001. Exchange-rate hedging: Financial versus operational strategies. *American Economic Review Papers and Proceedings* **91**, 391–395.

Anand, J., Kogut, B., 1997. Technological capabilities of countries, firm rivalry and foreign direct investment. *Journal of International Business Studies* **28**, 445–465.

Bodnar, G. M., Hayt, G. S., Marston, R. C., 1998. 1998 Wharton survey of financial risk management by US non-financial firms. *Financial Management* **27**, 70–91.

Broll, U., 1992. The effect of forward markets on multinational firms. *Bulletin of Economic Research* **44**, 233–240.

Broll, U., Eckwert, B., 2006. Transparency in the foreign exchange market and the volume of international trade. *Review of International Economics* **14**, 571–581.

Broll, U., Wong, K. P., Zilcha, I., 1999. *Multiple currencies and hedging. Economica* **66**, 421–432.

Broll, U., Zilcha, I., 1992. Exchange rate uncertainty, futures markets and the multinational firm. *European Economic Review* **36**, 815–826.

Carr, P., Madan, D., 2001. Optimal positioning in derivative securities. *Quantitative Finance* **1**, 19–37.

Chang, E. C., Wong, K. P., 2003. Cross-hedging with currency options and futures. *Journal of Financial and Quantitative Analysis* **38**, 555–574.

Dixit, A. K., Pindyck, R. S., 1994. *Investment under Uncertainty*. Princeton University Press, Princeton, NJ.

Drees, B., Eckwert, B., 2003. Welfare effects of transparency in foreign exchange markets: The role of hedging opportunities. *Review of International Economics* **11**, 453–463.

Eckwert, B., Zilcha, I., 2001. The value of information in production economies. *Journal of Economic Theory* **100**, 172–186.

Eckwert, B., Zilcha, I., 2003. Incomplete risk sharing arrangements and the value of information. *Economic Theory* **21**, 43–58.

Froot, K. A., Scharfstein, D. S., Stein, J. C., 1993. Risk management: Coordinating corporate investment and financing policies. *Journal of Finance* **48**, 1629–1658.

Gollier, C., 2001. *The Economics of Risk and Time.* MIT Press, Cambridge, MA.

Hines, J. R., Jr., 2001. *Tax sparing and direct investment in developing countries.* In: Hines, J. R., Jr. (Ed.), International Taxation and Multinational Activity. University of Chicago Press, Chicago, IL., pp. 39–66.

Kim, Y. S., Mathur, I., Nam, J., 2006. Is operational hedging a substitute for or a complement to financial hedging? *Journal of Corporate Finance* **12**, 834–853.

Kogut, B., 1983. *Foreign direct investment as a sequential process.* In: Kindleberger, C. P., Audretsch, D. (Eds.), The Multinational Corporation in the 1980s. MIT Press, Cambridge, MA., pp. 38–56.

Merton, R. C., 1973. Theory of rational option pricing. *Bell Journal of Economics and Management Science* **4**, 141–183.

Pantzalis, C., Simkins, B. J., Laux, P. A., 2001. Operational hedges and the foreign exchange exposure of U.S. multinational corporations. *Journal of International Business Studies* **32**, 793–812.

Pratt, J. W., 1964. Risk aversion in the small and in the large. *Econometrica* **32**, 122–136.

Smith, C. W., Stulz, R. M., 1985. The determinants of firms' hedging policies. *Journal of Financial and Quantitative Analysis* **20**, 391–405.

Stulz, R. M., 1984. Optimal hedging policies. *Journal of Financial and Quantitative Analysis* **19**, 127–140.

Stulz, R. M., 1990. Managerial discretion and optimal financial policies. *Journal of Financial Economics* **26**, 3–27.

Tufano, P., 1996. Who manages risk? An empirical examination of risk management practices in the gold mining industry. *Journal of Finance* **51**, 1097–1137.

Wong, K. P., 2003a. Currency hedging with options and futures. *European Economic Review* **47**, 833–839.

Wong, K. P., 2003b. Export flexibility and currency hedging. *International Economic Review* **44**, 1295–1312.

Wong, K. P., 2006. Foreign direct investment and forward hedging. *Journal of Multinational Financial Management* **16**, 459–474.

In: Foreign Direct Investment
Editor: Harrison G. Blaine, pp. 145-154
ISBN: 978-1-60456-921-6
© 2009 Nova Science Publishers, Inc.

Chapter 7

ENVIRONMENTAL REGULATIONS AND THE FLOW OF FOREIGN DIRECT INVESTMENT: A REVIEW OF THE POLLUTION HAVEN HYPOTHESIS

Raymond J. MacDermott
Virginia Military Institute. Lexington VA, USA

Abstract

This chapter will review what is known as the Pollution Haven Hypothesis. This hypothesis states a firm will move its production facilities to countries with relatively weak environmental regulations in order to capitalize on the lower production costs. Given the proliferation of environmental agreements both at the national and international level, their impact on international flows of investment capital is certainly of interest.

Over the years, a variety of approaches have been taken to empirically prove the Pollution Haven Hypothesis. These range from straightforward statistical comparisons to within-region studies to cross-border studies. Unfortunately, at this time there is no clear consensus as to the effects of more stringent environmental regulations on the flows of FDI.

One key issue is preventing this research from establishing a clear conclusion. That is, the difficulty in quantifying environmental regulations. The challenge here lies, first, in the subjective nature of measuring laws on the books. Beyond that, measuring the application of the laws on the books is even more elusive. A common approach is to use a proxy. However, finding a suitable one is difficult. Until a generally agreed upon approach can be found for dealing with the immeasurable nature of environmental regulations, true evidence of the Pollution Haven Hypothesis will continue to elude researchers.

I. Introduction

Foreign direct investment has been studied extensively in economics. The effects on FDI of trade agreements, tax policy and worker compensation are just a few of the areas that have been researched. Another area is that of the environment. The notion that the relative stringency of environmental regulations can influence foreign direct investment decisions is a particularly intriguing topic, for both academics and policy makers. More specifically, if a country has relatively weak environmental regulations, we expect it to be the location of more foreign investment.[1] This is known as the Pollution Haven Hypothesis.[2]

The Pollution Haven Hypothesis is based on comparative advantage. As environmental restrictions are enacted, the cost of production invariably rises. '(E)nvironmental regulations impose significant costs, slow productivity growth, and thereby hinder the ability of (domestic) firms to compete in international markets.' (Jaffe, et al, 133) This creates a source of "comparative advantage" for countries with weak environmental regulations that might induce some highly polluting industries to relocate.

We should address the notion of fairness. As in the case of low-wage countries, people often view 'pollution havens' as cheaters by keeping their environmental regulations below those in more developed countries. Is this the case? Walter and Ugelow (1979), one of the earlier works on the pollution haven hypothesis, frame the argument nicely.

> *Environmental quality is a matter of social choice and societies may differ, quite legitimately, in their views as to what constitutes an "acceptable" level of environmental quality. Societies afflicted with widespread malnutrition and disease, high infant mortality, low life expectancy, high illiteracy levels and endemic unemployment are not likely to place the same value on degradation of the natural environment as societies in which these kinds of problems have been overcome.*
>
> *(I)t is reasonable to infer that the demand for environmental quality is income-sensitive. ... If this is correct, it implies that high income countries will tend to have more rigorous environmental standards than poor countries. The latter, it is argued, have a variety of social priorities that take precedence. ... Pollution control uses up productive resources which could be applied to greater social advantage in one or more of these areas.*

There are several counter-arguments to the Pollution Haven Hypothesis. Many of these are similar to those found in other areas of foreign direct investment. For instance, while they may have appealing environmental regulations, many developing countries are limited host sites for FDI due to the limited availability of skilled labor and infrastructure, as well as high costs of transportation and oversight. This is also the case with low wage countries. In addition, the preferences of these developing countries are constantly evolving. As a result, their statuses as pollution havens may be temporary.

It should be noted this chapter is a review of the foreign direct investment approach to the Pollution Haven Hypothesis. The different empirical approaches are grouped into three categories and presented below. There are, of course, alternate approaches to the study of environmental regulations and firm location. While these are not discussed here, references are provided, where appropriate, for those readers who may want to pursue a more in-depth investigations of those studies.

The remainder of this chapter proceeds as follows. Section II presents a simple theoretical model justifying the Pollution Haven Hypothesis. This is followed by a discussion of empirical studies seeking to verify the hypothesis. Section IV concludes.

---

[1] Some have suggested that it is foreign direct investment that drives environmental regulation. See Bommer (1999) and Cole, Elliot and Fredriksson (2006) for more on this view.

[2] Neumayer (2001) offers up an alternate definition of the pollution haven. His definition states a country provides a 'pollution haven' if it sets environmental standards below the socially efficient level or fails to enforce its standards in order to attract foreign investment from countries with higher standards or countries that better

II. A Simple Model of FDI and Environmental Regulations

To display the effects of environmental regulations on foreign direct investment, we present a rather straightforward model of two countries, home (h) and foreign (f).[3] In this scenario, a firm has one production facility in the home country and an identical facility in the foreign country. All production is intended for sale in the home country. Goods produced in the foreign country and shipped back to the home country will face both tariffs (τ) and transportation costs (t). This is a two-stage production process. Firms will first determine the profit maximizing levels of output for the home and foreign plants.[4]

The production functions are:

$$
\begin{aligned}
Q_h &= A_h K_h^{\alpha h} L_h^{\beta h} E_h^{\delta h} \\
Q_f &= A_f K_f^{\alpha f} L_f^{\beta f} E_f^{\delta f}
\end{aligned}
\tag{1}
$$

where Q_i represents the output in country i, while K_i and L_i are the capital and labor used in country i. E_i represents the pollution emissions in country i. These are determined by the local government and can be considered a 'factor of production.' We see that as the local government enacts more stringent restrictions on pollution emissions, output decreases, all else equal.

Since the cost function is the same for facilities at home and abroad, subscripts are omitted:

$$C = \min(rK + wL) \text{ s.t. } Q = AK^{\alpha} L^{\beta} E^{\delta} \tag{2}$$

Solving for the first-order conditions and substituting into the production function yields:

$$Q = AK^{\alpha+\beta} E^{\delta} \beta^{\beta} \alpha^{-\beta} r^{\beta} w^{-\beta} . \tag{3}$$

Solving for K and L and substituting into the cost function produce:

$$C = \left(QA^{-1}E^{-\delta} r^{\alpha} w^{\beta}\right)^{\frac{1}{\alpha+\beta}} \left[\left(\beta^{-\beta}\alpha^{\beta}\right)^{\frac{1}{\alpha+\beta}} + \left(\beta^{\alpha}\alpha^{-\alpha}\right)^{\frac{1}{\alpha+\beta}} \right] \tag{4}$$

enforce their standards. This, of course, differs from the more 'traditional' definition based upon comparative advantage. This article will utilize the more commonly used definition, given above.

[3] The purpose here is to simply provide a sample model which shows, theoretically, that environmental regulations can influence investment decisions. There are, of course, many alternative models offering different conclusions. For instance, Eskeland and Harrison (2003) present a simple theoretical model which shows the effects on outward investment of environmental regulations imposed at home is ambiguous.

[4] This theoretical approach does not actually utilize flows of foreign direct investment. Rather, it is more in line with empirical studies utilizing data on employment of foreign owned affiliates (Bureau of Economic Analysis) to represent foreign direct investment such as Keller and Levinson (2002). However, it is satisfactory for our purposes.

If we assume constant elasticity of demand, the profit function can now be written as:

$$\Pi = \Phi(Q_h + Q_f)^{\varepsilon} - \Psi_h Q_h^{\frac{1}{\alpha_h+\beta_h}} - \Psi_f Q_f^{\frac{1}{\alpha_f+\beta_f}} - (t+\tau)Q_f \tag{5}$$

where $$\Psi_i = \left(A^{-1}E_i^{-\delta_i} r_i^{\alpha_i} w_i^{\beta_i}\right)^{\frac{1}{\alpha_i+\beta_i}} \left[\left(\beta_i^{-\beta_i}\alpha_i^{\beta_i}\right)^{\frac{1}{\alpha_i+\beta_i}} + \left(\beta_i^{\alpha_i}\alpha_i^{-\alpha_i}\right)^{\frac{1}{\alpha_i+\beta_i}}\right]$$

Since all production is intended for sale in the home market, foreign production faces both transportation costs and tariffs. These are incorporated into the foreign profit function as t and τ, respectively.

The first-order conditions yield:

$$\begin{aligned} \frac{\partial \Pi}{\partial Q_h} &= \varepsilon\Phi(Q_h + Q_f)^{\varepsilon-1} - \frac{1}{\alpha_h+\beta_h}\Psi_h Q_h^{\frac{1}{\alpha_h+\beta_h}-1} = 0 \\ \frac{\partial \Pi}{\partial Q_f} &= \varepsilon\Phi(Q_f + Q_f)^{\varepsilon-1} - \frac{1}{\alpha_f+\beta_f}\Psi_f Q_f^{\frac{1}{\alpha_f+\beta_f}-1} - (t+\tau) = 0 \end{aligned} \tag{6}$$

This can be solved numerically. However, if we assume perfect competition[5] in the home market, the following explicit solution can be derived:

$$\begin{aligned} Q_h &= \left(\frac{P}{\left(\frac{1}{\alpha_h+\beta_h}\right)\Psi_h}\right)^{\frac{\alpha_h+\beta_h}{1-\alpha_h-\beta_h}} \\ Q_f &= \left(\frac{P-t-\tau}{\left(\frac{1}{\alpha_f+\beta_f}\right)\Psi_f}\right)^{\frac{\alpha_f+\beta_f}{1-\alpha_f-\beta_f}} \end{aligned} \tag{7}$$

Comparative Statics:

What are the implications of this model? Let us first look at the impact of tightening environmental restrictions. According to our equation for Ψ_i in equation (5), a decrease in E_i, which corresponds to tighter environmental regulations, should cause Ψ_i to rise. Similarly, an increase in the domestic cost of factors, w_i and r_i, would cause Ψ_i to rise as well.

---

[5] This assumption is relaxed later.

What are the consequences for production? As Ψ_i rises, $\left(\frac{P}{\left(\frac{1}{\alpha_h + \beta_h} \right) \Psi_h} \right)$ in equation (7) falls. Assuming the exponent $\frac{\alpha_i + \beta_i}{1 - \alpha_i - \beta_i}$ is positive, we find tighter environmental regulations lead to a decrease in local production. Likewise, an increase in the domestic cost of labor or capital would cause local production to fall as well. And what about tariffs (τ) and transportation costs (t)? They appear only in the output of the foreign plant. As τ rises, Q_f falls while leaving Q_h unaffected.

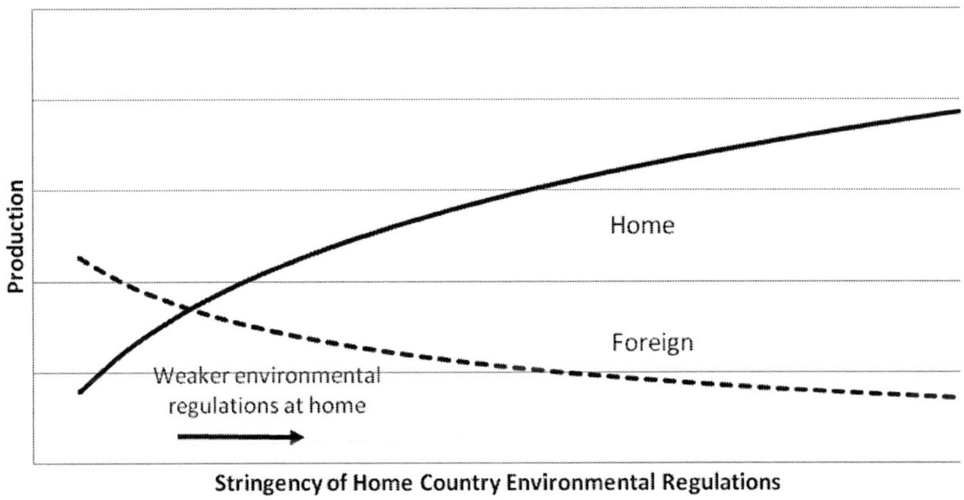

Figure 1. Output and Home Environmental Regulations.

One peculiarity of this model, as presented, is the disconnect between home and domestic production. Home production is determined entirely by home variables while foreign production is determined entirely by foreign variables. As a result, easing environmental restrictions at home (i.e. E_h rises) raises home production, while foreign production is unchanged. If we instead solve for the numerical solution to equation (6) under imperfect competition, this idiosyncrasy is eliminated. Figure 1 plots home and foreign production while allowing home environmental restrictions to vary, holding all else constant. We see that, as before, home production will rise. However, foreign production will fall. The numerical solution offers similar results for foreign environmental regulations and transportation costs (distance) as well as home and foreign wages and the cost of capital.

This analysis provides formal theoretical support for commonly accepted beliefs. We would expect an increase in environmental regulations at home to reduce domestic production and raise foreign direct investment abroad. A rise in the relative cost of factors of production would lead to similar results, as would a reduction in tariffs or transportation costs.

III. Literature on the Pollution Haven Hypothesis

We organize the foreign direct investment based studies of the Pollution Haven Hypothesis into three broad categories: [6]

1. statistical comparison of countries;
2. analysis of within-region variations in environmental restrictions; and
3. bilateral analysis.

Statistical Comparison

This approach investigates the Pollution Haven Hypothesis by making a direct comparison of the behavior of countries. The benefit of such an approach is the straightforward and intuitive manner in which it is conducted. On the other hand, some view this direct approach as a shortcoming because these types of studies sometimes utilize only 'basic' statistical methodology. As we will see, this approach finds little support for the Pollution Haven Hypothesis.

Wheeler (2001) contends if the Pollution Haven Hypothesis is valid, we should see pollution rising in poor countries because they are pollution havens. At the same time, pollution should be on the rise in wealthy countries as they relax environmental standards to remain cost-competitive. He plots FDI data from the World Development Indicators along with local metropolitan pollution emissions data[7] from 1988 to 1997 and searches for trends. The countries (cities) included are Mexico (Mexico City), Brazil (São Paulo), China (Urban Air Pollution Measures provide aggregate data on metropolitan pollution in China) and the U.S. (Los Angeles, Chicago, Houston, Atlanta and New York). He finds surprising results: rather than an expected increase, air pollution has declined in the major cities of all four countries. As a result, he concludes the 'race to the bottom' model is incorrect.

Eskeland and Harrison (2003) compare the behavior of U.S. multinationals at home to their counterparts in four developing countries: Mexico (1984-1990), Venezuela (1983-1988), Morocco (1985-1990) and Cote d'Ivoire (1977-1987). Using fuel and energy usage data as a proxy for emissions data,[8] they find 'foreign plants are significantly more energy efficient and use cleaner types of energy.'

This is followed up by testing whether the pattern of outbound U.S. investment can be explained by variations in abatement costs variations across industries. After all, if environmental restrictions led to higher costs of doing business, it should have been seen in the 'dirty' sectors. Utilizing data from the Manufacturers' Pollution Abatement Capital Expenditures and Operating Cost Survey (PACE)[9], Eskeland and Harrison (2003) test whether U.S. foreign direct investment is concentrated in industries with high abatement

[6] Trade based studies of the pollution haven hypothesis are a valid alternative. Tobey (1990), Low and Yeats (1992), van Beers and van den Bergh (1997), Mathys (2002), and Levinson and Taylor (2008) are just a few examples of this approach.

[7] The local environmental data comes from the National Environment Ministry (Mexico), Companhia de Tecnologia de Saneamento Ambiental (Brazil), the China Environmental Monitoring Center (China) and the Environmental Protection Agency (U.S.).

[8] Plant level emissions data for Mexico, Venezuela, Morocco and Cote D'Ivoire were not available. The authors use U.S. data on both energy usage and pollution emissions to justify their approach.

[9] This is a survey administered by the U.S. Department of Commerce. The 2005 report can be found at http://bhs.econ.census.gov/BHS/PACE/05_ma200pi.pdf

costs. In the end, they 'reject the hypothesis that patterns of US foreign investment is skewed towards industries with high costs of pollution abatement.'

Regional Analysis

This approach focuses on variations within a given region and generalizing the results to the international arena. The primary benefit of restricting focus to a single region is the consistency in measurement of environmental regulations. Keller and Levinson (2002) point out 'the difficulties inherent in quantifying the stringency of national environmental standards. Even if one could accurately measure stringency, countries differ on so many other grounds that it is hard to attribute any differences in international trade or investment to environmental regulations.' While there are benefits to concentrating on a single country, it is also the source of concern. Restricting focus to a single country or region may not be generalizable to the true variation in international environmental restrictions.

While there are a number of studies and approaches that investigate the impact of environmental differences within a region on new plant openings, we will restrict our attention to those that examine the effects of regional differences in environmental regulations on foreign direct investment. [10] As we shall see, this approach shows some promise of empirically verifying the Pollution Haven Hypothesis.

Keller and Levinson (2002) investigate the effects of differing U.S. state level pollution abatement costs on international investment patterns. They use FDI data from both the Bureau of Economic Analysis (employment of foreign owned affiliates) and the International Trade Administration (new foreign-owned factory openings) from 1977 to 1994. Fixed effects analysis of this data along with PACE data provides robust evidence that abatement costs have had moderate deterrent effects on FDI, thus providing evidence for the Pollution Haven Hypothesis

Dean, Lovely and Wang (2005) test the Pollution Haven Hypothesis using industry-level data by province in China. They utilize data on foreign equity joint venture projects in China from 1993 to 1996 and water pollution levy rates from the annual Chinese environmental census. Estimates from their conditional logit model suggest pollution levies do not significantly deter FDI from OECD countries. However, 'projects in highly polluting industries funded from Chinese sources (Hong Kong, Macao, Taiwan) are significantly deterred by pollution taxes.'

Bilateral Analysis

The final approach that will be presented uses foreign direct investment flows to several partner countries.[11] Its benefit is that it studies the effects of international variations in environmental regulations on foreign direct investment. As such, it is true to the traditional definition of the Pollution Haven Hypothesis. Unfortunately, this type of study suffers from several problems with the data. As mentioned above, quantifying environmental regulations

---

[10] A related stream of research, sometimes called industry location theory, investigates new plant openings. This approach often focuses only on domestic investment, though they generalize to draw conclusions on the pollution haven hypothesis. McConnell and Schwab (1990) study location decisions of the U.S. automotive industry. Levinson (1996) investigates new plant openings by U.S. state and Millimet and List (2004) focuses on the counties of New York State. Of these, only McConnell and Schwab (1990) finds any evidence of the pollution haven hypothesis.

[11] In all rights, Eskeland and Harrison (2003) could also be included in this section.

across countries as well as addressing the multitude of differences between countries beyond environmental regulations is quite challenging. That said, this approach has certainly shown promise in offering empirical confirmation for the Pollution Haven Hypothesis.

Letchumanan and Kodama (2000) takes a neo-technology approach which focuses on the role of technology in driving international industry location. They gather data on U.S. stock of FDI in both developing countries (Malaysia, Singapore, Thailand, and Philippines) and developed countries (U.S., Germany, and Japan). In addition, they utilize the EPA's Toxic Release Inventory to rank industries by pollution intensity. They find the correlation between pollution intensity and stock of FDI, both inward and outward, is positive for the developed countries. This suggests these countries are the recipient and source of significant levels of FDI in high pollution industries. At the same time, there is almost no correlation for developing countries. As a result, they conclude the Pollution Haven Hypothesis has no strong empirical basis.

Smarzynska and Wei (2001) use firm-level data on 534 U.S. multinationals located in twenty-four transition economies in Central and Eastern Europe.[12] They construct three measures of environmental stringency: participation in international treaties (index from zero to four); quality of air and water ambient emissions standards (index from one to three); and observed actual reduction in various pollutants, such as lead and CO_2. In addition to these, they incorporate corruption levels in the host country in a probit model and find 'some support for the "pollution haven" hypothesis, but the overall evidence is relatively weak and does not survive numerous robustness checks.'

Xing and Kolstad (2002) take a new approach. Attributing the failure of earlier studies to the difficulty in measuring environmental regulations,[13] they instead substitute measurable data on pollution: sulfur emissions. The justification for this is simple. According to the Pollution Haven Hypothesis, stronger environmental restrictions and foreign direct investment are negatively related. Likewise, stronger environmental regulations and pollution emission are believed to be negatively related. As a result, if the Pollution Haven Hypothesis holds true, pollution emissions and foreign direct are positively related.[14]

They use FDI data on U.S. foreign direct investment in twenty-two countries (seven developing and fifteen developed) in six manufacturing sectors (from the *Survey of Current Business*). This data is split into high, medium and low abatement cost categories according to Jaffe et al (1995). Running OLS and instrumental variables, they find strong evidence of the Pollution Haven Hypothesis.

MacDermott (2006) studies the notion that eliminating trade barriers, such as through the NAFTA, will further encourage firms already considering a move to a country with weaker environmental regulations. The study uses industry-level data on U.S. foreign direct investment into twenty-two countries. Following the Xing and Kolstad approach, CO_2, SO_2

---

[12] This data comes from a firm-level data set based on the EBRD Foreign Investment Survey conducted in 1995.

[13] There are problems quantifying environmental laws. First, it is rather subjective to measure the laws on the books. A common approach is to simply add up the number of Multilateral Environmental Agreements the country has signed. This is a good first step, but problematic. This measure says nothing about the stringency of the agreements that have been signed. Further, there is often a disparity between the stringency of the laws on the books and the enforcement of those laws.

[14] FDI = f(Environmental regulation (-))
→Pollution = g(Environmental regulations (-))
→ Environmental regulations = g^{-1}(Pollution)
→FDI = h(Pollution (+))

and NO_2 data are used as proxies for environmental regulations. [15] A fixed-effects gravity model provides strong evidence of the Pollution Haven Hypothesis.

Spatareanu (2007) focuses on the difference in regulatory environments in home and host economies. This study utilized data on new subsidiaries established in sixteen Western and nine Central and Eastern European countries by the largest companies operating in Europe from 1998 to 2001.[16] Several measures of environmental restrictiveness are used including Stringency of the Environmental Regulations from the Global Competitiveness Report, PACE abatement costs, and pollution emissions from the Toxic Release Inventory collected by the EPA. A fixed effects logit model 'suggest that more stringent environmental regulations in the investor's country relative to those in the potential host country are positively correlated with the probability of investment as well as with the volume of FDI. The results also show that firms in industries with higher abatement costs tend to invest more abroad.'

IV. Conclusion

Many have called the Pollution Haven Hypothesis a puzzle because, contrary to its intuitive appeal, it has been a challenge to confirm empirically. While definite strides have been made, particularly in the bilateral analytic approach, the controversy continues to linger.

The greatest problem lies not in the analysis of foreign direct investment. Rather, it is in quantifying the restrictiveness of environmental regulations. One way around this is regional analysis where the focus is restricted to a single region where measuring environmental regulations is less of a burden. Another common approach is to substitute other measurable data as a proxy for the notoriously difficult-to-quantify environmental regulations. These include using abatement costs (such as in Keller and Levinson (2002), Spatareanu (2007)), participation in multilateral environmental agreements (Smarzynska and Wei (2001), Spatareanu (2007)) and substituting other measures such as energy usage or pollution emissions (Smarzynska and Wei (2001), Xing and Kolstad (2002), Eskeland and Harrison (2003), Dean, Lovely and Wang (2005), MacDermott (2006), Spatareanu (2007)).

In each case, the researcher is trying to deal with a significant problem in the best way possible. However, each approach has its shortcomings. Until the issue of quantifying environmental regulations can be rectified, the Pollution Haven Hypothesis will likely continue to be hotly debated.

References

Bommer, R. (1999). Environmental Policy and Industrial Competitiveness: The Pollution-Haven Hypothesis Reconsidered. *Review of International Economics,* **7**, 342-355.

Cole, M. A., R. J. R. Elliot and P. G. Fredriksson (2006). Endogenous Pollution Havens: Does FDI Influence Environmental Regulations? *Scandinavian Journal of Economics,* **108**, 157-178.

[15] The World Bank is the source of the CO_2 data while SO_2 and NO_2 are from the OECD Compendium of Environmental Data.

[16] This is from Amadeus, a commercial data base compiled by Bureau van Dijk.

Dean, J., M. Lovely, and J. Wang (2005). Are Foreign Investors Attracted to Weak Environmental Regulations? Evaluating the Evidence from China. *World Bank, Policy Research Working Paper* #**3505**.

Eskeland, G. and A. Harrison (2003). Moving to Greener Pastures? Multinationals and the Pollution-haven Hypothesis. *Journal of Development Economics,* **70**, 1-23.

Jaffe, A., S. Peterson, P. Portney and R. Stavins (1995). Environmental Regulations and the Competitiveness of U.S. Manufacturing: What Does the Evidence Tell Us? *Journal of Economic Literature*, **33**, 132-163.

Keller, W. and A. Levinson (2002). Pollution Abatement Costs and Foreign Direct Investment Inflows to U.S. States. *Review of Economics and Statistics,* **84**, 691-703.

Letchumanan, R. and F. Kodama (2000). Reconciling the Conflict between the Pollution-Haven Hypothesis and an Emerging Trajectory of International Technology Transfer. *Research Policy,* **29**, 59-79.

Levinson, A. (1996). Environmental Regulations and Manufacturers Location Choices: Evidence from the Census of Manufacturers. *Journal of Public Economics*, **62**, 5-29.

Levinson, A. and M. S. Taylor (2008). Unmasking the Pollution Haven Effect. *International Economic Review,* **49**.

Low, P. and A. Yeats (1992). Do "Dirty" Industries Migrate? *International Trade and the Environment,* **89-103.**

MacDermott, R. (2006). Trade Agreements and the Environment: An Industry Level Study of NAFTA and the Pollution Haven Hypothesis. *Global Economy Journal,* **6**.

Mathys, N. (2002). *In Search of Evidence for the Pollution Haven Hypothesis.* Mémoire de Licence, Université de Neuchâtel.

McConnell, V. and R. Schwab (1990). The Impact of Environmental Regulations on Industry Location Decisions: The Motor Vehicle Industry. *Land Economics,* **66**, 67 – 81.

Millimet, D. and J. List (2004). The Case of the Missing Pollution-haven Hypothesis. *Journal of Regulatory Economics,* **26,** 239-262.

Neumayer, E. (2001). Pollution Havens: An Analysis of Policy Options for Dealing with an Elusive Phenomenon. *Journal of Environment and Development,* **10**, 147-177.

Smarzynska, B. and S. Wei (2001). Pollution-havens and Foreign Direct Investment: Dirty Secret or Popular Myth? *Contributions to Economic Analysis and Policy,* **3**, **1-32**.

Spatareanu, M. (2007). Searching for Pollution Havens: The Impact of Environmental Regulations on Foreign Direct Investment. *Journal of Environment and Development,* **16,** 161-182.

Tobey, J. A. (1990). The Effects of Domestic Environmental Policies on Patterns of World Trade; an Empirical Test. *Kyklos,* **43**, 191-209.

van Beers, C. and J. C. J. M van den Bergh (1997). An Empirical Multi-Country Analysis of the Impact of Environmental Regulations on Foreign Trade Flows. *Kyklos,* **50**, 29-46.

Wheeler, D. (2001). Racing to the Bottom? Foreign Investment and Air Pollution in Developing Countries. *Journal of Environment and Development,* **10** 225-245.

Xing, Y. and C. Kolstad (2002). Do Lax Environmental Regulations Attract Foreign Investment? *Environmental and Resource Economics,* **21**, 1-22.

In: Foreign Direct Investment
Editor: Harrison G. Blaine, pp. 155-168

ISBN: 978-1-60456-921-6
© 2009 Nova Science Publishers, Inc.

Chapter 8

FDI AND LABOUR DEMAND ADJUSTMENT TO FACTOR PRICES AND DEMAND SHOCKS IN THE UK MANUFACTURING INDUSTRY

Qian Cher Li[1] ***and Sourafel Girma***[2]
[1]Department of Economics, University of Glasgow, U.K.
[2]Nottingham University Business School, U.K.

Abstract

This paper documents evidence of differential speed of labour demand adjustment among exporters, foreign multinationals (henceforth MNEs) and domestic non-exporting firms from the UK manufacturing industry. Our findings show that MNEs exhibit the fastest speed of employment adjustment to its optimal level, followed by exporters and then domestic non-exporters. Interestingly, the long-run adjustment of labour demand with respect to factor price and demand shocks is less pronounced amongst MNEs and exporters, consistent with the view that firms engaged in international commerce activities generate more skilled jobs that are more costly to dispose of. Moreover, exporting intensity also seems to matter; MNEs with limited export-market commitment are found to have more rigid labour adjustment in response to output and wages shocks in the long run. These findings may allay fears on the footloose nature of MNEs in the sense that jobs in MNEs (followed by exporters) are expected to be more secure on average in response to any shocks affecting long-run labour demand.

Keywords: foreign direct investment (FDI); exports; employment adjustment

JEL classification: F16; F23; J23

1. Introduction

There is now a growing body of empirical evidence that captures a strong and positive relationship between multinationality, exporting and business performance[1]. The stylised

[1] For the exports-performance nexus, see for instance, Bernard and Jensen (1995, 1999, 2004) for the US; Bernard and Wagner (1997) for Germany; Clerides *et. al.* (1998) for Columbia, Mexico and Morocco; Delgado *et. al.*

facts documented in the empirical literature are consistent with a number of recent theoretical models [e.g. Melitz, 2003; Helpman *et. al.*, 2004] that predict firms engaged in foreign direct investment (FDI) activities are more efficient/productive than those serving foreign markets through arms-length exporting alone, while the least efficient/productive firms will operate only in the indigenous market[2]. This apparent empirical and theoretical consensus goes some way to explaining why governments over the world intervene to encourage exports and FDI [Blomström and Kokko, 2003]. For example, *UK Trade & Investment*, the government organisation that supports companies investing in the UK as well as domestic exporters, has active branches in over 200 countries across the world.

One prominent motivation for encouraging inward FDI and international trade is based on the presumption that multinational and exporting firms stimulate aggregate productivity and employment, either directly through their own productivity and employment growth, and reallocations of resources [e.g. Bernard and Jensen, 2004][3]; or through an indirect spillover effect [e.g. Driffield and Taylor, 2000]. Nevertheless, in light of the labour-market impact of international trade and investment, there also has been widespread public concern regarding the "footloose" nature of multinational firms [e.g. Görg and Strobl, 2003], suggesting higher job insecurity associated with cross-border investment vis-à-vis foreign expansion of domestic firms. This must be worrying from policy makers' perspective given that substantially more public funds are used to attract MNEs than are devoted to encouraging domestic firms to enter export markets. For instance, between 1991 and 1995, about half a billion pounds was paid in grants for internationally-owned companies by the UK government under the *Regional Selective Assistance* scheme[4], costing around £17,500 per net job created. While it is of public interest to determine the optimal mix of resources allocated to encourage exporting and FDI, it appears that there is a dearth of work analysing the relative labour-adjustment behaviour of multinational subsidiaries and exporters on which to base informed policy decisions.

The purpose of this paper, therefore, is to contribute to the effort to bridge this gap in the literature. In particular, it examines the relative role of distinct international commerce activities in moderating the employment adjustment of firms. The empirical setting of this paper is the UK manufacturing industry, which represents an interesting case study given that the UK is the top inward investment destination in Europe and the fifth largest exporter in the world.

The rest of the paper is organised as follows. Section 2 provides a brief discussion of the related literature; Section 3 describes the empirical model and the dataset employed in the analysis is presented in Section 4; Section 5 discusses the estimation results and the last section concludes.

(2002) for Spain; Baldwin and Gu (2003) for Canada; Girma *et. al.* (2004) and Greenaway and Kneller (2004) for the UK. For the positive impact of (inward) FDI on firm performance, see Harris and Robinson (2003) for a review of the literature, and in particular, Doms and Jensen (1998), Aitken and Harrison (1999), Conyon *et. al.* (2002), and Griffith and Simpson (2004).

[2] Most recently some studies attempt to empirically test Helpman *et. al.*'s hypothesis (*op. cit.*) and have found supporting evidence: the productivity distribution of FDI firms dominates that of exporters, which in turn dominates that of domestic non-exporters, such as Girma *et. al.* (2005) for the UK; and Wagner (2006) for Germany.

[3] In particular, they are able to show that increased export opportunities are associated with both intra- and inter-industry reallocations that account for 40 per cent of TFP growth in the US manufacturing. Thus, the higher productivity levels and faster growth rates found in exporters provide an important reallocative channel for explaining aggregate productivity growth.

[4] See http://www.dti.gov.uk/regional/evaluationRSA91-95.pdf

2. Literature Review

It is often felt that international trade and investment are exerting an increasingly significant impact on the labour market (particularly as far as the source country is concerned), as part of the inevitable process of globalisation. For instance, Driffield and Taylor (2000) and Gaston and Nelson (2002) provide reviews of the empirical and theoretical literature of inward FDI and its labour-market impact in the host country, particularly in light of wage-inequality, skill-upgrading as well as the deterioration of labour-market conditions for unskilled workers; Girma (2005) examines the acquisition FDI and its impact on employment dynamics in the UK manufacturing industry. On the other side, turning to trade, Bernard and Jensen (1995, 1997) provide plant-level evidence from the US manufacturing, of the labour-market outcomes of exporting, mainly in the context of technology differentials, wage gap, and within plant skill-upgrading. From a microeconomic perspective, despite a relative abundance of work looking at the role of FDI and exporting in transforming some features of the workforce, there is a deficiency of research focusing on the dynamic adjustment process of labour demand *per se* in firms engaged in international commerce activities and therefore facing demand shocks from international markets.

Traditional international trade theory suggests that international trade can increase the equilibrium elasticity of labour demand. This is hypothesised to occur by means of increasing the product-demand elasticity for the industry as well as the constant-output elasticity of substitution between labour and other variable factors of production [e.g. Hamermesh, 1993]. Therefore, this theory would imply that labour demand elasticities are higher in MNEs and exporters, relative to domestic non-exporters [Hatzius, 2000; and Slaughter, 2001]. By contrast, human capital theory suggests a different story. This theory assumes that firms tend to invest in the development of firm-specific human capital, since higher skilled personnel usually brings about higher returns to both the firms (in terms of higher profits) and the employees (in terms of higher wages). Therefore, employment may turn out to be more rigid and the level of separation between employers and employees lower for high skilled workers than for low skilled ones. As MNEs and exporters tend to employ a more skilled workforce relative to domestic (non-exporting) firms[5], one might expect jobs in these firms engaging in international commence activities to last longer and their labour demand to be more rigid and stable. Indeed, Görg and Strobl (*op. cit.*) have found some evidence in line with this view and conclude that MNEs seem to be more likely to create new jobs only if they expect them to last in the long run; while domestic plants base their recruitment decisions more on shorter term considerations. Also Fabbri *et. al.* (2003) estimate labour demand equation for production and non-production labour for the UK plants, and find that over time wage elasticity of the demand for production labour is rising more rapidly in multinational subsidiaries. Moreover, Naveretti *et. al.* (2003) provide a cross-European perspective to compare the adjustment process of employment between MNEs and national firms; and their results show that employment adjusts significantly faster in MNEs although they tend to have a more rigid labour demand in response to wage shocks. Nevertheless, it is surprising that there is a

[5] On the use of more skilled labour in MNEs, for more detailed discussions, see Driffield and Taylor (*op. cit.*); Gaston and Nelson (*op. cit.*); and Griffith and Simpson (*op. cit.*). From the perspective of trade, see Bernard and Jensen (1999); Yeaple (2005); and Roper *et. al.* (2006) for a most recent discussion of a higher demand for skilled workers (and thus a higher average skill level of the workforce) in exporting firms, as a result of adopting technologies favouring the highly skilled.

distinct lack of studies comparing the effects of inward FDI and exporting activities on employment adjustment in a unified framework.

3. The Empirical Model

In order to assess the speed and magnitude of employment adjustment, we consider a dynamic labour demand model that can be derived from a Cobb-Douglas production function. In the absence of adjustment costs, a price-setting and cost-minimising firm facing a constant-elasticity demand function would choose to set employment according to the following log-linear conditional labour demand equation:

$$n_{it}^{*} = \beta_1 + \beta_2 w_{it} + \beta_3 y_{it} + D_t + f_i + \varepsilon_{it} \qquad (1)$$

where n^* is the log of desired level of employment for firm i at time t; w is the log of real wages; y is the log of real output; D is a vector of time dummies; f represents the firm-specific fixed effects and $\varepsilon_.$ the disturbance term. The time dummies account for factors such as technical changes in government regulatory and/or tax policies that are common to all firms and that affect labour demand[6]. If employment adjustment is costly, then in the short run actual employment, say n_{it}, will deviate from n_{it}^{*}, the desired level of employment. In a framework of dynamic optimisation, under quadratic adjustment costs (e.g. Hamermesh, *op. cit.*), a reduced form of the dynamic labour demand equation with AR(2) representation can be written as:

$$n_{it} = \beta_1 + \sum_{l=1}^{2} \alpha_l n_{it-l} + \beta_2 w_{it} + \beta_3 y_{it} + D_t + f_i + \varepsilon_{it} \qquad (2)$$

The speed of employment adjustment is measured by $1 - \sum_{l=0}^{2} \alpha_l$, and the long run elasticity of labour demand with respect to wages, for example, is $\dfrac{\beta_2}{1 - \sum_{l=0}^{2} \alpha_l}$. To allow for differential speed of labour adjustment and demand elasticities across firms grouped by international commerce activities, we introduce two dummy variables, viz., *MNE* and *EXP*, where *MNE* takes the value of 1 if the firm being considered is a foreign multinational, and 0 otherwise; and *EXP* is equal to 1 for an exporter, and 0 otherwise. These two dummies are then interacted with the lagged dependent and independent variables.

---

[6] Theory suggests that the price of capital also has an impact on employment. However, due to the presence of time dummies, this is not included in the current model, assuming that all firms face the same price of capital at any given time and it will only change through time.

The problems arising from estimation of dynamic models such as that represented by Equation (2) (particularly prevalent in short panels) are frequently discussed in the econometric literature [e.g. Anderson and Hsiao, 1982; Arellano and Bover, 1995]. In particular, in the presence of fixed effects and lagged dependent variables, the OLS estimator will no longer be consistent as a result of the well-documented endogeneity problem. We therefore adopt the estimation technique of generalised method of moments (GMM) developed by Arellano and Bond (1991). This would entail first-differencing Equation (2) and employing lagged levels of employment, wages and output as instruments. Meanwhile, care should be taken to check the validity of those instruments via the Sargan test of overidentifying restrictions and the serial correlation test as suggested in Arellano and Bond (*op. cit.*).

4. The Data

This paper draws on the *OneSource* data, a large electronic database derived from the accounts that companies are legally required to deposit at Companies House[7]. These data contain information on firm-level employment, physical capital, output and wages in a consistent way across time and across firms. Companies with employees less than 50 and those are dissolved or in the process of liquidation are excluded[8]. The data were also screened to keep only those firms for which there exists a complete set of information on output and factors of production. Our analysis is restricted to firms whose main activity is manufacturing, and they are classified into three groups, viz. MNEs, domestic exporters, and domestic non-exporters[9]. For each of them, we have from 957 up to 3540 observations each year during the period 1990-1998, adding up to 51598 observations in total. The panel is unbalanced both in the sense that there are differentiated numbers of observations amongst enterprises, and that these observations correspond to different points in time.

Table 1 provides the frequency of distribution of the companies by type of international commerce activities and Table 2 gives summary statistics of some variables of interest. It seems apparent that MNEs are on average larger than their domestic counterparts and enjoy higher level of employment and output. It is equally worth noting that, as indicted by the log of labour cost per employee, the level of wages is invariably the highest in foreign subsidiaries[10], which may be taken as a proxy for the highest skill intensity, although the skill mix unfortunately cannot be directly measured for lack of information in our dataset.

[7] The *OneSource* CD-ROM entitled "U.K. companies, Vol. 1" (for Oct., 2000) was used for this study. Further details of this dataset can be found in Oulton (1998) and Girma (2005).

[8] Note, although firms with less than 50 employees are under-represented in this non-stratified sample, this may not be problematic in current analysis since larger domestic firms are compared with MNEs and exporters, which are generally found to be large as well.

[9] Notably this grouping is based on different degree/intensity of internationalisation (assuming different skill composition of labour and distinct wage shocks between national and foreign markets), from indigenous non-exporters (the baseline group), domestic exporting firms, to subsidiaries of multinational firms. Admittedly, MNEs may also engage in exporting activity; nevertheless, these are classified as FDI firms only so as to ensure these three groups are mutually exclusive, given multinationality being the most distinguishable feature of MNEs (as opposed to arms-length exporting alone).

[10] Similar empirical findings are also available in Aitken *et. al.* (1996) for Mexico, Venezuela and the US; and Driffield and Taylor (*op. cit.*) for the UK. Also Gaston and Nelson (*op. cit.*) provide a theoretical treatment on this skill-FDI linkage.

Meanwhile, these statistics also echo the consensus in the literature of trade in that exporters are generally larger, have a higher level of output and pay higher wages[11].

Table 1. Number of firms by type of international commerce orientation

Firm type Year	Non-exporters	Exporters	Multinationals	Total
1990	2,609	1,040	957	4,606
1991	2,890	1,238	1,007	5,135
1992	3,094	1,393	1,035	5,522
1993	3,319	1,550	1,090	5,959
1994	3,428	1,677	1,133	6,238
1995	3,540	1,809	1,178	6,527
1996	3,392	1,850	1,166	6,408
1997	2,493	2,175	1,057	5,725
1998	2,386	2,081	1,011	5,478
Total	27,151	14,813	9,634	51,598

Table 2. Summary statistics

Firm type	Statistics	Log employment	Log wages	Log output
Non-exporters	mean	4.35	2.67	8.56
	median	4.25	2.68	8.36
	std. dev.	1.32	0.44	1.38
	skewness	0.64	-0.12	0.75
Exporters	mean	4.63	2.69	8.88
	median	4.54	2.71	8.74
	std. dev.	1.14	0.39	1.13
	skewness	0.41	-3.48	0.69
Multinationals	mean	5.12	2.77	9.54
	median	5.06	2.78	9.43
	std. dev.	1.28	0.34	1.37
	skewness	0.39	-2.81	0.49

Source: the *OneSource* (authors' own calculations)

5. Main Findings

In Table 3 we report the estimated parameters using the dynamic panel data methods. The interpretation of the results is based on the GMM estimate, but here we also report the OLS and within-group estimates for comparison purposes. The interacted terms of $MNE\ /EXP$ and the adjustment coefficients (the α s) are negative and statistically significant, indicating firms engaged in international commerce adjust their labour demand significantly faster than

[11] See for example, Bernard and Jensen (1995); Girma *et. al.* (2004); Baldwin and Gu (2004); and more recently, Silvente (2005).

their solely national counterparts. The ranking of the speed of adjustment here is perhaps not surprising: MNEs adjust their labour demand to its optimal level most rapidly, and domestic exporters adjust significantly faster than non-exporters. The adjustment advantages conferred by multinationality are intuitively appealing: having the option of relocating activities or shifting employment in their affiliates across countries can substantially reduce MNEs' costs associated with hiring and firing personnel; meanwhile, given that MNEs tend to enjoy more benefits from governments and unions in host countries, they are able to bargain with labour from a more privileged position and are therefore less constrained[12]. As to domestic exporting enterprises, being frequently larger than non-exporters[13], they may also have more resources and flexibility to adjust with lower costs and more ease than firms operating solely in domestic market, given the well-documented evidence on the superior performance of exporters [see Footnote 1 for more details]. To put it another way, the fact that exporters have successfully overcome entry barriers into more competitive international markets (often proxied by sunk costs in the microeconomics literature related to trade), is a manifestation *per se* of their pronounced cost advantages over non-exporting firms.[14]

Table 3. Estimation results for the employment equation

	OLS	Within group	GMM
Employment (t-1)	0.942	0.412	0.849
	(0.026)***	(0.006)***	(0.049)***
Employment (t-2)	-0.094 (0.019)***	-0.053 (0.005)***	-0.229 (0.023)***
	(0.019)*** (0.019)*** (0.019)*** (0.019)***	(0.005)***	(0.023)***
Employment (t-1)*EXP	-0.007 (0.042)	-0.011	-0.575
	(0.042)	(0.010)	(0.049)***
Employment (t-2)*EXP	-0.005 (0.031)	0.010 (0.009)	0.412 (0.032)***
	(0.031)	(0.009)	(0.032)***

[12] In addition to these cost advantages, other distinctive characteristics of MNEs as documented particularly in the business management literature, which may also contribute (at least indirectly) to their faster speed of labour adjustment, include better risk diversification strategies, more and better investment opportunities, as well as some other firm-specific assets such as technological know-how, superior managerial capability, brand names, etc. [e.g. Shaked, 1986].

[13] Size advantage of exporters is frequently documented in the micro literature, for instance, Aw and Hwang (1995), Bernard and Jensen (1999), Bernard *et. al.* (2003), Baldwin and Gu (2004), and Gourley and Seaton (2004).

[14] Here the notion of sunk costs is extensively investigated in both theoretical and empirical research, such as Roberts and Tybout (1997), Melitz (2003), Girma *et. al.* (2004), to name just a few.

Table 3. Continued

	OLS	Within group	GMM
Employment (t-1)*MNE	0.015 (0.037)	0.030 (0.012)**	-0.665 (0.056)***
	(0.037)	(0.012)**	(0.056)***
Employment (t-2)*MNE	-0.028 (0.026)	0.003 (0.010)	0.328 (0.036)***
	(0.026)	(0.010)	(0.036)***
Wages	-0.177 (0.017)***	-0.478 (0.007)***	-0.471 (0.040)***
	(0.017)***	(0.007)***	(0.040)***
Wages* EXP	-0.023 (0.022)	-0.016 (0.009)*	-0.130 (0.038)***
	(0.022)	(0.009)*	(0.038)***
Wages* MNE	-0.017 (0.027)	0.086 (0.015)***	0.060 (0.101)
	(0.027)	(0.015)***	(0.101)
Output	0.139 (0.013)***	0.523 (0.004)***	0.470 (0.023)***
	(0.013)***	(0.004)***	(0.023)***
Output* EXP	0.012 (0.017)	0.001 (0.006)	0.123 (0.027)***
	(0.017)	(0.006)	(0.027)***
Output* MNE	0.011 (0.017)	-0.049 (0.009)***	0.048 (0.045)
	(0.017)	(0.009)***	(0.045)
No. of observations	36,525	36,525	29,714
R-squared	0.97	0.66	
Sargan test (p-value)			0.793
AR(1) test (p-value)			0.000
AR(2) test (p-value)			0.880

Notes: (i) robust standard errors in parentheses; (ii) time and industry dummies included in all models to control for time and industry effects; (iii) ***significant at 1%, ** significant at 5%, *significant at 10%.

With respect to the extent of employment adjustment to output and wage shocks, the GMM results indicate that exporters have higher short-run elasticities, therefore less rigid labour demand. By contrast, neither the output nor the wage elasticity for MNEs is statistically different from that of domestic non-exporters in the short run.

So far we've identified that MNEs adjust their labour demand at a faster speed on the one hand; and nevertheless, they do not seem to have a more elastic labour demand in the short run on the other hand. To reconcile this apparent inconsistency, we investigate long-run responses and our main findings are reported in Table 4.[15]

[15] Here the asymptotic standard errors of long-run elasticities are calculated by means of delta method.

Table 4. Short-run and long-run elasticities of labour demand

	Non-exporters	MNEs	Exporters
Adjustment speed	0.380***	0.717***	0.544***
Short-run output elasticity	0.470***	0.518	0.592***
Long-run output elasticity	1.235 *** (0.088)	0.722*** (0.074)	1.089*** (0.051)
Short-run wage elasticity	-0.471***	-0.411	-0.601***
Long-run wage elasticity	-1.239*** (0.123)	-0.574*** (0.132)	-1.106*** (0.070)

Notes: (i) calculations based on estimated coefficients in the differenced GMM regression reported in Table 3; (ii) for non-linear combinations as in the case of long run elasticities, asymptotic standard errors are included in parentheses; (iii) ***significant at 1%, ** significant at 5%, *significant at 10%.

Despite the insignificant discrepancy between MNEs and non-exporters in the short run, domestic non-exporters exhibit the highest long-run elasticity with respect to output whilst MNEs show the lowest one. A similar pattern emerges when comparing long-run values of the labour demand elasticity with respect to wages. To check the robustness of our results, two labour demand functions have also been estimated for exporters and MNEs separately and we find that the rank orders of all the parameters of interest are in agreement with those reported in Tables 3 and 4.[16]

With regard to the long-run magnitude of adjustment as measured by factor price and output elasticities, we conjecture that the heterogeneity among different groups may be accounted for by their different market power and most importantly, distinct skill composition of their workforce[17]. Overall labour demand may be most rigid in MNEs, which may be partly explained by their highest level of market power[18] and most rigid product demands; moreover, they enjoy the highest intensity of skilled labour: skilled jobs are created on a long-term basis and are costly to be disposed of. The evidence here is in accordance with the theory discussed by Hamermesh (*op. cit.*) and the conclusion drawn by Görg and Strobl (*op. cit.*). In a similar vein, since exporting enterprises have higher skill intensity relative to non-exporters, they exhibit a more rigid labour demand.

Thus far, our analysis has not distinguished between the exporting intensity of exporters and exporting multinationals[19]. However, it can be argued that the extent of export-market participation might matter for the adjustment of domestic labour demand. For example, a multinational company with limited exports and greater commitment to serving the domestic market is likely to be less footloose. It follows that the last empirical question we seek to answer is whether exporting intensity matters amongst different modes of internationalisation.

---

[16] To save space, these results are not reported here but are available upon request.

[17] Refer to Footnote 5 for a discussion and evidence on the use of more skilled workforce in FDI and exporting firms respectively. Meanwhile, this skill-upgrading could also be contributable/attributable to wage inequality, and technology advancement in MNEs and exporters, all of which are explicably interrelated [Driffield and Taylor, op. cit.].

[18] A discussion of the firm-specific advantages associated with multinationality is available in Footnote 12.

[19] See Footnote 9 for an explanation of the grouping criteria.

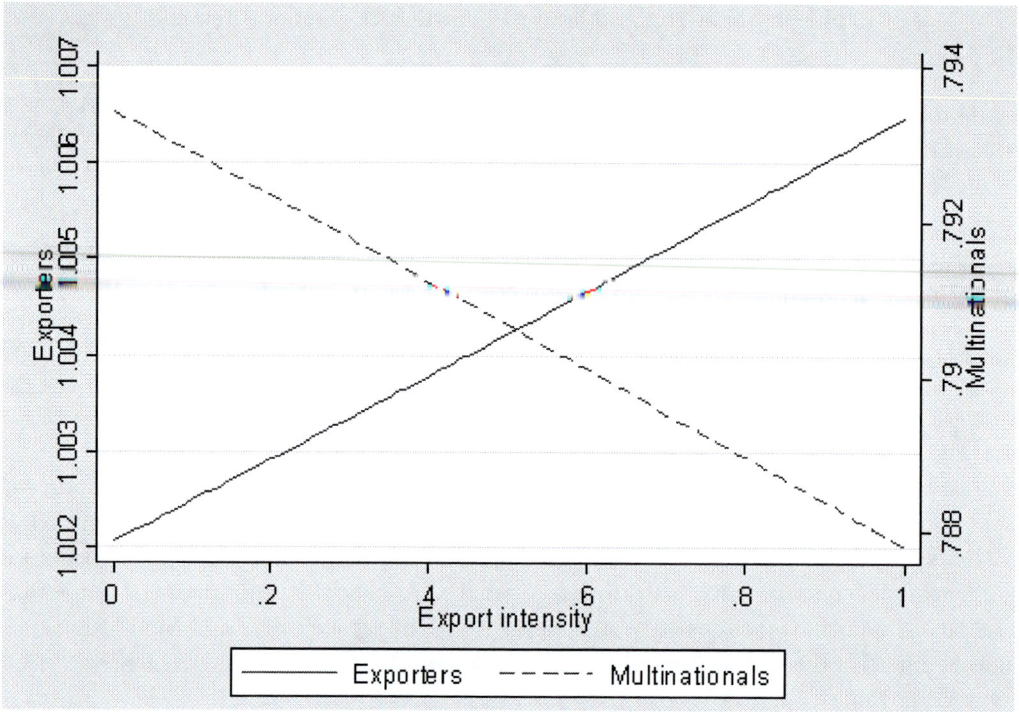

Figure 1. LR elasticity w.r.t. output and export intensity.

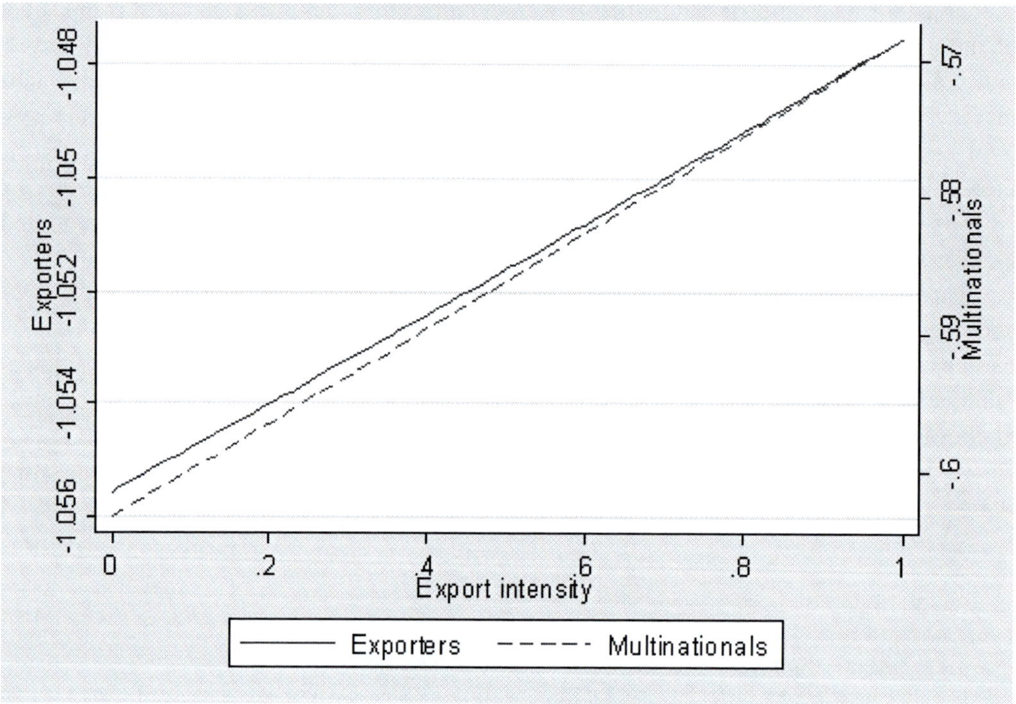

Figure 2. LR elasticity w.r.t. wages and export intensity.

Note: Figures 1 and 2 are based on the GMM estimates reported in Table 5.

Table 5. Employment adjustment and exporting intensity

	Exporters			MNES		
	OLS	Within group	GMM	OLS	Within group	GMM
Employment (t-1)	0.892	0.424	0.914	0.880	0.415	0.919
	(0.061)***	(0.014)***	(0.093)***	(0.040)***	(0.016)***	(0.103)***
Employment (t-2)	-0.068	-0.068	-0.400	-0.090	-0.061	-0.345
	(0.048)	(0.012)***	(0.056)***	(0.023)***	(0.013)***	(0.057)***
Wages	-0.217	-0.517	-0.513	-0.234	-0.397	-0.257
	(0.026)***	(0.016)***	(0.043)***	(0.037)***	(0.016)***	(0.089)***
Output	0.163	0.513	0.487	0.192	0.489	0.338
	(0.020)***	(0.009)***	(0.033)***	(0.023)***	(0.009)***	(0.046)***
Employ (t-1) * EXP_INT	-0.018	0.008	0.151	-0.012	0.000	0.080
	(0.016)	(0.005)	(0.020)***	(0.005)**	(0.002)	(0.011)***
Employ (t-2) * EXP_INT	0.014	-0.010	-0.128	0.006	-0.004	-0.064
	(0.013)	(0.004)**	(0.017)***	(0.004)	(0.002)**	(0.008)***
Wages * EXP_INT	-0.006	0.002	0.028	-0.008	0.006	0.024
	(0.009)	(0.005)	(0.009)***	(0.004)**	(0.002)***	(0.008)***
Output * EXP_INT	0.004	0.000	-0.021	0.006	0.001	-0.015
	(0.006)	(0.003)	(0.006)***	(0.003)**	(0.001)	(0.005)***
No. of observations	11,245	11,245	9,440	7,175	7,175	5,999
R-squared	0.97	0.92		0.97	0.92	
Sargan test (p-value)			0.178			0.274
AR(1) test (p-value)			0.000			0.000
AR(2) test (p-value)			0.604			0.668

Notes: (i) EXP_INT denotes export intensity; (ii) robust standard errors in parentheses; (iii) time and industry dummies included in all models to control for time and industry effects; (iv) ***significant at 1%, ** significant at 5%, *significant at 10%.

Nevertheless, we are not aware of any theoretical work that provides a prediction on the employment adjustment effects of exporting intensity among domestic exporters or MNEs. To explore these issues empirically, we re-estimate the dynamic labour demand models by interacting the regressors with exporting intensity. The findings are given in Table 5, which seem to indicate the importance of accounting for the firm-level exporting intensity (again based on the GMM results). For ease of interpretation, Figures 1 and 2 chart the implied long-run output and wages against exporting intensity, for both exporters and multinationals. Consistent with our conjecture, multinationals with limited export-market commitment have more rigid labour adjustment schedules: their long-run (domestic) labour demand elasticity with respect to output and wages[20] is inversely proportional to exporting intensity. Domestic firms with higher propensity to export have also a less elastic wage elasticity. However, in contrast to MNEs, domestic exporters with higher exporting intensity exhibit faster labour adjustment in response to output shocks.

[20] Here we are referring to the absolute values of the wage elasticities.

6. Conclusion

This paper provides microeconometric evidence of differential labour demand adjustment patterns amongst exporters, foreign multinationals and indigenous non-exporters for the UK manufacturing sector. It is found that FDI firms exhibit the fastest speed of employment adjustment to its optimal level, followed by exporters, which could possibly be attributed to a diminishing level of adjustment costs from MNEs, exporters to domestic non-exporting firms. Interestingly, turning to its long-run magnitude in terms of elasticities, the adjustment of labour demand with respect to factor price and demand shocks is less pronounced amongst MNEs and exporters, consistent with the view that firms engaged in international commerce activities have more market power, more rigid product demands; and perhaps most importantly, generate more skilled jobs that are more costly to dispose of. Lastly, our findings also suggest that it is important to control for exporting intensity of the firms with international-market exposure; for instance, MNEs with limited export-market commitment are found to have more rigid labour adjustment in response to output and wages shocks in the long run.

These empirical findings can address some of the public concerns on the footloose nature of MNEs: jobs in MNEs are expected to be more secure on average in that they adjust more easily and less costly to wage changes; also they are more reluctant to change the composition of their workforce in response to any shocks affecting their long-run labour demand. Nevertheless, a caveat of this study is that it does not explicitly control for the skill mix within firms given limitations of the dataset. It is hoped that suitable data would be available in the future to address this issue.

References

Aitken, B. & A. Harrison (1999). Do Domestic Firms Benefit from Direct Foreign Investment? *American Economic Review* **89**: 605-618.

Aitken, B., A. Harrison & R.E. Lipsey (1996). Wages and Foreign Ownership: A Comparative Study of Mexico, Venezuela, and the United States. *Journal of International Economics* **40**: 345-371.

Anderson, T.W. & C. Hsiao (1982). Formulation and Estimation of Dynamic Models Using Panel Data. *Journal of Econometrics* **18**: 47-82.

Arellano, M. & S. Bond (1991). Some Tests of Specification for Panel Data: Monte Carlo Evidence and an Application to Employment Equations. *Review of Economics Studies* **58**: 277-297.

Arellano, M. & O. Bover (1995). Another Look at the Instrumental-Variable Estimation of Error-Components Models. *Journal of Econometrics* **68**:29-52.

Aw, B.Y. & A.R. Hwang (1995). Productivity in the Export Market: A Firm Level Analysis. *Journal of Development Economics* **47**: 313-332.

Baldwin, J. & W. Gu (2003). Export-Market Participation and Productivity Performance in Canadian Manufacturing. *Canadian Journal of Economics* **36**: 634-657.

Baldwin, J. & W. Gu (2004). Trade Liberalisation: Export-Market Participation, Productivity Growth, and Innovation. *Oxford Review of Economic Policy* **20**: 372-392.

Bernard, A.B., J. Eaton, J.B. Jensen & S. Kortum (2003). Plants and Productivity in International Trade. *American Economic Review* **93**:1268-1290.

Bernard, A. & J.B. Jensen (1995). Exporters, Jobs and Wages in US Manufacturing: 1976-1987. *Brookings Papers on Economic Activity, Microeconomics* **1995**: 67-119.

Bernard, A. & J.B. Jensen (1997). Exporters, Skill-Upgrading, and the Wage Gap. *Journal of International Economics* **42**: 3-31.

Bernard, A. & J.B. Jensen (1999). Exceptional Exporters Performance: Cause, Effect or Both? *Journal of International Economics* **47**: 1-25.

Bernard, A. & J.B. Jensen (2004). Exporting and Productivity in the USA. *Oxford Review of Economic Policy* **20**: 343-357.

Bernard, A. & J. Wagner (1997). Exports and Success in German Manufacturing. *Review of World Economics* **133**: 134-157.

Blomström, M & A. Kokko (2003). The Economics of Foreign Direct Investment Incentives. CEPR Discussion Paper No. 3775. Available at SSRN: http://ssrn.com/abstract=390667

Clerides, S., S. Lach & J. Tybout (1998). Is Learning by Exporting Important? Micro-Dynamic Evidence from Columbia, Mexico and Morocco. *Quarterly Journal of Economics* **113**: 903-948.

Conyon, M.J., S. Girma, S. Thompson & P.W. Wright (2002). The Productivity and Wage Effects of Foreign Acquisition in the United Kingdom. *Journal of Industrial Economics* **50**: 85-102.

Delgado, M.A., J.C. Fariñas & S. Ruano (2002). Firm Productivity and Export Markets: A Nonparametric Approach. *Journal of International Economics* **57**: 397-422.

Doms, M.E. & J.B. Jensen (1998). Comparing Wages, Skills and Productivity Between Domestically and Foreign Owned Manufacturing Establishments in the United States. In R. Baldwin, R. Lipsey, & J.D. Richardson (Eds.), *Geography and Ownership as Bases for Economic Accounting*. University of Chicago Press.

Driffield, N. & K. Taylor (2000). FDI and the Labour Market: A Review of the Evidence and Policy Implications. *Oxford Review of Economic Policy* **16**: 90-103.

Fabbri, F., J.E. Haskel & M.J. Slaughter (2003). Does Nationality of Ownership Matter for Labour Demands? *Journal of the European Economic Association* **1**: 698-707.

Gaston, N. & D. Nelson (2002). Integration, Foreign Direct Investment and Labour Markets: Microeconomic Perspectives. *The Manchester School* **70**: 420-459.

Girma, S. (2005). Safeguarding Jobs? Acquisition FDI and Employment Dynamics in U.K. Manufacturing. *Review of World Economics* **141**: 165-178.

Girma, S., D. Greenaway & R. Kneller (2004). Does Exporting Increase Productivity? A Microeconometric Analysis of Matched Firms. *Review of International Economics* **12**: 855-866.

Girma, S., R. Kneller & M. Pisu (2005). Exports versus FDI: An Empirical Test. *Review of World Economics* **141**: 193-218.

Görg, H., & E. Strobl (2003). Footloose Multinationals? *Manchester School* **71**:1-19.

Gourlay, A. & J. Seaton (2004). Explaining the Decision to Export: Evidence from UK Firms. *Applied Economics Letters* **11**:153-158.

Greenaway, D. & R. Kneller (2004). Exporting Productivity in the United Kingdom. *Oxford Review of Economic Policy* **20**: 358-371.

Griffith, R., & H. Simpson (2004). Characteristics of Foreign-Owned Firms in British Manufacturing. In Blundell, R., D. Card & R. Freeman (Eds.), *Seeking a Premier*

Economy: the Economic Effects of British Economic Reforms, 1980-2000. University of Chicago Press.

Hamermesh, D.S. (1993). *Labour demand.* New Jersey: Princeton University Press.

Harris, R.I.D. & C. Robinson (2003). Foreign Ownership and Productivity in the United Kingdom: Estimates for UK Manufacturing Using the ARD. *Review of Industrial Organisation* **22**: 207-223.

Hatzius, J. (2000) Foreign Direct Investment and Factor Demand Elasticities. *European Economic Review* **44**: 117-143.

Helpman, E., M.J. Melitz & S.R. Yeaple (2004). Export versus FDI with Heterogeneous Firms. *American Economic Review* **94**: 300-316.

Melitz, M. (2003). The Impact of Trade on Intra-Industry Reallocations and Aggregate Industry Productivity. *Econometrica* **71**: 1695-1725.

Navaretti, G.B., D. Checchi & A. Turrini (2003). Adjusting Labour Demand: Multinational versus National Firms: A Cross-European Analysis. *Journal of the European Economic Association* **1**: 708-719.

Oulton, N. (1998). Competition and the Dispersion of Labour Productivity amongst UK Companies. *Oxford Economic Papers* **50**: 23-38.

Roberts, M. & J.R. Tybout (1997). The Decision to Export in Colombia: An Empirical Model of Entry with Sunk Costs. *American Economic Review* **87**: 545-564.

Roper, S., J.H. Love & D.A. Higon (2006). The Determinants of Export Performance: Evidence for Manufacturing Plants in Ireland and Northern Ireland. *Scottish Journal of Political Economy* **53**: 586-613.

Shaked, I. (1986). Are Multinational Corporations Safer? *Journal of International Business Studies* **17**: 83-106.

Silvente, F.R. (2005). Changing Export Status and Firm Performance: Evidence from UK Small Firms. *Applied Economics Letters* **12**: 567-571.

Slaughter, M.J. (2001). International Trade and Labour-Demand Elasticities. *Journal of International Economics* **54**: 27-56.

Wagner, J. (2006). Exports, Foreign Direct Investment, and Productivity: Evidence from German Firm Level Data. *Applied Economics Letters* **13**: 347-349.

Yeaple, S.R. (2005). A Simple Model of Firm Heterogeneity, International Trade, and Wages. *Journal of International Trade* **65**: 1-20.

In: Foreign Direct Investment
Editor: Harrison G. Blaine, pp.169-188
ISBN: 978-1-60456-921-6
© 2009 Nova Science Publishers, Inc.

Chapter 9

ON THE RELATIONSHIP BETWEEN OFDI AND CHINA'S ECONOMIC STANDARD* —TEST OF THE DUNNING'S THEORY OF FDI

Zhang Weifu*
School of International Business & Economics
Nanjing University of Finance & Economics, Nanjing, China 210046

Abstract

This paper sets up a demonstration model to testify the adaptability of the Dunning's theory of FDI in China at first, the result indicated that China is still in the second phase of the whole process. And then the paper analyzed the effect of FDI on Chinese economical growth by utilizing the co-integration and error correction model. Empirical results show that there was a stable positive equilibrium relationship between Outflow FDI and China's economic growth in the long or short run. Through the Granger causality test, it was found that China's economic growth was the reason for Outflow FDI, and conversely, the conclusion wasn't true.

Key words: OFDI; Dunning's theory of FDI; Co-integration analyses; Granger causality test

International direct investment includes Outflow FDI and inflow FDI. In fact, attracting inflow foreign direct investment and outflow FDI are both methods of taking part in international economic activities. In the course of economic development, attracting inflow foreign direct investment and promoting Outflow foreign direct investment are co-existed in the developed and developing countries. China is a developing economic country, also attracting the most amounts of inflow FDI in the world, but relative little Outflow FDI. That

* Acknowledgements: This research is sponsored by the humanities and social sciences research project of National Ministry of Education, China (06A790051) and National Natural Foundation Program ,China(70673032).
* E-mail address: cwf-01@163.com. Phone:(86-25) 52136305, (86) 13951783132; . Address of Author: School of International Economics and Trade, Nanjing University of Finance and Economics, Nanjing Xianlin New District. R.P.C. Zipcode:210046

fact indicates, Chinese economic development Standard and status in the world are not in line with Outward FDI, which impairs the ability of balance of China's Foreign exchange and also makes against exerting the ability of comparative advantage and fostering the ability of continual development. This paper sets up a demonstration model to testify the adaptability of the Dunning's theory of FDI in China at first, and the result indicated that China is still in the second phase of the whole process. And then the paper analyzed the effect of FDI on China's economic growth by utilizing the co-integration and error correction model. Empirical results show that there was a stable positive equilibrium relationship between Outflow FDI and Chinese economic growth in the long or short run. According to the Granger causality test, it was found that Chinese economic growth was the reason for Outflow FDI, and conversely, the conclusion wasn't true.

1. The Characteristics of Chinese Outflow FDI

China's foreign direct investment storage quantity, amounts to 57.2 billion US dollars to 2005, capital stock invests19.73 billion US dollars, the profit invests 27.04 billion US dollars again, and other invest 10.43 billion US dollars. The investment distributes in the global 163 countries and regions, to Asia's investment 40.63 billion US dollars, accounts for 71%, Latin America accounts for 20%, but mainly concentrates to Asia's investment to the Chinese Hong Kong area, accounts for 63.8%. The investment involves the commercial service, the wholesale and retail, mining industry, the transportation and storage, manufacturing industry, real estate and so on, commercial service industry investment accounts for the entire investment 28.9%.The statistical data indicates China's outflow FDI has the representative characteristics of the developing countries.

1.1. Outflow FDI Has a Bigger Undulation, Lacks the Continuous Nature

From 1990, Chinese outflow FDI presented the major rises and falls during the different year. After Deng Xiaoping south patrolled, Chinese outflow FDI attained a large growth, promoted the increase of outflow FDI and inflow FDI, and had the intense political nature. The increased range maximum value in 2001 and the increased range minimum value in 2002 differs above 600%, indicated the systematic characteristic and the continuous nature of the Chinese outflow FDI are serious insufficient, also explained our country's enterprise outflow FDI lacked each kind of superiority which in the traditional FDI theory pointed out, thus the enterprise lacked the motive and self-consciousness of outflow FDI, depended upon the country's preferential policy to promote passive investment. After 2001, outflow FDI largely increased, firstly because Chinese international investment environment had been improved after taking part in WTO. Secondly because China encountered the international trade barriers, presented the non-customs duty and the serious tendency after taking part in WTO, and forced our country's enterprises to enhance the level of outflow FDI. And also because, had a part of investments which aimed to dodge the cost enhancement which the domestic manufacturing industry element of production price's rise. According to the present situation, in next several years, our country's foreign direct investment will be able to present rational growth. Because the intrinsic causes and external environment which promote Chinese enterprises outflow FDI are unceasingly mature and Chinese enterprise's investment goal and the direction also will be clear day by day.

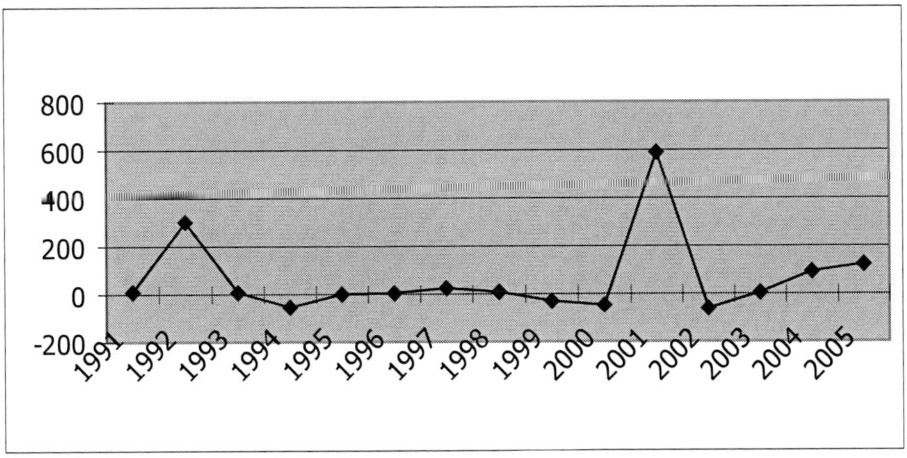

Source: before 2000, the data comes from the United Nations trade and the development conference various years' "World Investment Report", later data comes from the Chinese department of commercial affairs.

Figure 1. The change of outward FDI.

1.2. Chinese outflow FDI Has the Nature of Eluding Trade Barriers, and Lack the Nature of Seeking Technologies

Looked from Chinese enterprise goals of outflow FDI, belong to the customs duty dodging direct investment to account for a greater proportion. In 2005, Hong Kong, Cayman, the Virgin Islands which were three big eluding taxes investments amounts to 47.43 billion US dollars, accounts for the Chinese foreign direct investment storage quantities 82.9%, presented high region centralized. In 2005, in the outflow FDI also had 28% to flow to Hong Kong, 42% flows to Cayman, 10% flows in Virgin Islands, indicated dodge tendency which the tax revenue still had further continues. Also had a part in the inflow above three places investments to return to mainland China by the foreign capital name, used the mainland foreign capital preferential policy, formed the circulation of capital strange circle to pursue the preferential policy "the domestic capital turns to foreign capital, foreign capital turns to domestic capital "

Looked from Chinese outflow FDI intercontinental flows, Asia and Latin America become the Chinese greatest investment place, mainly concentrates regarding Asia's investment to Hong Kong, Latin America invests mainly concentrates to two archipelagoes, is the person arteries relations close and the same national culture correlation to Hong Kong's investment, in recent years to central Asian nation investment by resources seeking primarily, but invests many regarding two archipelagoes ambulant investment. To European and North America's investment I mainly by technical seeking primarily, to Africa's investment is by the natural resource and labor force seeking primarily, invests to Oceania by strategic resources seeking primarily.

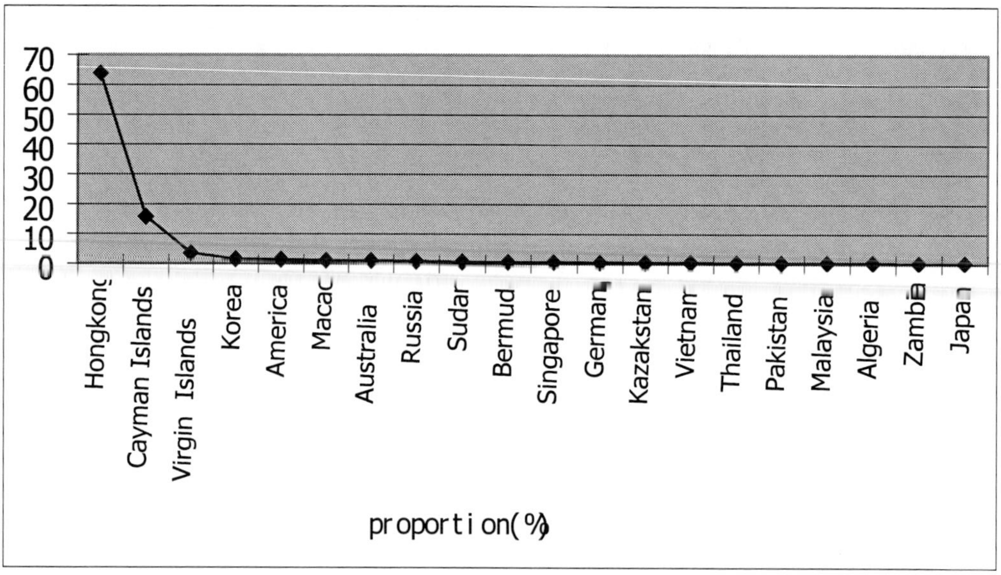

Source: According to 2005 Chinese outward FDI bulletin data ordering.

Figure 2. Proportion of Chinese outward FDI to various regions.

Table 1. China outflow FDI storage quantity intercontinental distribution list in 2005

Continent	**Investment storage quantity (billion dollar)**	**Proportion (%)**	**Continent**	**Investment storage quantity (billion dollar)**	**Proportion (%)**
Asia	40.63	71	Africa	15.9	2.7
Latin America	11.48	20	North America	2.68	0.47
Europe	1.598	2.8	Oceania	2.45	0.43

Material origin: According to 2005 Chinese outflow FDI bulletin data ordering.

1.3. Chinese Outflow FDI Mainly Concentrates to the Low Attachment Value Service Industries

Looked from the distribution of Chinese outflow FDI profession storage quantities, mainly concentrate to the lower technical level and the lower attachment value commercial service industry, the wholesale and retail sales profession, these are one kind of typical commercial existence type investments, some part of investments which enter mainland China through the commercial service way to carry on return to the type investment. In recent years, has enlarged to the strategic resources investment, is important reason which the mining industry investment proportion increases. But after joined the WTO, the trade frictions increase and our country exports bitter experience increasing trade barriers have urged the increase in manufacturing industry investments, was connected with development of the transportation and the storing industries.

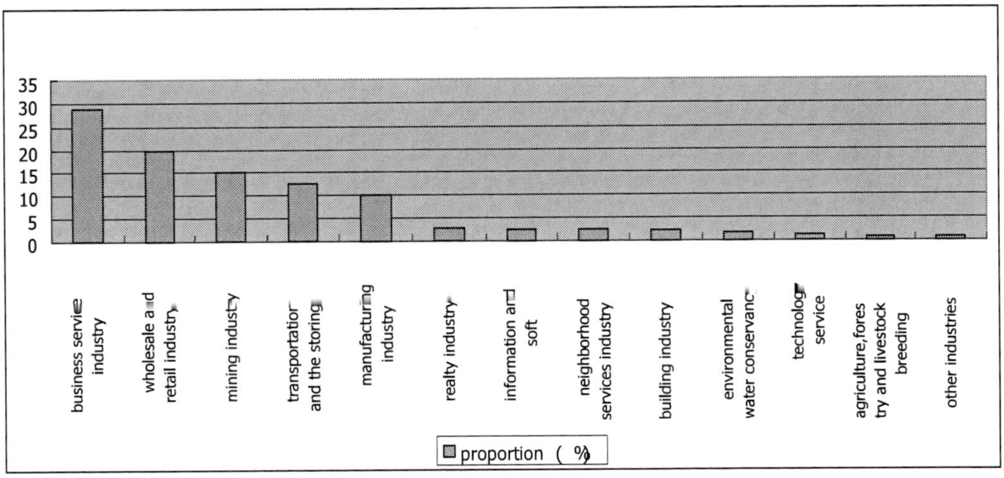

Source: According to 2005 Chinese outflow FDI bulletin data ordering.

Figure 3. Chart of the proportion of Chinese outward FDI to various industries.

1.4. Chinese Outflow FDI Belongs to the Model of the National Impetus Type

Looked from the body of Chinese outflow FDI, the central national enterprise's investments account for the investment storage quantities 83.7%, on the one hand manifested the central national enterprises or the central national holding companies have the foreign direct investment scale superiorities, the profession monopoly superiority and shoulder the security responsibility of the national strategy industries, on the other hand also indicated the state-owned enterprises were the country "goes out" the strategic faithful performer, enable Chinese outflow FDI to have the obvious country's drive, the enterprises lack the initiative.

Table 2. The main body constitution of Chinese outflow FDI

main body of Investment	2003 (billion dollar)	2004 (billion dollar)	Rate of increment (%)	2005 (billion dollar)	Rate of increment (%	Investment storage quantity (billion dollar)
Central national enterprise	2.098	4.525	115.7	10.203	126.1	47.875
Region enterprise	0.757	0.973	28.53	2.058	11.5	9.33

Material origin: According to 2005 Chinese outflow FDI bulletin data ordering.

Looked from two years (2004, 2005) different investments main body's investment current capacity rate of increment, the central national enterprise's investment growth scope was still greatly higher than the regional enterprise, indicated that our country was insufficient to pay attention to the outflow FDI of massive mid- and small-scale enterprises and the privately operated enterprises, how to promote the privately operated enterprises "to go out" is government's next step of work key.

2. Brief Review of Relative Research Literature

2.1. Review about Classic International Direct Investment Theory

The international direct investment theory was produced in the 20th century 60's, which is the result of the international economy theory attention because of the international direct investment unprecedented development. At present, the international direct investment mainstream theory mainly includes Hymer's the monopoly superiority theory[1], Buckley, Casson and so on[2], Internalization Advantage Theory, Dunning' international direct investment theory[3], Vernon the life cycle theory and Kojima[4], Kiyoshi comparative superiority theory and so on[5]. Monopoly superiority theory explained the World War II latter section of times US large-scale foreign investment behaviors well, but this theory is unable to explain the developing countries' foreign direct investment phenomenon. Internalization Advantage Theory actually is Ronald. Coase "the enterprise theory" and extends in the international direct investment domain application, Internalization Advantage Theory only shows the reason of the enterprise' s outflow FDI, certainly could not explain the enterprises the direction to international market interior development and the position choice of host country well. The product life cycle theory indicates that the enterprise chooses different ways of international labor division, based on different production stages which have the production and the competition condition, this theory similarly also only can partially explain the FDI behavior, yet cannot reasonably explain FDI in developing countries. The marginal industry shift theory indicates that investment country should successively transfer its industry which already be in or soon be in the comparative inferiority, but this theory only could explain the vertical division of labor between the developed country and the developing nation, this theory is contradictory to the phenomena that many developing countries' industrial structure promotion and traditional industry outward investment because of Using international direct investment. Dunning' international direct investment theory is still most comprehensive and widely acceptance up to the present. It not only explains the cause of FDI, moreover have pointed out the flow direction of FDI, simultaneously founded the unified theory system which is about the international trade, the foreign direct investment and the international cooperation arrangements[6].Had pointed out three main international economy division forms and its' conditions which mutually transform .But Dunning' international

1 Hymer.S.,1976.International Operation of National Firms: A Study of Direct Foreign Investment .MIT press

2 Buckley .P. and M. , Casson ,1976.The Future of the Multinational Enterprise London:Macmillan ,p.69. Rugman, A. M.,1981. Inside the Multinationals: the Economics of International Markets. London: Croom Helm ,p28

3 Dunning.J.H., 1977 .Trade ,Location of Economic Activity and the Multinational Enterprise :A Search for an Eclectic Approach, First Published in B. Ohlin Per Ove Hesselborn and Per Magnus Wijkman ed. The International Allcoation of Economic Activity, London:Macmillan. Dunning.J.H., 1981. International Production and the Multinational Enterprises .Allen&Unwin.

4 Vernon. Raymond,1966."International Investment and International Trade in Product Cycle ." Quarterly Journal of Economics ,May.Vernon. Raymond,1974.Location of Economic Activity ,in John H..Dunning ed.., Economic Analysis and the Multinational Enterprises.

5 Kojima,Kiyoshi,1978.Direct Foreign Investment :A Japanese Model of Multinational Business Operation .London :Croom Helm.

Kojima,Kiyoshi,1982. Macroeconomic Versus International Business Approach to Foreign Direct Investment .Hitosubashi Journal of Economics,23.

Kojima,Kiyoshi,1985. Japanese and American Direct Investment in Asia :A comparative Analysis. Hitosubashi Journal of Economics,26

6 Clegg, J.,1987.Multinational Enterprises and World Competiton .London :Macmillan,P2.

direct investment theory is also unable to explain outflow FDI of developing countries that some enterprises have not simultaneously have three kinds of superiorities in the developing countries.

American economist Lewis first has made a more systematic explanation on the developing country enterprise's foreign direct investment. Comparing with the developed countries ' multinational corporation, except to dodge the barrier to the import countries' market and to protect the market of exports and to reduce the production cost, he thought its unique place is to be able to disperse risk which is caused by the instability of female countries' political economy. Simultaneously he also thought the developing countries' enterprises had technical superiorities of the small-scale production, waa suitable to invest these countries which have a lower level of income and the small capacity of market[7]. After 1980s, the developing countries' direct investments flow to the developed countries at the progressively speed.In1990s, English economical scholar Cantwell, JshnA & Tolentino, ParEstrella proposed the technical innovation promotion theory, namely these foreign direct investments are in order to be close to the technology markets and use the technical overflow effects and the organization managerial experiences.

2.2. Explanation about Dunning's International Direct Investment Stage Theory

In 1980, Dunning advanced the stage theory of foreign direct investment, by reviewing the relations about 67 countries OFDI and Economic Standard。He divided one country outflow FDI into four stages according to one country average per person GNP, one country's outflow and inflow FDI are to be various at different stages, thus further had developed its international eclectic paradigm theory, also has given the explanations to the developing countries' outflow FDI[8].

The Dunning's theory indicates one country net outflow FDI will be experienced four development phases, as one country economy development and the enhancement of the average per person GDP level.

At the first stage, average per person GNP does not surpass 400 US dollars, which is the most impoverished country in the world. As the domestic enterprise does not have the advantage of the property rights and the interior, cannot make use of the foreign geographical advantage, therefore does not have foreign direct investment. Because this country lacks the advantage of the economical scale and the market conditions, the comparative few foreign direct investments enter, therefore one country's net FDI is zero or a negative value.

At the second stage, average per person GNP is in 400 - 2,000 US dollars. As the enhancement to the domestic economy level of development, the expansion to market scale, the improvement in investment environment, the augment in geographical superiority, foreign direct investments enter at the increasing rapid. As the advantage of the domestic enterprise's property rights and the interior are to be limited, this country's foreign direct investment was still only a negative value, mostly the developing countries are at this stage.

[7] Lewis T. Wells, Third world transnational enterprise, Chinese edition, translation company in Shanghai, 1986

[8] Dunning.J.H., 1981. International Production and the Multinational Enterprises .Allen&Unwin.

At the third stage, average per person GNP is in 2,000 - 4,750 US dollars. One country's economic strength will have a bigger enhancement at this stage, the domestic partial enterprises started to have the advantage of property rights and the interior, outflow FDI will be increased at the rapid speed, and the speed will surpass the speed of inflow FDI. Although outflow and inflow FDI have a large-scale, the net current capacity is only a negative value. The majority emerging industrialized countries are at this stage.

At the fourth stage, average per person GNP surpasses 5,000 US dollars. The most developed countries are at this stage, they have stronger advantage of property rights and the interior, and can utilize each kind of superiority of the host country from the global strategy division of labor angle, therefore net FDI is a positive value.

In 1988, Dunning also proposed the theory of the 5th stage. Net FDI is still a positive number at this stage, but the absolute value already starts to drop. Compares with the first 4stages, the influence of economy development phase is greatly been weaken at the 5th stage, but more is decided by the overlapping investment between the developed country.

Following the Dunning theory, we can describe a country economy level of development by average per person GNP, can express the status of a country participation international direct investment by net FDI, can divide different countries into 5 groups according to the phase of different economy development, describing the relations between outflow FDI and the national economy level of development, also may follow the dynamic evolution course between a country the economy level of development and the enhancement to participation the international direct investment, may be divided 5 stages, international direct investment and economic standard present the "J "structure in the first 4 stages.

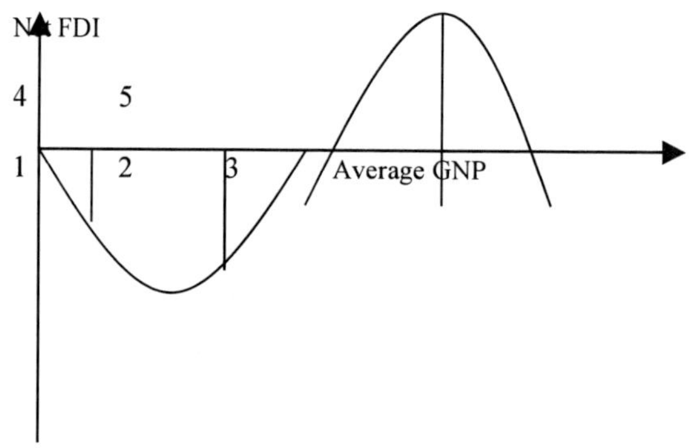

Figure 4. foreign direct investment development period grams.

2.3. Reviewing Correlation about Chinese Outflow and Inflow FDI

The researches about this question, mainly concentrate to FDI and the performance of Chinese economic development, the fruit of research is extremely rich, mainly may be divided into following several kinds:

Firstly, some studies about the technical overflow effect, which is caused by FDI in China. At present, some researches about this question all generally considered the multinational corporation's FDI have the vertical technical overflow effect on the developing country, Qin Xiaozhong made use of 39 professions data which were the national third industry general survey in 1995, carried on the measurement analysis, indicated FDI had the overflow effect which was our country economic development and the technology advancement[9]. Shen Kunrong made use of the data of 1996, and analyzed the relevance of FDI and the economic development, also indicated that FDI/GDP was increased a percentage point, the total essential factor productivity(TFP) would enhance 0.37 unit [10].Zhou yan studied FDI of Zhejiang Province, also confirmed FDI had the overflow effect[11] .Some studies ' common grounds about the technical overflow effect, which bring FDI into the production function as the investment variable, considered inflow FDI should be able to enhance China's TFP, could have the effect on the ontogenetic technical overflow and the technology advancement, thus became the factor of ontogenetic economical growth, the findings indicated FDI had the technical overflow effect and the demonstration effect to our country manufacturing industry[12,13,14,15,16,17,18,19].

Secondly, some studies about the effect on macroscopic economy and regional economy which is caused by FDI in China. Jiang Xiaojuan thinks the multinational corporation direct investment not only to increase the Chinese capital scale, moreover has affected China's market mechanism, has introduced the competitive system[20]. Wang Xinhua and some other scholars had selected 7 indexes, and inspected the effect on FDI in the national 31 provinces and cities, the findings also indicated the effect on FDI was also various under the different foundation condition and the external environment[21]. Li Xuehui and some other scholars had analyzed the relation of FDI and the level of wage ,and considered FDI should enhance the level of wage[22]. Xuan ye and some other scholars also analyzed the relation of FDI and the level of wage, the findings also indicated FDI should enhance the price of labor force and land, so on conducts the real diagnosis research take the Jiangsu Province different urban district as the sample to FDI and the wage level, the result had also indicated FDI truly enhanced foreign capital collection element of production the and so on central area labor force and land price, moreover followed the flowage of labor force , also proliferated the

---

9 Qin xiao zhong, analysis about technology overflow effect on inward FDI in China, Modern Economic Research, 1998(4):47-49

10 Shen kunrong, Overflow effect on inflow FDI in China, Journal of Finance, 2000(3):103-110

11 Zhou yan, Research about the overflow effect on outflow FDI, Inquiry into Economic Problems,2002(6):60-62

12 Cheng Huifang, Foreign Direct Investment and Open Endogenous Economic Growth Economic Research Journal,2002 (10) : 71-78

13 Chen Taotao , How Capacity Gaps between Foreign and Domestic Firms Shape Industry-to-industry Spillover of China's FDI, Social sciences in China,2003(4):33-42

14 Chen Taotao , How Capacity Gaps between Foreign and Domestic Firms Shape Industry-to-industry Spillover of China's FDI, Social sciences in China,2003(4):33-42

15 Pan wenqin, The Spill-over Effects of FDI on China's Industrial Sectors:A Panel Data Analysis , the Journal of World Economy, 2003(6)

16 Shen kunrong, The analysis about Spill-over Effects of FDI, Journal of Finance, 2000 (3)103-110.

17 Bao Qun & Lai Mingyong ,The dynamic measurement and explanation of FDI technology outflow, Statistical Research,2003(6).

18 Yan bing, analysis about the Spill-over Effects and correlative factors of FDI, Economic Review,2006(1)

19 Zhang yu, the ownership structures of foreign enterprises and the spill-over effect on FDI. World Economy study,2006(11)

20 Jiang Xiaojuan, Foreign Investment,Market Structure and Competitive Behavior of Foreign Investment Company, Economic Research Journal, 2002(9).

21 WANG Xin-hua WANG Zhao-yang ,Empirical Study on the Evaluation of the Effect of Introducing FDI in 31 provinces of China, Journal of international Trade,2006(6)

22 Li xuehui, Xu luodan, Analysis about the effect of inflow FDI on the level of wage, NanKai Economic Studies,2002(2)

wages effect[23].More researches thought FDI promoted the Chinese macroscopic economy, and hastened economical scale expansion, and optimized economic structure, and enhanced the competitive ability of foreign trade[24,25,26,27]. Simultaneously have pointed out the different regional characteristics of FDI (such as the investment of Exports Oriented, the investment to imports substitution), which bring the different influences to the development of regional economy[28,29,30,31,32,33,34,35]

Thirdly, studies about the industrial and the regional performances of FDI. This kind of research mainly chose typical industry, and analyzed industrial upgrade and the renewal of product and the improvement to industrial competitive abilities[36,37,38,39,40].

The most studies all considered FDI has the positive effect to the industrial development. Some studies about regional performance of FDI mainly analyzed the difference of eastern part, middle and the western area in China[41].Ge Shunqi analyzed the performance and potential of FDI, according to Comparing to 31 provinces and cities in China. The result indicated the performance and potential of FDI were various between western area and

---

23 Xuan Ye and Zhao Shudong, The Effect of FDI on Wage Rate --An empirical study of Jiangsu Province, NanKai Economic Studies,2005(1)

24 Jiang Xiaojuan, foreign economy in China---attributing to growth,upgrade and competition, Chinese People's University publishing house, 2001 version

25 Jiang Xiaojuan, the growth of exports and the structural change in China: Foreign investment enterprise's contribution, NanKai Economic Studies,2002(2)

26 Zhang weifu, The research about international industrial capital shift and Chinese world manufacturing center, Chinese finance economical publishing house ,2005 version.

27 Wei Houkai, Effects of Foreign Direct Investment on Regional Economic Growth in China, Economic Research Journal,2002(4): 19-26

28 Wu Jian, Regional Discrepancy of FDI in China and its effect on Economic Growth, Economic Research Journal,2002(4): 27-35

29 Yu Jinping, FDI Policy, National Welfare and Economic Development, Economic Research Journal,2004(5): 49-57

30 Dic Lo; Assessing the Role of Foreign Direct Investment in China's Economic Development: Insights from Sectoral-regional Analyses, Economic Research Journal, 2003(9):40-48

31 Gao Tieme, Kang Shulong, Dynamic Analysis of the Impacts of FDI on Chinese Economy, the Journal of World Economy,2006(4):22-30

32 Mi yunsheng, Research about the regional difference and influence of Chinese FDI disposition efficiency region difference ----A analysis is based on panel data, Finance & Trade Economics 2006(11)

33 CHEN Quan-gong ,A Contrastive Analysis of FDI in Hubei and Zhejiang, Journal of Wuhan University of science and technology,2006(1)

34 Jiang Xiaojuan, Research about the gradient shift of our country's foreign capital investment ,China industrial Economy,2004(4)

35 Chen Taotao , How Capacity Gaps between Foreign and Domestic Firms Shape Industry-to-industry Spillover of China's FDI, Social sciences in China,2003(4):33-42

36 Li yongjun, Research about profession distribution determining factor of FDI, Journal of World Economy, 2003(7)

37 He JIE, The spill-over effect on FDI to Chinese industry sector further precise quantification, Journal of World Economy, 2000(2)

38 Yao Yang, Zhang Qi, An Analysis of Technological Efficiency of Chinese industrial firm , Economic Research Journal, 2001(10).

39 WANG Shu-li, Cui Hui-li ,Industrial Distribution and Optimization of Japan's Direct Investment in China, Journal of Wuhan University of Technology (Social Science Edition),2005(2)

40 Xiong jun,Zhou yinheng, Research about spill-over effect on FDI to our country's industrial sector, Industrial Technology & Economy ,2005(5)

41 Wang Chengqi, Zhang Jianhua Ai Hui, Foreign Direct Investment,Regional Difference and China's Economic GrowthJournal of World Economy, 2002(4)

eastern area[42]. Hu Yichao utilized the non-parameter DEA method, has appraised our country various provincial introduction efficiency of FDI with two phases which was from 1998 to 2000 and from 2001 to 2003,finally indicated various provincial introduction efficiency of FDI were probably existed in different provinces and cities and in the different phases[43].Xu Chunqi analyzed various provinces and cities 'the achievement index and the potential index based on the high achievement index of FDI, and has studied the relevance to the achievement index and the potential index[44].

Fourthly, the influence of FDI is existed in Chinese imports and exports. The most research believed that, FDI promoted the Chinese foreign trade ,in particular the development of industrial finished product trade, but partially studies indicated FDI also has causes the tendency which the Chinese trade condition was worsen[45464748].Zhang erzhen devised the index of competitive ability in Opening economy, and calculated the competitive abilities of extroversive economy, the findings indicated FDI has the influence of promotion to the competitive abilities of extroversive economy in China[49]. Zhang Weifu, selected some economic indexes (the scale of foreign trade, the structure of foreign trade, the quality of foreign trade) which FDI possibly affects, the findings indicated FDI had the benefit to the development of the long triangle area foreign trade according to the relevant analysis[50].

Nowadays, some studies gradually increases about the absorbent ability and superior scale of FDI, which become a hot spot.

At present, the domestic scholars mainly focus on the position choice question about outflow FDI in China. Some studies primarily introduced experiences and put forward the proposals, Wang Jinzhen has analyzed the Chinese enterprise "go out" the strategic choice and the arrangement step, from the angle to the government management[51]. Cheng Huifang, has analyzed the position of outflow FDI according to using the model of gravitation, considers the economical scale and average GDP and the bilateral trade quantity and so on which are positive correlative to Chinese outflow FDI, but are negative correlative to the distance to host countries[5253]. This findings, while has stronger direct-viewing, due to lacking

---

[42] Comparative research about the performance and potentials of FDI is in Chinese various provinces and cities. Journal of World Economy, 2004(1)

[43] Hu yichao,Leiming, Appraisal and Analysis of the Efficiency in Absorbing FDI in China, The Journal of Quantitative & Technical Economics,2006(5) .

[44] Xu Chunqi, Li Jianping ,On the Evaluation of FDI Performance and Rethinking of FDI Performance Index and FDI Potential Index, Journal of Finance,2006(8)

[45] Yang wei, The correlative analysis about FDI and Chinese imports & exports, Journal of World Economy, 2000(2)

[46] Wang shaoping,feng fuyue, The trade effect and regional difference about FDI, Journal of World Economy, 2006(8)

[47] Wang weiling,Luo xiaoming, Comparative Research about our country's exports trade of two kind of FDI pattern, World Economy Study,2006(9)

[48] Zang Wei-fu WU Qi, Experimental Study On FDI and China's Foreign Trade, international trade Journal,2005(12)

[49] Zhang erzheng,,Zhang Wei-fu, Study on the Competitiveness of Nanjing Open-Economics,2002(Supplement)

[50] ZHANG Wei-fu, ZHANG erzheng, Experimental Study On FDI and Yangtze River delta manufacturing industry development, Forum of World Economy and Politics,2005(5)

[51] Wang shizheng, Experience and questions and policies of outflow FDI in China, World Economy Study, 2004(4):37-47

[52] Tingben, J. Shaping the World Economy, Appendix □, "An Analysis of World Trade Flows." New York: Twentieth Century Fund,1962.

[53] Cheng huifang,Ruan xiang,Analysis of the selection of position of outward FDI by using the gravity model in China, Journal of World Economy, 2004(11):23-30

of the studies about the foreign capital policies, the cultural laws, the social systems and so on in host counties, the certain disparity existed in academic studies and the reality. Cai rui thought the supplementary relations were existed between Chinese outflow FDI and foreign trade by the regressive analysis based on the theory of marginal industrial shift , indirectly explained the Chinese outflow FDI should flow to those counties which have a big scale to foreign trade with China[54] .

The synthesis of domestic studies about Chinese outflow FDI main results can be detectable, these studies mostly based on taking the theory of western classics FDI, using pure data computation and the logical inference, these studies are short of the analysis of the investigation, still have the certain disparity with the realistic situation.

At present, some study fruits about Chinese outflow and inflow FDI have acquired, but the positive analysis about the relationship between the phase of economic development and the international direct investment is lack, strengthens to this question research will be advantageous to point out the characteristics and the tendency of the international economic division of labor.

3. On the Relationship between OFDI and China's Economic Standard

3.1. Examination about the Phase of China's OFDI

China's average per person GNP breaks through 1,000 US dollars in 2003 , about nearly 2,000 US dollars in 2006 , according to the present level of economic development and Dunning's cycle theory about international direct investment, China's international direct investment should be in the second stage or third stage.

Make the following model to confirm the conclusion that China's international direct investment should be in the second stage or third stage.

3.1.1. Variable and Data Access

Chinese net outflow FDI is a dependent variable which can be expressed by $NFDI$; The investment tendency variable is from 1984 to 2006 which is a independent variable which can be expressed by $Trend$ .At first, analyze the tendency of outflow FDI by making a unitary linear regressive model based on the data net outflow FDI, and then use average per person GDP which can be expressed by $RGDP$ as a dependent variable to analyze the relation between net outflow FDI and the level of economy.

3.1.2. Data Examination and Result Analysis

The regressive result about $NFDI$ and $Trend$:

$$NFDI = 88.69 - 30.584Trend \tag{1}$$

(3. 104) (-14. 06)

54 Cai rui,Liu quan, Are international direct investment and trade supplementary in China?

$$R^2 = 0.908 \qquad F(1,22) = 197.82$$

Independent variable coefficient's T statistic and F statistic are both Remarkable and R^2 is also great, which explain this regressive model's result is quite ideal. From this regressive model's result, we can conclude that Chinese net outflow FDI will increase 30.584 units every year from 1984 to 2006. According to past yeas' net outflow FDI, we may make out the decreasing trend to net outflow FDI, also know China's outflow FDI is still in the second stage of the investment development cycle

Dunning's theory about the cycle of the investment development also point out, a country's net quantities of outflow FDI presents the J shape curve distribution the foreign direct investment cost presents the J curve distribution in the first four stages, will return to the horizontal axis in the fifth stage. Build a non-linear regressive model ,according to China's net quantities of outflow FDI from 1984 to 2006.

$$NFDI_t = \alpha + \beta RGDP_t + \gamma (RGDP_t)^2 \tag{2}$$

Net quantities of outflow FDI in t year can be denoted by $NFDI_t$, Corresponding year average GDP can be denoted by $RGDP_t$.

According to Dunning's theory about the cycle of the investment development, $\beta \prec 0$ and $\gamma \succ 0$ should be satisfied in formula (2), namely along with the enhancement to average GDP(人均GDP), a country's net quantities of outflow FDI should obey a J shape curve distribution.

According to 22 years data's non-linear regressive, the result is as follows

$$NFDI_t = 97.53 - 1119.8 RGDP_t + 481.9 (RGDP_t)^2$$
$$(5.435) \quad (-12.342) \quad (9.781)$$

$$R^2 = 0.978 \qquad F(2,19) = 328.78$$

Looked from the above regressive result, $R^2 = 0.978$, indicated the goodness-of-fit of model is very high, T examination was also more remarkable, had demonstrated average GDP indeed China's explained the change of net outflow FDI.

Looked from the coefficient sign ,two variables coefficients conform to Dunning theory of the development cycle "J curve" supposition, therefore may judge, China's international direct investment is still in the second stage.

3.2. Analyze the Effect of Outflow FDI on China's Economic Growth by Utilizing the Co-integration

At present, domestic majority of scholars explain the relation between outflow FDI and the economic level of development from a qualitative angle. Partial scholars explain the relation between outflow FDI and the economy level of development by using the regressive method, but very few scholars point out whether have co-integration relation and causal relation. The paper analyzes the effect of outflow FDI on China's economic growth by utilizing the co-integration and error correction model, also analyzes the causal relation between outflow FDI and the economic level of development.

3.2.1. Variable and Data Access

Quantities of outflow FDI are expressed by $OFDI$, which can reflect a country's ability of outflow FDI. Average per person GDP is expressed by $RGDP$, which can reflect a country's the economic level of development. In order to make the monetary unit of $RGDP$ and $OFDI$ is consistent, with the same year multiplied by same year Renminbi to US dollar exchange rate(The exchange rate standard originates from website of the People's Bank of China).Because the logarithm transformation certainly does not affect co-integration among the primitive variables, moreover the logarithm transformation often may eliminate the different variance phenomenon, therefore first carries on the logarithm transformation to A and B, and separately uses $LN(RGDP)$ and $LN(OFDI)$ expressed the logarithm transformation average per person GDP and the outflow FDI amounts, then analyze their relations.

3.2.2. Unit Root Examination of Time Series A and B

As the condition of existence of co-integration relation is that two variables of time series must be satisfied $I(d)$, before examining the co-integration relation of $LN(RGDP_t)$ and $LN(OFDI_t)$, first examine the stability of $LN(RGDP_t)$ and $LN(OFDI_t)$ by using the method of ADF unit root examination.

Table 3. Result of time series $LN(RGDP_t)$ and $LN(OFDI_t)$ unit root examination

variable	ADF Statistic	τ (5%)	AIC	SC	Examination form (c,t,k)	Conclusion
$LN(OFDI)$	-1.705	-3.6920	-7.4636	-4.412	(c, t, 1)	non-steady
$LN(RGDP)$	-1.945	-3.6920	-4.5432	-7.362	(c, t, 1)	non-steady
$\Delta LN(OFDI)$	-2.624	-3.7119	-6.2314	-4.685	(c, t, 1)	non-steady
$\Delta LN(RGDP)$	-2.621	-3.7119	-5.3791	-7.579	(c, t, 1)	non-steady
$\Delta^2 LN(OFDI)$	-3.625	-3.0521	-7.4568	-4.2681	(c, t, 1)	steady
$\Delta^2 LN(RGDP)$	-3.324	-3.0521	-4.5782	-7.2546	(c, t, 1)	steady

Intercept, trend variable and lag order numbers are described by c,t,k ,first and second difference is described by Δ and Δ^2. The k value is based on the minimum value to AIC and

SC. k value is AIC and SC when they are in the minimum and τ is equal in t value of the regression analysis.

Looked from the above table, time series $LN(RGDP_t)$ and $LN(OFDI_t)$ are stable after second order difference, satisfying the condition of co-integration of two variables, possibly exist the relation of co-integration between two variables.

3.2.3. Time Series $LN(RGDP_t)$ and $LN(OFDI_t)$ Co-integration Relations Test

The above unit root test indicates that variable A and B are possible to exist co-integration relations, to determine whether co-integration relations are existed, to test two variables according to Engle-Granger two steps test methods, the test of procedure and the step is as follows

The first step, with the 0LS method estimating equation, may obtain:

$$LN(OFDI_t) = \beta_1 + \beta_2 LN(RGDP_t) + \varepsilon_t \tag{3}$$

$$LN(\hat{O}FDI_t) = \hat{\beta}_1 + \hat{\beta}_2 LN(RGDP_t) \tag{4}$$

$$\hat{\varepsilon}_t = LN(OFDI_t) - LN(\hat{O}FDI_t) \tag{5}$$

The second step is to test the integration of time series. If time series is the stable time series after the d order difference, the time series is d order integration, and may consider co-integration relation is existed between $LN(RGDP_t)$ and $LN(OFDI_t)$.

According to above methods, we utilize the actual data of average GDP and outflow FDI from 1984 to 2006, and can obtain the following result by EViews5.0 software:

$$LN(OFDI_t) = 1.1920 + 0.2109\,LN(RGDP_t) \tag{6}$$

$$(18.120)\quad(39.921)$$

$$R^2 = 0.981 \quad Adjusted\ R^2 = 0.9678 \quad F = 414.765$$

Error series $\{\varepsilon_t\}$ can be obtained, and its functional relation is as follows:

$$\hat{\varepsilon}_t = LN(OFDI_t) - 1.1920 - 0.2109 LN(RGDP_t) \tag{7}$$

The value in the parenthesis respectively is the t statistics in (6) formula, the result of each test statistic indicates the equation has well fitted value.

According to Engle-Granger test methods, if co-integration relation is existed in time series $LN(RGDP_t)$ and the $LN(OFDI_t)$,time series $\{\varepsilon_t\}$ must be integration.

We test the time series $\{\varepsilon_t\}$ according to ADF unit root test, the result is as follows

Table 4. The result of Error term unit root test

ADF Test Statistic	-1.9614	1% Critical Value	-2.7057
		5% Critical Value	-1.9067
		10% Critical Value	-1.6257

As the value of test statistic is −1.9614 which is below the value of 5% significance level, which indicates co-integration relation is existed between time series $LN(RGDP_t)$ and $LN(OFDI_t)$. we also can know the co-integration coefficient is 0.4321. Indicates the economical growth and outflow have the long-term balanced relations, also average GDP increases 1%, and outflow FDI can grow 0.2019%.

3.2.4. The Causality Test between Average GDP and Outflow FDI

3.2.4.1 Error Correction Model Establishment

The above co-integration test indicates that co-integration relation is existed between average per person GDP and outflow FDI, namely two has the long-term balanced relations, but this kind of long-term balanced relations whether is the causal relation, must wait for further confirms.

As many time series are not steady in the real life, some "false regression" can be existed if directly uses the regression analysis. Because error correction model can not only present the long-term balanced relations, and also can manifest the influence of the variable short-term change. We will analyze the short-term and long term relations between outflow FDI and economic development according to error correction model.

According to error correction series $\{\varepsilon_t\}$, we construct the error correction model of the economic growth and outflow FDI.

$$\Delta \mathrm{LN}(\mathrm{OFDI}_t)=\beta_0+\beta_1\Delta \mathrm{LN}(\mathrm{RGDP}_t)+\sum_{i=1}^{p}\left(\theta_i \Delta LN(OFDI_{t-i})+\delta_i \Delta LN(RGDP_{t-i})\right)+\lambda\varepsilon_{t-1}+\mu_t \quad (8)$$

After many times' regression analysis, may obtain the following regression equation

$$\Delta \mathrm{LN}(\mathrm{OFDI}_t)=0.5216\Delta \mathrm{LN}(\mathrm{OFDI}_{t-1})+0.1847\Delta \mathrm{LN}(\mathrm{GDP}_{t-1})+0.1529\varepsilon_{t-1} \quad (9)$$

Data estimate analysis result, following table:

Table 5. The estimate result of error correction model

Variable	coefficient	STD error	t-statistic	prob
ΔLOFDI(-1)	0.5216	0.1416	5.1475	0.0002
ΔLGDP(-1)	0.1847	0.0391	2.9684	0.0140
$\varepsilon(-1)$	0.1529	0.0694	1.8538	0.1014

R-squared	0.6140	Mean dependent var	0.0618
Adjusted R-squared	0.5938	S.D. dependent var	0.0313
S.E. of regression	0.0204	Akaike info criterion	-7.6266
Sum squared	0.0062	Schwarz criterions	-7.4782
Log likelihood	46.098	F-statistic	12.447
Durbin-Watson stat	2.4379	Prob (F-statistic)	0.0006

Looked from the result of the EViews5.0 software, error correcting term $\varepsilon(-1)$ can pass the examination in 10% significance level, other two difference terms also can pass the examination in 5% significance level, and the D-W value is 2.4379,which indicated error term μ_t does not have the autocorrelation. Looked from the equation of (9), the undulation of $\Delta\text{LN}(\text{OFDI}_t)$ may divide into two parts: The short-term undulation, the preceding issue of OFDI rate of increment has the promoted action to the latter issue of OFDI rate of increment, and the short-term influence reaches as high as 52.16%, lags an issue of RGDP growth also have the certain influence to the OFDI growth, but affects is relatively smaller, is 18.47%.

3.2.4.2. Granger Causality Test

The above analysis indicates that co-integration relations are existed between outflow FDI and average per person GDP, namely two has the long-term balanced relations, but this kind of long-term balanced relations whether mutually constitute the causal relation, namely outflow FDI whether can promote the economical growth, the economy growth whether can lead to the outflow FDI of Chinese enterprise, or two all has, this needs further to carry on Granger causality test ,for this purpose, we establish following analysis model:

$$\text{LN}(\text{OFDI}_t)=\delta_0+\sum_{i=1}^{k}a_i\text{LN}(\text{OFDI}_{t-i})+\sum_{i=1}^{k}\beta_i\text{LN}(\text{RGDP}_{t-i})+\mu_t \quad (10)$$

$$\text{LN}(\text{RGDP}_t)=\sigma_0+\sum_{i=1}^{k}\gamma_i\text{LN}(\text{RGDP}_{t-i})+\sum_{i=1}^{k}\lambda_i\text{LN}(\text{OFDI}_{t-i})+\nu_t \quad (11)$$

Looked from above equation, ν_t and μ_t are not correlation error term .If the estimated coefficient of lag term $LN(RGDP)$ as a community in statistics is different from zero in equation (10), and also the estimated coefficient of lag term $LN(OFDI)$ as a community in statistics is not different from zero in equation (11), and then indicates the unidirectional Granger causality relation from $LN(RGDP)$ to $LN(OFDI)$.

Whereas, If the estimated coefficient of lag term $LN(RGDP)$ as a community in statistics is not different from zero in equation (10), and also the estimated coefficient of lag term $LN(OFDI)$ as a community in statistics is different from zero in equation (11), and then indicates the unidirectional Granger causality relation from $LN(OFDI)$ to $LN(RGDP)$. If the estimated coefficient of lag term $LN(RGDP)$ as a community in statistics is different from zero in equation (10) and (11) ($\sum \beta_i \neq 0$, $\sum \lambda_i \neq 0$), and then indicates bidirectional causal relation between $LN(OFDI)$ to $LN(RGDP)$.

Using Eviews5.0 software, may calculate the F statistic and the corresponding probability, passes through the repeatedly experiment, and takes the biggest lag order number to the model is 2, the result of analysis is as following table:

Table 6. Result table of Granger causality test

Null Hypothesis	Obs	F-Statistic	Probability
LGDP does not Granger cause LOFDI		8.2496	0.01102
LOFDI does not Granger cause LGDP	20	3.4782	0.48880

The analysis result of the Grainger causal relation indicates that the Granger causality is existed from $LN(RGDP)$ to $LN(OFDI)$ in 5% significant level, but the probability is small from $LN(OFDI)$ to $LN(RGDP)$ in 5% significant level, namely outflow FDI is not the reason that economy grows, but the growth of economy may promote outflow FDI of Chinese enterprise.

This test result indicated Chinese outflow FDI amount will assume the tendency which gradually rise along with the economical growth, which is in consistent with Dunning theory of international direct investment, namely the advantage which the enterprise will have is more obvious along with a national economy level of development enhancement, and then this national outflow FDI amount also gradually will increase, but the outflow FDI will increase certainly cannot promote the domestic economy level of development.

4. Main Conclusion

This paper sets up a demonstration model to testify the adaptability of the Dunning's theory of FDI in China and to testify the causal relation between outflow FDI and economical level of development. The main conclusion is as follows:

The result of linear and the non-linear regression analysis between net outflow FDI amount and the economy level of development indicates Chinese outflow FDI is still in the second stage of Dunning theory of the investment cycle. At present, the massive negative value of outflow FDI is consistent with Chinese economy level of development.

The paper analyzed the effect of FDI on Chinese economical growth by utilizing the co-integration, error correction model and the causality test. Inclusions are as following:

First, the result of unit root test indicates that the co-integration is existed between $LN(RGDP)$ and $LN(OFDI)$, namely the long-term stable balanced relation is existed between Chinese outflow FDI and average per person economical growth, and co-integration coefficient is 0.2109. These inclusions indicate the positive relation is existed between Chinese outflow FDI and average per person economical growth, and also demonstrate Chinese average per person economical growth has the more tremendous influence to outflow FDI in China.

Second, as the size of long-term coefficient of error term can reflect the deviation to long-term balanced adjustment dynamics, from the estimated long-term coefficient of error term in the error correction model, adjustment dynamics is ordinary. Looked from the short-term, the positive relation is existed between the short-term undulation of the average per person GDP and Chinese outflow FDI, but the coefficient is not very high.

Third, looked from the Granger causality test, it was found that Chinese economic growth was the reason for Outflow FDI, and conversely, the conclusion wasn't true.

References

[1] Aitken,B.& Harrison,A."Do Domestic Firms Benefit From Foreign Direct Investment? Evidence from Venezula",*American Economic Review*, 1999(89),605-618.

[2] Balasubramanyam.V.N.,Salisu,M.,Sapsford,D .Foreign Direct Investment and Growth in EP and IS countries. *Economic Journal*.1996,106,92-105

[3] Bloomsom , M.Kokko.A .Multinational corporations and spillovers, *Journal of economic Surveys*. 1998, 12(3),247-277.

[4] Borensztein.E, De Gregorio.J, Lee.J.w, How does Foreign Direct Investment Affect Economic Growth, *Journal of International Economics Surveys*,1998,12(3),247-277.

[5] De Gregorio.J, Economic growth in Latin America ,*Journal of Development Economics*. 1992, 39, 59-83.

[6] Javorcik,Beata,Smarzynska:"The composition of Foreign Direct Investment and Protection of Intellectual Property Rights: Evidence from Transition Economics",*European Economic Review* 2004, 48(1)39-62.

[7] John.H.Dunning. International Production and the Multinational Enterprises「M」,George Allen and Unwin, 1981, 439.

[8] Konings,Jozef:"The Effects of Foreign Direct Investment on Domestic Firms",*Economics of Transition*,2001, 619-633.

[9] Gao Tiemei, Kang Shulong, Dynamic Analysis of the Impacts of FDI on Chinese Economy, *the Journal of World Economy*,2006(4):22-30

[10] Lai Mingyong, Bao Qun, Peng Shuijun and Zhang Xin, Foreign Direct Investment and Technology Spillover: A Theoretical Explanation of Absorptive Capability, *Economic Research Journal*, 2005(8):95-105

[11] Dic Lo, Assessing the Role of Foreign Direct Investment in China's Economic Development: Insights from Sector-regional Analyses, *Economic Research Journal,* 2003(9):40-48

[12] Wei Houkai, Effects of Foreign Direct Investment on Regional Economic Growth in China, *Economic Research Journal*, 2002(4) : 19-26

[13] Wu Jian, Regional Discrepancy of FDI in China and its effect on Economic Growth, *Economic Research Journal*, 2002(4) : 27-35

[14] Yu Jinping, FDI Policy, National Welfare and Economic Development, *Economic Research Journal*, 2004(5) :49-57

[15] Zhao guqing, The Dynamic Economic Analysis on GDP-FDI Nonlinear System in China, *Journal of Quantitative & Technical Economica*,2006(2):51-60

INDEX

C

D

E

F

G

H

I

J

K

L

M

N

O

P

Q

R

S